one light still shines

one light still shines

My Life Beyond *the* Shadow *of the* Amish Schoolhouse Shooting

Marie Monville *with* Cindy Lambert

ZONDERVAN

One Light Still Shines

This title is also available as a Zondervan ebook. Visit www.zondervan.com/ebooks.

This title is also available in a Zondervan audio edition. Visit www.zondervan.fm.

Requests for information should be addressed to:

Zondervan, *Grand Rapids, Michigan 49530*

ISBN 978-0-310-33866-6

International Trade Paper Edition

Author is represented by Ambassador Literary Agency, Nashville, TN 27205.

Cover photography: Getty Images®
Interior photography: Getty Images®
Interior design: Katherine Lloyd, The DESK
Editorial: Sandy Vander Zicht, Bob Hudson, Sarah Kuipers

Printed in the United States of America

13 14 15 16 17 18 19 /DCI/ 22 21 20 19 18 17 16 15 14 13 12 11 10 9 8 7 6 5 4 3

To Dan, Abigail, Bryce, Carson, DJ, and Nicole —

I cherish you.

You are vibrant proof of God's great love for me,

and on the hard days,

your presence reminds me why I breathe.

contents

prologue: the secret

I'd like to tell you a love story.

I could tell another story instead. I could recount a gruesome, premeditated murder. I could describe unspeakable acts. I could take you behind the scenes into the shielded private world of my Amish neighbors as they mourned the horrific losses of their daughters, granddaughters, nieces, sisters, and friends. I could speculate about secrets deeply buried in a troubled heart. I could attempt to decipher the clues of brokenness and irrational, twisted thinking as the man I loved, the man I thought I knew, descended into a silent madness.

I've been asked to tell those stories time and time again. But those stories are not mine to tell.

I was not at the crime scene. I was not privy to murderous plans. I cannot violate the privacy of my beloved Amish neighbors who showed me nothing but tenderness and grace when their own hearts had been shattered. I did not know there were dark secrets inside my husband, Charlie, nor did I know there were clues to watch for. And I simply cannot fathom the darkness that invaded Charlie's head or heart.

The only story I have to tell is my own. Although an unspeakable tragedy invaded my life and thrust me into a sudden storm of darkness, my story always has been and continues to be one of miraculous love.

It has taken me years to find my voice to write this story. Not because I couldn't find the words — I never lacked for words. But because, until recently, I was unable to see the *reason* to write my story. In fact, I could not comprehend why my story would matter to anyone but my family, closest friends, and a few local church groups still feeling their own way through the aftermath of the tragedy.

If the "outside" world wanted to know about the Amish schoolhouse shooting, the Internet had far more information than I would ever know. And apart from the shooting, I knew there was nothing about me that was remarkable in the least. In fact, I'd led a thoroughly unremarkable life, and since the shooting I had done my very best to avoid the media at every turn. When headlines about "the shooter's wife" still surfaced two, three, four years after the shooting, I'd cringe at the label that had stolen my name and shake my head in disbelief that anyone could still be interested in the woman in the background.

It wasn't until the fifth anniversary of the October 2, 2006, Nickel Mines Amish schoolhouse shooting that I realized the importance of telling my story to the world, when once again the anniversary brought the spotlight back on my family. Rather than diminishing, the level of interest in my story, along with invitations to speak, was increasing. The questions I was asked were shifting from the details of the event itself to questions about how I'd emerged from such a tragedy with joy and wholeness. How, after Charlie's heinous acts, had I been able to trust my heart to a man again, enough to actually remarry? Where had I found the strength to blend my family with another? How had my faith survived such a horrific ordeal? How had the tragedy changed me?

For the first time, I understood that the hunger of those interested in hearing my story was not *really* about me at all — it was about the experience of loss or pain or struggle or mystery in the lives of my listeners. *Their* lives were also filled with sudden storms and dark places. What they were searching for within my story was the secret to navigating through their own darkness.

They were hungry for a story of hope. What they knew of my experience had been so abhorrent, so incomprehensibly shocking and shattering, that they longed to discover how I'd managed to go on breathing, much less walking and living and even loving again.

And *that* was a story I could tell, not because I was at all remarkable, but because the secret to go on living — and more than that, to go running toward life, laughing and singing and loving, vibrantly alive even when every circumstance threatens to drown you in darkness — was remarkable news I had to share. I'd been given a precious gift in my darkest moment. I could not keep it to myself.

Once I knew the reason to tell my story, I found my voice to share it.

I won't keep you in suspense. I'll tell you right now, before you even have to turn the page. The secret is this:

No matter how tragic your circumstances, your life is not a tragedy. It is a love story. And in your love story, when you think all the lights have gone out, one light still shines.

Step into my story and I'll show you how to see that light.

part one

Darkness Falls

1

the call

As a little girl I loved swinging. There was no feeling quite like drinking in a sun-kissed day with the freedom to soar as high as I wanted, imagining I could touch the clouds. What was up there beyond the blue ceiling over my world? Sometimes when the sun was caught just behind the clouds, its dazzling rays caught my heart and I thought I could almost see heaven. Then, just as I was sure I'd flown higher than I'd ever flown before, the earth's invisible arms would slow me and pull me back earthward once again.

Maybe on the next swing I'll get closer, I'd think, as I tilted my head back, dark curly hair flying in the wind of my ascent, legs extended straight as an arrow in front of me. I worked to gain momentum for the next rush toward heaven. I was like the pendulum on my aunt's antique grandfather clock, rocking from earth toward heaven but always back again.

Of course, I had no way of knowing that I would grow into an adult with an even deeper longing to peer into the glorious heights of that homeland of heaven — where some of my most beloved people now live. I was just a little girl living in the peaceful village of Georgetown, Pennsylvania. If that name calls to mind images of its D.C. namesake, try instead to imagine the polar opposite. Try swapping the ding-dong of closing Metro doors for the clip-clop of horses' hooves, and you'll have a more accurate soundtrack for my quaint little hometown of six hundred.

My dad was the neighborhood milkman, just like Grandpa and Great-Grandpa before him. As I swung in the backyard of our little yellow house, all I could see in every direction were rolling hills dotted with farms and barns and silos. Maybe that description wouldn't seem so out of the ordinary if my childhood years had been in the early 1900s when the agrarian life was the national norm, but I was a child of the 1980s, born in '77, and even at a very young age I realized how unique it was to have next-door neighbor girls who wore bonnets and rode in horse-drawn buggies, who read stories by lantern light after dark, and whose fathers and brothers plowed their fields with the leather strap of a horse-drawn plow tight across their muscled backs.

It's a challenge even to locate Georgetown on a map unless you live in the area. Residents of Georgetown may have any one of four different zip codes, corresponding with Bart, Christiana, Paradise, or Quarryville. As a child, my street address was Quarryville, while my grandparents up the street were in Paradise. Yet when my family walked the one-third of a mile to visit them, we'd pass the post office labeled Bart. It's all rather confusing for an "outsider" but makes absolute sense to those of us in Lancaster County.

The neighborhood is composed of as many Amish as English residents (*English* being the term used by the Amish to refer to everyone else). This means cars on the road often make way for horse-drawn buggies, and the closest thing we have to a local celebrity may be Antique John, the area Amish bishop who's so well known that many refer to him as the mayor.

For my entire life, right to this day, Georgetown truly has been an idyllic country setting. In this rural town, early each morning and again in the evening, you can hear the hum of diesel motors powering the cooling systems for the milk tanks. (Yes, my Amish neighbors do use diesel motors for this purpose.) The cows are milked twice a day, with the warm milk being collected in large, wheeled cans or piped to the milk houses. It's collected in a tank, where it's cooled and then kept at around 35 degrees Fahrenheit. An agitator (a long arm with paddles) continually stirs the milk to speed the cooling process, creating a familiar, predictable melody that permeated my childhood. Like a bedtime lullaby, it assured me that all was right in the world.

And for twenty-eight years I thought it was, until I received the phone call that shattered my world.

~

How could I know, on that pristine Indian-summer morning of October 2, 2006, that in mere moments my world would cave in?

Sunlight bathed our family room, and the vivid blue sky was perfectly framed by the French patio door leading onto our porch. The tree just beyond was ablaze in vibrant crimson and amber; the leaves were especially beautiful that year. I had opened the windows a few inches and was enjoying the gentle breeze dancing around me as I tidied the kitchen. Eighteen-month-old Carson, my youngest of three, was taking his morning nap, right on schedule. He and I had just returned from the prayer group I led at a nearby church, where our team of moms had spent the morning praying for our children and the staff of the public elementary school in our district.

That morning around 8:30, Charlie and I had walked our two

oldest, Abigail, seven, and Bryce, five, to the bus stop. Afterward, he'd left for a work appointment in my grandfather's blue Chevrolet pickup, since Charlie's Jeep wasn't running.

I had just poured myself a cup of coffee when the phone rang. I picked it up in the kitchen. It was 11:00 a.m.

"Marie, it's me."

And that was all it took for me to sense some unfathomable evil lurking just steps away. I'd never heard Charlie's voice sound like this before, not in almost ten years of marriage. Something was horribly wrong.

"Charlie, what's going on?" My entire body was suddenly alert, my heart racing and my hands trembling. Had something happened to my dad? The kids? An accident? His voice was tense with ... with what? Grief? Pain? Fear?

"I'm not coming home."

Have you ever felt a depth of cold so bitter it leaves you feeling hypothermic — stunning your soul, leaving your body shivering in confusion? In such a moment, the heart has little time to contemplate or question; it's struggling merely to grasp the devastation. I felt life being pulled from my body, as if by a vacuum. My breathing, which had stopped, resumed in shallow, ineffective breaths, which left my lungs screaming for air. Every sense, every nerve ending, was on full alert.

"What are you talking about?" I said. "What do you mean you aren't coming home?"

There was something he needed to do, he said. Something he should've taken care of a long time ago, and he was going to do it today.

There was almost no way to respond to the words he spoke or the dark, threatening implications behind them. The years we'd shared, memories made, and promises spoken flashed before me, and my heart began to crumble. Could this be real?

Most of the things he said in our brief conversation made no sense. *Why* wasn't he coming home? Then he told me that the police were already there — but I had no idea where *there* was. Even so, my pulse quickened with the fear that our lives had just changed forever. I struggled with all of my senses to understand what was going on, to find words to stave off some disaster that I couldn't grasp.

"I left a letter for you," he said. "It's on top of the dresser, under a magazine. I'm sorry it has to be this way, Marie." Charlie's voice was so odd, so flat and lifeless.

"Charlie, whatever it is, just come home. We'll talk about it and figure it out."

My plea went unanswered. The last words I ever heard from him were assurances of his love for our family and me. And then, abruptly, he hung up.

I ran to the bedroom, lifted the magazine, and grabbed the letter scrawled in Charlie's small, tight handwriting on three pages. My hands were trembling.

Marie,

I don't know how you put up with me all these years. I am not worthy of you. You are the perfect wife. We had so many good memories together as well as the tragedy with Elise.

My heart lurched. Elise had been our firstborn child. She had died in our arms only twenty minutes after birth, nine years ago — just one year after we married.

It changed my life forever. I haven't been the same since. It affected me in a way I never felt possible. I am filled with so much hate, hate toward myself, hate toward God, and unimaginable emptiness. It seems like every time we do something fun I think about how Elise wasn't there to share it with us and I go right back to anger.

I turned to the second page, this one rambling and confusing to me: first, tender, loving words about me, followed by painful words trying to express Charlie's confusion, anger, and shame. Each word I read made me dread the next word more.

I turned to the third and final page — afraid to read on, afraid not to — and then I ran for the phone again. I dialed 911.

"Yes, my name is Marie Roberts. My husband just called me on his cell phone and told me that he wasn't going to be coming home and that the police were there and not to worry about it. I have no idea what he is talking about, but I'm really scared. I don't think he's coming home."

"What makes you think he's not coming home?"

"Because he left me a letter and I think it's a suicide note."

I suspected, by the questions the dispatcher asked, that he knew more than I did — that he had information he wasn't sharing with me. He had me read the letter over the phone. I concentrated on calming myself, remaining composed, as I read the final paragraph aloud.

I am so sorry, Marie, I never wanted it to be this way ... I am sorry to put you and the kids in this position but I feel that this is the best and only way. I love all of you and that's why I am doing this. Your lives will be better without me. Please tell mom and dad and brothers that I love them, thank you.

At some point the dispatcher transferred me to the state police dispatcher, who had me describe the GMC pickup and asked more questions. Our conversation lasted minutes but felt like hours. I just wanted to hang up in case Charlie tried to call back. I didn't want to miss the chance to hear his voice, to influence whatever was unfolding. But the dispatcher kept saying that he needed to keep me on the phone.

Finally, he let me hang up. I stared at the silent phone until a suffocating feeling drove me outside to the porch. Sirens began to sound in the distance, and then helicopters passed directly overhead. They were low, clearly preparing to land not far away. I knew it was bad, and instinctively I knew it was about Charlie. But that was all I knew. An overwhelming sense of dread was mounting within me. I'd never known such tension, as if every molecule of my being was stretched beyond capacity, suspended, awaiting the snap that would surely break me into pieces.

I found myself praying. The pleading that had gone unanswered by Charlie was now directed to one who, I knew, heard every word. I simply asked God to help; I could find no other words.

At that moment everything I knew about my life changed. My quiet "normal" existence ended, and I was faced with a choice — a crisis of belief. Would I throw myself into the arms of my Savior, believing that everything I'd heard, read in the pages of the Bible, and experienced with him up to now was true? Or would I succumb to fear, believing my life was over and accepting this as the end?

It occurred to me that this was my moment to "walk on water." Even though I couldn't see anything to stand on, I felt challenged to trust that God would meet me in the midst of this outward storm and inward sinking. I went back inside our home. Everything looked so normal. *A family lives here, children, a husband, a wife,* I tried to assure myself. Yet two worlds were colliding, one fighting in opposition to everything I had known, believed in, and trusted. As I attempted to absorb this contradiction in the quiet solitude of my living room, I stretched my arms out wide, open to the heavens, and I re-surrendered my family and myself to God's care.

"Oh, God, whatever you can do with this situation, in any place you can bring good from bad, wherever you've declared a victory, let it be."

I knew that the enemy would believe he had the victory through whatever losses those sirens were now rushing toward. But I decided that this would *not* be the end for me or for my children. Satan would not triumph. We were not going down in defeat.

Suddenly I found myself standing with a boldness and confidence I had never known. I began declaring Bible verses of God's promises of care and protection over my household. I called out for the provision of the Lord and told him I trusted his ability to bring good out of any situation. I felt like the teenaged Mary, who yielded herself to an unknown future by saying, "May your word to me be fulfilled" (Luke 1:38).

I had no idea what was unfolding with Charlie, but in a moment of sacred stillness as the world raged around me, I vowed this would not be the day that my children looked back on in the belief that it had destroyed their lives forever. This was not the end. We would not be victims. I did not know how he would bring it about, but God filled me with an absolute assurance that we were going to be victorious.

2

invasion

My walk-on-water moment still shines crystal clear in my memory. I can see myself praying with boldness over my family and home as I'd never prayed before. Scripture verses, long treasured quietly in my heart, now poured out effortlessly. I knew in those moments that I was experiencing a truly supernatural infusion of boldness. Anyone who knew me would have correctly described me as timid and reserved — until that moment.

If self-confidence is a shout, then I had always been a whisper.

The transformation in me from my barely uttered, front-porch, heavenward plea for help to the audacious declarations of God's presence and victory over my children, our lives, and our future, was so dramatic, so sudden, and so unlike my own style of spiritual expression that I knew God's powerful presence had literally invaded my living room. It was an invasion I desperately needed if I was going to survive this other invasion, this descent of darkness that had just broken into my peaceful life.

I'd made the call that mattered most — I'd called on God Almighty himself.

The next call I made was to my mom. When you've been

blessed with loving parents, when you've known open arms and trustworthy hearts and selfless care since the day you were born, then reaching for that place of safety is as natural as breathing. I told Mom what little I knew, and she was on her way.

Mom came. Such a simple sentence for such a powerful act, but it reveals volumes about the trust between parent and child I had always known. Mom and Dad had always been there for me. I didn't wonder when I called *if* she would come. That was a given. In the same way, my call to God that morning had not been simply a hope or a wish tossed into the wind; it had been a daughter's call to the heavenly Father. I'd known he would come, just as I'd known Mom and Dad would come, even if I didn't know how he would show himself. But he'd come so fast, so dramatically, that my confidence in his power was now heightened.

Mom had been at work at a store in Quarryville, less than seven miles from my home, and she was by my side in a heartbeat. Together we listened to the whirring of helicopters overhead and the blaring siren of Bart Fire Hall, easily heard for miles around as it beckoned volunteer firefighters to the unnamed emergency. The scene at the fire hall when the siren sounded was one I'd seen many times from childhood on. At this very moment, Amish volunteers were arriving at the fire hall by foot-powered scooters, their fastest means of immediate transportation, while English volunteers were arriving by car and truck. Amish and English worked side by side here in Georgetown to help their neighbors in times of crisis. But as the siren blared on and on, my mother's eyes and mine locked. How many emergency vehicles could possibly be needed? We shared the unspoken agony of knowing that some tragedy involving Charlie was unfolding, but we didn't have a clue as to what that tragedy might be.

My grandpa, who lived next door with my grandma, stopped in. Grandpa had a police scanner in his kitchen. "There's been a shooting of some kind near White Oak Road," he told us. He had no inkling that Charlie was somehow involved — he was just explaining the emergency sirens and helicopters. Mom and I read each other's eyes, silently agreeing to not yet burden my elderly grandparents with the anxiety we were suffering. We thanked him for the news, listened for a few moments as he speculated about what might be going on, and sighed with relief as he headed back across the yard to his own house.

"Mom, I can't just sit here," I said. "I've got to drive up there to see what I can find out."

"No, Marie," Mom said, "stay here in case the police call back. Besides, if Carson wakes up to all these sirens and you aren't here, he'll be scared. You stay. I'll drive up toward White Oak Road and see if I can find someone who can tell me what's happening."

Mom left, and I missed her presence immediately. But somehow, in her absence, a holy presence made itself known. I was not alone. I checked on Carson who was still napping soundly, undisturbed by the sounds of helicopters and sirens, his sleeping face so peaceful. The world he would awake to would be drastically different from the one he'd known this morning. Would he still have a father? I shuddered at the thought.

Mom was soon back. "The roads are blocked and emergency vehicles are everywhere. No one can get through." I could have turned on the radio and probably gotten at least some bits and pieces of information, but I didn't. The burden of not knowing seemed easier to bear than whatever news I might hear over the air.

And then I saw them through the window — three cars pulling into my driveway. One was a police car, the other two unmarked, but they were clearly together on an official visit. Part of me wanted to run to the door, fling it open, and know everything. But that part was overruled. I stood frozen in the living room, heard the car doors open and close, heard footsteps on the porch, yet still I did not move. Whatever news they carried with them, I knew I did not want it to invade our lives. But then the knock. I had no choice. The invasion was upon me.

I opened the door to somber faces.

"It's Charlie, isn't it?" I heard myself say.

"Yes, ma'am."

"He's dead, isn't he?"

"Yes, ma'am, he is."

I held the door open and stepped aside, nodding for them to enter, an odd calm settling over me. A few detectives in suits and several uniformed officers entered my home while a few remained outside.

"This is my mom, Nadine Welk," I said as Mom and I sat down side by side on the couch in the living room. Two of the men, detectives in suits, sat on the chairs facing us. They began by asking us questions but quickly concluded that Mom knew nothing about what had happened, and I knew nothing beyond the letter Charlie had left me and his cryptic call, both of which I'd already relayed to 911. How kind God was to send me compassionate detectives, because I still recall the gentleness and empathy of their voices, their eyes, as they began relating details no one would ever want to know. The specifics of death and destruction they recounted made my soul sick. It could not be true. And yet it was.

Charlie, one detective explained, had entered the one-room Amish schoolhouse at Nickel Mines, less than two miles from our home, that morning at about 10:25 a.m. He took ten girls hostage, ages seven to twelve, and sent the boys home. He also allowed the schoolteacher and her sister, who was pregnant, to leave, then barricaded himself and the remaining girls inside, reinforcing the doorway and windows with lumber to cut off any hope of escape or rescue. I listened in stunned horror to the officer's words, the images too unbearable to absorb. Charlie, my Charlie, the daddy who cuddled with Abigail and romped with Bryce and Carson, had ordered the girls to line up, then bound the feet of these precious little Amish girls and, one by one, shot them, execution-style. Then Charlie had turned a gun on himself. My husband was dead. At least three little girls were dead, while the others, all gravely wounded, were already in nearby hospitals, their conditions not yet known.

The officers in my home had just come from the schoolhouse. I did not want to believe that such a thing had even happened, much less that it had been done by my own husband, but the looks on the faces of these men left me no choice. They had witnessed the aftermath of the massacre, and now they carried those images within them. I could feel the weight of the burden they carried — the same weight that now pressed against my chest. The air was being sucked out of the room, replaced with a heaviness that seemed to slow time itself.

The terror and suffering endured by those innocent girls pierced my heart. It pierces me still. Sometimes the memory of it still causes an almost incapacitating weakness that overwhelms me. Inside that schoolhouse, something in Charlie spilled over in volcanic destruction, spewing a molten flow of immeasurable grief across the Amish community I knew, respected, and loved. These were our kind and gracious neighbors. We'd spent our lives surrounded by their farms, enjoying their produce. Charlie, my dad, my grandpa, my great-grandfather — four generations of men in my family — had collected milk from these Amish farmers and carried it to local dairies. We knew their names, their faces, their waves and nods.

Normally, I neither listened to the news nor watched movies depicting violence and cruelty. I had guarded my heart from evil as best I could and had maintained a stance of purity for myself and for my children. It had always disturbed me to think that sin of great magnitude could exist within the hearts of humankind. But now the intimate knowledge of evil — something from which I had worked to insulate my sensitive spirit — was invading the most private area of my life. My own husband? The gentle man in whose arms I slept? This was unfathomable. Here I sat on our dark-green plaid couch in the living room — the very same couch where I'd sat surrounded by Charlie's love — listening to the officer's descriptions of horrific evil at Charlie's hands.

I had never had what some might call a vision, yet I know that God alone gave me the images that came to me as I sat still amid the detective's haunting words. In my mind I saw myself as a tulip petal falling away from the flower — still full of color but dying. As the petal fell, I saw the hand of God come and scoop it up — right before it hit the floor — and then he cradled me securely. God was here; he was with me. I didn't know how it would happen, but I felt certain of his promise that he would help me through everything. I would be carried through my weakness and into his strength.

There wasn't time for me to slip into the denial stage of grief or to try to rewind my life to a place of wholeness, untouched by this blackness. "I have just a few more questions for Marie, alone," the detective said, so my mom stepped away, busying herself in the kitchen. The questions went on and on, deeply personal questions about our marriage, Charlie's state of mind, his childhood, his parenting, his schedule, his friendships, his interests and habits. My answers felt lame in light of this tragedy. Charlie was a quiet, hardworking man, a solid provider, a faithful and loving husband, a playful and loving father, a churchgoing Christian his entire life, a loving son and son-in-law.

I showed the detective the note Charlie had left, and we went over it word by word, trying to make sense of it, looking for hidden meaning, searching for clues that might somehow explain such a heinous act. The detective asked about Charlie's reference to Elise, our premature daughter who had lived only twenty minutes, nine years before. I spoke of our grief and explained that Charlie had deeply mourned this loss but had kept it bottled up inside.

"Like many men," I explained, "Charlie was not verbal about his feelings."

But rage? No, I'd never witnessed it. Violence? Never. Aggression? In no way. Nothing revealed a man on the brink of mass murder.

"We walked our children to the bus stop together just this morning," I explained, "like we often do. He hugged them goodbye, as usual. In every way, this was an ordinary day until I got his call."

"Where are your children?" the detective asked.

"Abigail is seven. She's at school. Bryce is five and at morning kindergarten. He'll be stepping off the bus at the end of the driveway soon."

"You'll want to have a counselor present when you tell them about your husband."

My stomach lurched, and a wave of panic flooded me. Mom had returned to my side; her presence calmed me. We needed to make an immediate plan for Abigail and Bryce, to shield them from hearing about any of this from any source but me. We arranged for my aunt to meet Bryce at the bus and take him next door to my grandparents' home. We didn't want him to be frightened, seeing his home filled with police. Mom agreed to go to Abigail's elementary school, get her out of class, and then take both children to my parents' home until I could follow. She and Dad lived only two minutes away, just down the street from the Bart Fire Hall, still in the house we'd moved to when I was nine years old. For Bryce and Abigail, an afternoon playing at their grandparents' home was nothing out of the ordinary and always fun, and at this point I wanted to do all I could to keep their lives normal for as long as possible. Mom would call two friends of hers who are counselors and have them at her house, ready when it came time to tell my children that their father was gone. I pushed that thought aside; it was too horrible to contemplate right now.

Then Mom called Dad, who was out driving his eighteen-wheel tanker on his milk route. The only way to reach him was to call his dispatch office and have them radio for him to call my house. Mom and I agreed that we didn't want him to hear about Charlie's acts over the radio. We wanted to be the ones to tell him. We knew it might take him up to an hour to arrive.

He called back in just a few minutes. Mom answered and told him that there was some kind of emergency involving Charlie. "Ken, don't turn on the radio, don't make any other stops," she told him. "Just go park the truck and get to Marie's as fast as you can."

The time had come to call Charlie's parents. It fell to me to share this news that no mother or father should ever have to hear. I'll never forget their cries of shock and sorrow as their hearts were rent.

There is something very real about the sound a heart makes

as it's torn apart. It's not heard by the human ear but is felt by the body. Life and breath are forced out, and for a few moments you're aware of reality but feel vacated from it, as if outward expressions of living have stopped.

As I hung up the phone, I was in that frozen state when, once again, God met me profoundly, bringing an indescribable strength I couldn't have expected. While drawing me back to earthly reality, God awakened me to his provision. I felt his love pour over me, giving me mental clarity and the energy to move, to fight, to live. I would draw from this well continually over the hours, days, and weeks to come. It was a lifeline of peace to my heart.

I looked at my mom and saw her strength. She gave me confidence to walk through this because she wasn't visibly shaken, distraught, or bewildered. She was calm. She had a plan, and she was acting upon it, modeling for me what God had planted in me before this news had come. Just as I had embraced God's presence in the moments before Mom had arrived, now seeing her exhibit the same strength solidified the new boldness I felt inside.

The police asked to search our home, so as Mom and I made our arrangements and calls, they rummaged through my dresser drawers, closets, cabinets, and under and behind the furniture. The sounds of doors and drawers opening and closing, of heavy footsteps and furniture scraping across the floor echoed through the house. I watched as our family computer was carried out of the house and into a detective's car. I knew that after the police finished searching our home and questioning me, I would need to pack our belongings and leave the house.

"How long do you think I have until the media arrives?" I asked an officer.

"I'm surprised they're not here already," he replied. He advised me to pack quickly and offered to stay until I was ready to leave. Mom left to pick up Abigail just as the other officers left, but that officer remained, still and quiet. His protection was profoundly moving. I felt guarded and secure as he became for me an outward sign of God's immovable strength, shielding me from harm.

In my earthly world, I had just been abandoned and left to answer for someone else's actions. At the same time, I was being sheltered and surrounded by an impenetrable strength. This came not just from the police force but also through the spiritual reality that superseded my natural circumstances.

Then my dad arrived. He stepped through the door, concern and questions clear in his face, gentleness and strength in his eyes. He still knew nothing of the events that had unfolded, but he'd parked next to the remaining police car and nodded to the officer now standing by the window. I don't know what I expected of myself, but I was shocked by the calm of my own voice as I announced from across the room, "Dad, Charlie is dead. He took the Amish school hostage, shot ten girls, and took his own life. The media is likely to show up any minute, and we need to get out of here and over to your place. We need to pack up. Fast."

Dad's entire countenance changed before my eyes. His color faded, his eyes widened and searched my face, his body recoiled as if he'd taken a blow, and for a moment he stood frozen. I'll never forget his stunned silence in the wake of my rapid-fire delivery of crushing news.

I took a rattled breath and softened my tone. "Dad, we must go. I need you to help me." My voice now sounded small in this chasm of shock.

My precious dad, always steady and dependable and solid. He seemed to grow taller before my eyes and stepped into action without a single question. We barely spoke as I rushed through the house, gathering clothing and necessities, handing everything over to him as he made trip after trip to my car, packing it in and coming back for more. I wasn't sure how long we'd be gone or where we'd end up, but miraculously we soon had everything we needed packed into my car. I buckled little Carson, still groggy from being woken from his nap, into his car seat and jumped behind the wheel of my car. Dad climbed into the passenger seat beside me, and we nodded goodbye to the policeman guarding my house and took off for my parents' home.

I would guess that not even three hours had passed since Charlie had called me. In that brief time, I'd been widowed, my children made fatherless, my community assaulted, my home searched, my husband's name disgraced, and my naive innocence shattered. Almost everything that this morning had been a certainty was now in question.

Almost everything.

One thing was now more rock-solid certain than ever before in my life — my faith in a loving heavenly Father. In fact, far more than merely confirmed, my faith had multiplied in that short time. God had never seemed so tangible, so miraculously present, as he was to me now.

It is a mystery, this gift called faith. I had not mustered it on my own; it had simply been given to me. The boldness to pray, the Scriptures filled with promise and victory, the image of the tulip petal caught and cradled in the loving hand of God, the supernatural inner strength now coursing through my being, each of them a gift as real as the policeman guarding my home, my sleepy son securely tucked into his car seat, my mother's strength to plan and act, and my father's solid presence by my side in the car.

Such are the makings of my love story. God's gifts are far too easy to miss when all hell is breaking loose, when the blackness of evil comes crashing into our lives. How tempting, how natural, to see only the ugliness as it threatens to gobble up the goodness, wreaking havoc on the life we've known. But that blackness doesn't have the power to steal away those good gifts. It merely dims our view of them. The God-given riches of our lives are still there, and we must call upon his Light to pierce the shadows so we can see his love gifts all around us. This black day, God had pierced the darkness just enough for me to see his presence.

But now it was time to flee. My job for the moment was to keep my hands steady on the steering wheel and my foot on the gas toward a hiding place for my family, away from the telescopic camera lenses that would soon attempt to search out my children, my family and friends, and every detail of our lives.

The invasion was upon me. A brutal massacre had opened the floodgates, and now a nightmare was rushing toward me. I knew it as surely as I knew that God was with me. Yet knowing the one truth did not cancel out the other. Somehow the two truths had to coexist.

I had no idea how. I simply knew that it was so.

3

threshold

I sat in my parents' family room listening to Abigail, Bryce, and Carson playing in the backyard, enjoying the beautiful Indian-summer afternoon. They were still blissfully unaware that their lives had been forever altered just a few hours before, that they would never again see their daddy. How long would it be, I wondered, after the crushing blow I was about to deliver, before I heard the sound of their laughter again? When would they return to playing like this, so carefree?

I dreaded having to share the news with them. How could I tell them that the daddy who loved them so very much — who had walked them to the bus stop this very morning, kissing them goodbye — had done something so evil? The reality was difficult enough for me, for any adult. How could they possibly bear this ugly truth?

I watched them through the broad windows lining the wall of the family room as they tossed a big beach ball around with my mom and dad, their laughter floating into the house, carried by the breeze. This gave me some time to gather my wits and talk with the two counselors, friends of my mom, who now sat across from me. I knew there was no way around what must be done. My children had to know the truth, and now was the time, here in this safe and familiar place, surrounded by their loving family.

"This is what I'm thinking," I said. I studied the faces of the two counselors, watching for signs of approval or caution. "I want to tell the children just a little bit at first, and then gradually over the course of the week I will tell them everything. Abigail and Bryce need to know the full account before they go back to school. It would be unbearable for them to hear something about their own father on the playground and not know whether it's true."

They needed to hear it from me; I had no choice.

"I don't think they need to know all the details at once. Carson is too young to hear some of these things. But Abigail and Bryce must know the whole truth within the week."

The counselors agreed. We talked about word choices and the possible reactions the children might have.

No matter what I have to go through, I told myself, *I am determined to do everything possible to protect my children. I will fight for them, I will cover them, and I will love them through it all.* Focusing on that purpose gave me the strength to stand and take the first step.

I walked to the door and called to the kids and my parents in the backyard, "Can you come in? I need to talk to you about something." I did my best to keep my tone warm, gentle, and even, although inside I felt the complete opposite. I did not want to do this. Telling the kids would propel us into a future we couldn't escape. But I immediately recognized my faulty thinking. There *was* no place of escape, and there would be no benefit to prolonging this limbo in which my life was falling apart and theirs was seemingly still intact.

I stood on the threshold of two separate worlds, about to reveal to my children that one of those worlds had been destroyed.

They came to me, leaving behind the innocence of carefree play, warm sunshine upon their faces, leaves dancing through the breeze overhead, and they crossed over into my world. I closed the door behind them. There was no going back.

I thought of the countless times during my years with Charlie that I had complained inwardly about laundry and dishes, tight finances, and lack of deep communication. Those things seemed trivial now. I thought about the hopes and dreams my heart held for my children's future and wondered how vibrant life could possibly survive the chaos of death. I felt a mother's responsibility deeper and sweeter than I'd ever known before. Charlie's choices were crushing. I couldn't undo them, but I was free to make my own. My choice was for our family to face this new reality together, holding on to one another, and find our way through it with all the trust, strength, and love we could share.

As the kids skipped and bounced into the room, a breeze softly danced through the open windows, and with it I felt the peace of Jesus envelop me. He was the whisper woven through this autumn day. *Do you trust me? Do you really trust me? Will you entrust them to me?* he seemed to say.

I did trust him, but at the same time I did not. I did not trust so fully as to remove the weight of the moment and lay it at his feet. I didn't know how. My heart yearned to trust like that. While I sensed that God was encouraging my heart to embrace his power, his provision, and his protection, I was nevertheless terrified. My words and actions would either add to the misery of the choices Charlie had made or help free my children from the weight of this mountain pressing down upon us. Over and over my heart cried out to the Lord, "Give me *your* words."

This moment felt like the final seconds before the space shuttle reenters earth's atmosphere, when the heat shield must be perfectly positioned, everything covered, so that it doesn't erupt in flames. God had to cover every inch of us or this would be the end.

Mom sat on a chair along the wall of windows. Dad stood next to her. Their nearness was comforting, as if they were willing me strength, and I knew that their spirits were at that very moment praying for me, praying for my children. Dad's eyes met mine. While sad, they were filled with deep love. I knew that, if he could, he'd take all our pain upon himself to spare us the suffering ahead.

I led the kids to the sofa, and we all four sank into soft blue cushions that cradled us. The counselors sat on another sofa across the room. Carson climbed into my lap; Abigail and Bryce nestled in on either side. I leaned down and rubbed my cheek against Carson's hair, so soft, so sweet. He leaned back into me, and I breathed deep of this last solitary moment before we would cross over to the other side. I swallowed hard and cleared my throat.

"I have something very sad to tell you."

Abigail's eyes met mine instantly, reading my pain in a heartbeat. She stiffened as if bracing herself for a blow. Bryce looked at me quizzically at first, then a shadow of fear darkened his eyes. Carson toyed with his pacifier. This was the moment. No turning back.

"Today Daddy made some very bad choices, some people got hurt, some people died, and he died too." One sentence. That's all it took.

"I'm so sorry." I did my best to keep my voice gentle and warm, wanting them to feel wrapped with love, but I could feel my throat constricting. "You're not going to see your daddy anymore." Tears, fresh and hot, fell from my face onto Carson's head and ran down the tendrils I had just caressed.

The eyes of Abigail and Bryce, now huge and round, held pain too great to express. As my tears fell, my children did not utter a sound. Time stood frozen, within us and around us. My children, like me, were now marred by this day.

No one moved. It seemed as though everyone around us was holding their breath, waiting to see what the rest of this life would look like and how the kids would respond. Silence filled the room.

Then Carson broke the stillness. He began smiling at his siblings, first at Bryce, then Abigail, and back at Bryce again, as if he'd noticed their sudden sadness and wanted them to be happy again. He was my always-happy child. My eighteen-month-old did not comprehend the moment the way seven-year-old Abigail and five-year-old Bryce clearly did, but whatever he grasped led him to try to connect with his brother and sister. He leaned over and rested his head against Abigail.

I had said the words no parent would ever want to tell a child. And we had survived.

But the hardest part, I suddenly realized, was yet to come. For the past few hours I had dreaded this conversation, thinking it would be the hardest part, but now I understood that just because we had made it through this moment did not mean that the danger was over. I had no idea what was going on inside of my children in these first few minutes, nor did I know what might happen as I shared more details in the days to come. But undoubtedly, there would be many times over the next few days, weeks, months, maybe even years that would be even harder. The added weight of that realization threatened to undo me.

I wanted to take upon myself every bit of the sorrow they felt. My shoulders were wider than theirs, my love for them ran deep, and I felt my heart breaking again, this time by the magnitude of their loss.

Physically, I was still sitting on a blue sofa in a sun-drenched family room surrounded by my hurting family, but emotionally I was suddenly standing above a raging fire, flames licking at my legs, trying desperately to lift my children safely over the blaze.

Silently, my soul cried in agony, "God, you have to *fix* this! Their lives are not supposed to look like this. They are not supposed to know such pain or be enveloped by such agony."

What came in the next moment was as unexpected as my vision of the tulip petal, just as tangible, just as life changing.

I looked up and my eyes fell upon the open window. Outside, the sun still shone bright and warm. I felt a breeze surround me. Jesus was here. Into my soul he whispered these words:

"I am not going to *fix* it. I am going to *redeem* it."

As those words rang in my mind, I knew that I was on holy ground, in the presence of the Almighty. Tension immediately melted away from my shoulders — I hadn't realized how tightly my body had fused to the couch. I began to relax; I took one deep, ragged breath, then a second that came easier. It felt good to breathe this clear air in and let it fill me. I exhaled and inhaled again. When I breathed in, it was as if I got a little more of Jesus, and when I breathed out, the heaviness left.

All of this took place in mere seconds. Mom, Dad, and the counselors hadn't moved or spoken. They'd seen and heard nothing, yet everything had changed. I held on to the quiet comfort of this moment, my children pressed safely against me, knowing that soon the world would erupt. But in this precious moment, we were in the eye of the storm, and it was a safe place to be. Jesus had not left us. He would not. He was close and tangible. I didn't want to forget, when the eye passed and the winds raged and I groped for something to cling to, the way he felt inside me now. I didn't want to forget that he would still be there.

Then Carson crawled off my lap, asking, "Bryce, wanna play?" Bryce looked at me as if to check whether this was allowed, and at the same moment, the sliding glass door opened and a tidal wave of family members flooded the house. I was in a sea of warm hugs and tender words and loving hearts wanting to help us, support us, and be love to us.

The winds were picking up; this storm was far from over. A hurricane was threatening my heart. I knew that in the days to come I would find myself returning again to quiet conversation with my children. There was much yet to say. I would need to speak with them individually and relate the details of Charlie's actions in a way appropriate for their age and understanding. I knew it would be hard every time, that my heart would be continually pierced by the words I spoke and the damage done by those words. But that moment, as I huddled with my children, hope took hold of this mother's heart. Jesus had whispered to my soul. He had promised to redeem this horror. Redemption would come.

We spent the rest of the afternoon and evening at my parents' house, surrounded by aunts and uncles, grandparents, and close friends. A gray mist still hovers over my memories of the rest of that day, but I vividly remember bits and pieces. It wasn't long before the media discovered where we were. The phone rang a lot, primarily media wanting some response. I didn't want to be interviewed, so I wrote a short paragraph that my pastor read to the reporters. We kept the television and radio off; my family was determined to protect me from the trauma of having the crime and its aftermath replayed before me time and time again.

My brother, Ken, found one reporter sneaking through the shrubs in my parents' yard, camera in hand. When Ken confronted him, he unleashed a torrent of questions, but my brother's ominous scowl sent him scurrying away. A few photographers lurked in the field behind my parents' property. They must have had telephoto lenses, given their distance, but the men of my family were vigilant in their protection of our privacy.

My loved ones told me the names of the three girls who had died: Naomi Rose Ebersol, age seven, Marian Stoltzfus Fisher, age thirteen, and Anna Mae Stoltzfus, age twelve. The next day, I would learn that Lena Zook Miller, age eight, and Mary Liz Miller, age seven, also did not survive their injuries, while the five other injured girls were still hospitalized: Rachel Ann Stoltzfus, age eight, Barbie Fisher, age eleven, Sarah Ann Stoltzfus, age twelve, Esther King, age thirteen, and Rosanna King, age six.

I recoiled as I heard each name. These families who had lost their daughters or who were now sitting by the girls' bedsides as they fought for their lives were not strangers. I'd biked past their farms in my youth. We bought produce from their roadside stands. Charlie had formed relationships with these families in the past seven years of milk hauling, and my father, grandfather, and great-grandfather had known and served these families through our family milk-hauling business. Every spring I visited the Fishers' greenhouse to buy plants for our flower beds and vegetable seeds for our own gardens. These were our peaceful, kind neighbors, people we respected and appreciated. We knew their faces and their names, as they knew ours. To this day, I have no words adequate to express the grief of knowing that it was my husband who so brutally victimized these good families.

As I sat surrounded by extended family and friends, weeping together at the incomprehensible loss, I knew that the victims' families too were gathered doing the same. I could envision their kitchens and porches filled with aunts and uncles, grandparents and cousins, brothers, sisters, and friends — a sea of black and gray and green and blue, of white bonnets and black hats, all the trademark garb that so fascinates the hordes of tourists. To me, these people were far more than a peculiar society living a plain and simple life. They were individuals, part of the fabric of my community and my life since the day of my birth.

My Charlie had murdered their children?

My Charlie had *murdered* their children!

How would they ever bear to see me again? Would we need to move away? Would the sight of my children sicken them by reminding them of the man who'd taken their own children from them? Would they resent that I still had my children when they'd been robbed of theirs? Would they blame me, believing I'd known they were in danger but hadn't protected them? Would they think I'd sat passively by and ignored the signs and clues of Charlie's rage?

I asked myself the same questions. Had I been blind? Were there clues I'd missed — that my entire family had missed? It was a question explored in every room of my parents' home that day. We all spoke of Charlie, comparing notes for any telling signs. But we all came up empty. Every encounter, every story, every memory painted a picture of the same man I'd known and loved for ten years. Quiet and kind, responsible and hardworking, gentle and playful with our own children and his young cousins.

Those of us who knew him best knew that there was sadness as well, especially in the wake of the death of our firstborn, Elise. But that had been nine years ago. I'd worried about Charlie being lonely, not having any deep friendships with other men, but Dad described Charlie as well liked by the other truckers and the customers, the kind of guy they joked and laughed with and were always happy to see. It was clear to all of us that whatever had been going on inside of Charlie had been hidden from us all. I took some small comfort in knowing that if I'd been blind, I'd been no more blind than all the others who'd known and loved and worked alongside him, day in, day out, for years. But it was not a comfort that lasted. What had I missed?

My spirit sensed waves of guilt and shame building just off the shore of my life, roaring toward me in a churning rush. Yet God's presence, so tangible to me this day, somehow stood between those waves and me. He was a wall of protection that would not allow them to hit me. I knew this was miraculous. Without him guarding me, I would have undoubtedly been swept out into that violent, stormy sea and taken under by a current I would have been helpless to fight against. *His name is Immanuel, God with us.* I'd heard that truth from the pulpit countless times. Now I was living it.

The media's descent on my parents' home intensified as the afternoon wore on. The phone calls were coming more quickly, and a few reporters had even knocked on the door. My brother, Ken, posted himself on the front steps. *That will scare them away*, I remember thinking. Ken was an imposing figure. Thirty-one years old, with a solid, muscular frame, he claimed his spot like a menacing bouncer prepared to toss aside anyone daring to venture into the yard. He naturally projected an intimidating presence. I'd always joked that he was someone I wouldn't want to run into in a lit alley, let alone a dark one. A few years before, he'd started shaving his head — that just added to the image. I felt safe with my big brother standing guard, and knowing Kenny (a nickname my sister and I alone were allowed to call my big brother) as I did, he'd probably needed to find some purpose, some job to do, since he was never much for just sitting still and talking. I later learned that the police, concerned for our privacy, soon blocked off our street to all but our neighbors, keeping the onslaught of media vans from even entering our line of sight. I owe them a debt of gratitude.

I soon found that I lacked the energy for conversation. In search of solitude, I withdrew to the kitchen. The children were once again out back, and my dad was tossing a ball around with them. Dad, taking care of my kids. Dad, modeling for me what God, my heavenly Father, was doing for us all.

In my solitude, I reached for God and offered him my tortured thoughts. *I haven't done anything wrong,* I tried to assure myself, *but I was Charlie's closest connection. What kind of man would execute little girls? How could my Charlie be that man? God, what did I miss? Could I have stopped this? How can I explain what he did?*

I felt deserted, left behind to bear the world's judgment and questions alone, and I felt that weight pressing me down. But even in my weakness, I knew that the Lord would come in strength. It was my duty to be willing, obedient, and devoted to him, trusting his heart and walking in confident expectation of his provision in all forms. I remembered a verse, 2 Corinthians 12:9: "My grace is sufficient for you, for my power is made perfect in weakness." In my insufficiencies he would be sufficient. I needed to allow God to be responsible for working out my healing and the healing of my children. The pressure of it all was not for me to bear.

I didn't know how, but I knew that God was profoundly at work.

I was sitting alone at the kitchen table, watching the breeze playing with the deep red maple leaves on the driveway out front, when I first saw them — a small group of five or six Amish men walking down the street. Black hats, black pants with suspenders strapped over their solid-color shirts, blue, gray, and green. For a moment I thought I was going to be sick; my stomach lurched as a wave of dread washed over me. I stood and stepped toward the window, half-hiding myself behind the curtain. I panicked. They were coming here!

I rushed from the kitchen, looking for Dad, and found him in the backyard with the kids again.

"Dad, a group of Amish men are coming down the street. What should we do?" I couldn't think. I was afraid to face these men, afraid to see the pain in their faces, afraid of the anger they must feel, the questions they must have for me.

"It's okay, Marie," Dad said. "I'll go out and talk to them. You stay inside."

I returned to the kitchen and again half-hid myself behind the curtain.

The Amish men stood in the street in front of the house for a moment, then stepped forward onto my parents' driveway. My mouth went dry. I watched as Dad walked down the driveway to talk with them — to these men who were not strangers, but rather neighbors he had known a long time. No doubt they had just left their own weeping families. I could only imagine what was going through my dad's head as he neared those who had sustained tragedy and devastation at the hand of his son-in-law.

Now these men stood face-to-face with my dad. I couldn't breathe.

And then the most unimaginable act.

An Amish man with a long gray beard stepped toward my father and opened his arms wide. My father fell into those arms, his shoulders heaving, held and comforted by a friend.

Grief met grief.

My heart knew that I too was being held in this embrace. A cry deep within me made its way to the surface, and I wept in astounded relief, in shared sorrow, in pure communion with my Father God who was painting before my eyes a masterpiece of grace.

My world went silent except for the sound of my own crying as I watched this scene play out through the windowpanes. I couldn't hear a word being spoken but didn't need to — the gestures told the story. Heads nodding, hands clasping, the men offered more embraces as they stepped in closer to one another. My dad placed his hand on the shoulder of one of the men, and their eyes met as they spoke and listened to one another. Dad was among brothers, sharing grief and comfort.

I don't know how much time passed as the men talked and wept together. It could not have been long, but I didn't tear my eyes away for even a moment. I knew I was witnessing an exchange filled with mutual love and concern, an embrace of my entire family from the entire Amish community.

Finally, the men stepped back amid handshakes and nods of farewell. They turned, walked slowly down the driveway, and retreated down the street, this band of Amish men shoulder to shoulder, this troop of grace framed by red maples. Dad stood still and watched them go, then turned and headed back to the front door. I dried my tears with a handful of tissues pulled from my pocket, took a deep breath, and headed to the living room just as Dad closed the front door behind him.

My entire family gathered around Dad, waiting for him to speak, to share the words he'd heard. Mom stepped into Dad's arms, and they held each other for a moment; then Dad looked at me. His face, to my surprise, was filled with light in spite of red-rimmed eyes.

"Marie." Dad spoke so softly that I stepped closer to him. "They came out of concern for you, for the children, for all of us. They asked if you were okay, if the children were safe. They wanted to know what they could do for you. They asked how they could help." Dad looked around the room, speaking to the entire family now, his voice choked with emotion. "Every one of those men had a family member in the schoolhouse this morning. Can you believe they came to express their concern for *us*? They wanted us all to know that they have forgiven Charlie and that forgiveness embraces us all. They spoke no words of anger, not the slightest hint of resentment, only assurance, concern, and comfort."

How can I describe the sound at that moment in my parents' living room? It was as if the room itself inhaled in amazement, then exhaled in relief. Or was that just my own breathing, amplified by my heart? I stood speechless, too stunned to respond. These men whose families had been ravaged by my Charlie were concerned about me? Their hearts were moved for *my* children while their own little girls lay dead and injured? They wanted to know how they could help *us*?

How does a fractured heart hold such a gift?

My soul drank it in but could not contain in. It flowed through my veins, spilled over, filled the very air I was breathing, infused me with the brilliant light of God's presence. I now understood the light in Dad's face.

The Amish could have chosen hate or blame, yet they chose *love*. They freely gave love in its purest form — they poured grace unimaginable and divine mercy generously into our lives. Before my eyes, the gospel was being powerfully lived out. They had come to my door to reach across the threshold, extending unconditional love.

part two

Night Vision

4

the milkman's daughter

The image of the Amish embracing my father stirred all my earliest memories of visiting Amish farms and families alongside my dad. How fitting that God should choose that image to breathe comfort into my nightmare.

I was too young to remember the first time I was lifted into the cab of Dad's eighteen-wheel tanker milk truck. My parents tell me I was a toddler, bubbling with excitement and so fascinated with the gauges and levers that I wanted to touch them all. But even at that age, I was so eager to please that I obeyed and did not touch them. By the time I was five I often rode alongside my dad for a full day on his route, as I would well into my teens, progressing from wide-eyed passenger to wage earner.

My great-grandfather, Lloyd C. Welk, started the business of hauling milk from the farms to the dairy back in 1963. He'd drive his delivery truck along the winding dirt roads of Lancaster County, Pennsylvania, stopping at farms, Amish and English alike, picking up milk in cans and taking them to the local bottling plant in Lancaster. His son, my grandfather Lloyd W. Welk, followed his dad into the business, as did my own father, Ken. By the time my father was a paid driver, my great-grandfather had enlarged the fleet to twenty-one trucks, some of them shiny eighteen-wheel tankers, others a shorter version called straight trucks. Over those same years, many of the farms had grown as well. Rather than delivering the milk to the bottling plant, our trucks now delivered it to large corporate dairies that supplied butter, milk, cream, ice cream, and even nondairy bottled drinks to stores well beyond the boundaries of Pennsylvania.

Visiting a dairy was a highlight for me as a child. The dairy's lunchroom refrigerator would always be stocked with a variety of flavors, and we were invited to help ourselves to choices like iced tea, chocolate milk, fruit punch, or orange juice. There was always one to drink and one to take for the ride home.

I still remember the excitement of driving along as a little girl, just my dad and me, together on a haul. Dad's invitations to join him made me feel special, grateful that he enjoyed me enough to want to share his big world with me. The gently rolling hills dotted with barns and silos and carpeted with fields of corn, tobacco, alfalfa, soybeans, and more, changed with the seasons. As Dad identified the crops for me and explained the cycles of farming, I was sure he must be the smartest man in the world. I loved bouncing in the front seat of the eighteen-wheeler, watching the precision with which Dad backed down long winding lanes and around barns and outbuildings without ever bumping into anything. He was so expert a driver that he could shift gears without using a clutch, simply judging by the sound of the engine.

When we pulled into the perfectly manicured Amish farms, Dad would unload the hose from the back of the trailer and hook it up to the farmer's milk tank. The milk in the farmer's tank first needed to be measured (with a long measuring stick) and the reading converted into pounds. Then the milk was agitated and sampled to measure its fat content and ensure against bacteria before loading it onto the trailer.

While the milk was loading, Dad and I would often venture out into the barn, looking for puppies or kittens or just to chat with the farmer. I loved the bright flower gardens, tended with such care, neatly planted along their farm lanes and around their homes and barns. After Dad loaded the milk, he disconnected and put away the hose, then rinsed the milk residue out of the farmer's milk tank by hand with a garden hose. Then after a friendly wave between my dad and the farmer, off we went to the next farm.

I was fascinated by the many differences between these Amish families and my own. They always worked and played together, children in the field next to their parents, planting tobacco, hoeing weeds, and harvesting crops. Older boys threw bales of hay onto the wagon or pulled rocks from the tilled ground before planting. The tireless work ethic of the Amish, shared and passed down by so many of the Swiss and German immigrants in the area, was always in evidence on the neat, tidy farms we visited. Hard work was understood at any age and respected. More than that, it seemed to be enjoyed.

My parents had a large garden every summer — not as extensive as those of most of our Amish neighbors, of course, but sizable. My siblings and I were expected to help plant seeds, pull weeds, and harvest vegetables, but I confess we did not do it with the same joy the Amish families seemed to have. For me this was a chore, and I did not particularly enjoy the time spent stooped over pulling weeds or stemming string beans. I wondered: Why did the Amish kids not seem to mind?

I was thankful that I didn't wear the same styles of clothing as the Amish girls my age. Their solid-colored dresses were made of cotton-polyester blends, which couldn't breathe on hot summer days filled with outdoor adventures. On top of the dresses they wore an added layer of fabric — an apron, which I didn't imagine was a blessing when the temperature climbed into the 90s! But I never saw complaint on their faces.

The sweet and gentle nature of the Amish children was always evidenced by their genuine attitudes of service toward one another in whatever task they were assigned. Although they were generally quiet in public, their eyes danced and sparkled as they smiled and waved from the backs of their buggies as cars passed. Though it was a scene I saw daily, I never tired of the sight of those adorable, innocent faces framed in black bonnets for girls or brimmed hats for boys.

On the whole, Saturday afternoons in the Amish community are set aside for preparation for Sunday's church activities. Stone driveways are raked to remove debris and remnants of the past week's farm duties. Lawns are manually mowed — no gas-powered mowers here. The older girls in the household typically take on this task while the men work in the field or barn. Sundays are spent attending church and fellowshipping, so horse-drawn buggies abound on the roads. Each bishop leads two separate congregations, alternating his Sundays between them. On the Sunday when one congregation doesn't have a church service, they spend their day visiting family and friends, sharing meals together. Many Sunday evenings are filled with volleyball games, hymn sings, and time enjoying neighbors' conversation and company. Just as they work so hard together all week, they relax and refresh together as well.

My family life, it seemed to me, held few similarities to theirs. Raised the middle child of three siblings, I was destined to be a peacemaker. Ken was the eldest, born in 1974, three years before me. Vicki came along four years after me. Despite our age differences, we often played together. After all, our little town of Georgetown was out in the country, so we didn't have friends within walking or biking distance. Our school friends, like us, were bused in from miles of rural countryside where even visiting a "next-door" neighbor would often require a parent's willingness to drive us kids. It was always a treat when aunts and uncles would visit and bring cousins to play with us.

From the time I was born until the summer after third grade, we lived in a little yellow house next to a large Amish farm belonging to the Esh family. Our ranch-style house was close to the road, but the Eshes had a long lane that ran along the right side of our property and beyond, down their hill and back up again to their big gray house and their expansive two-story white barn. I'd swing in my backyard, overlooking their cows and horses, their two silos, and many acres of farmland. I remember the summer day when their grandfather gave my cousin and me a ride in his buggy up the farm lane; the upholstered interior was softer than I had imagined. Bouncing on the seat as the wheels jostled over the bumpy driveway was great fun!

There was an electric wire along the top of their fence, powered by the diesel generator (not uncommon on Lancaster Amish farms to not only cool the milk but also power the fences), which helped keep the cows and horses within their enclosure. When we were playing baseball, my siblings and I took turns retrieving any balls hit into the field, hoping the fence wasn't turned on. We tried to stay clear of the wire so we wouldn't have to find out! One afternoon, Ken was at bat and sent the ball sailing over my head and over the fence.

Vicki and I looked at each other. "It's your turn to get the ball, Marie," Vicki said. "Ken got the last one."

"I know that, Vicki," I said, not appreciating my little sister telling me what to do. I trotted toward the fence.

"I already touched the wire, Marie," Ken called. "Didn't shock me. It's off."

"Okay," I said, mildly surprised that my older brother was giving me a helpful tip. Yet at the fence, I hesitated.

"What's the matter — you scared?" Ken chided. "I told you, it's off. Go ahead and grab it. You'll see."

I grabbed the wire.

I screamed as a shock I will never forget jolted me backward. I'm not sure which hurt worse — the electric shock or the fact that my brother had set me up for pain.

"Kenny!" I cried. "How could you! I trusted you!"

But Ken was unrepentant. He probably couldn't even hear me over his laughter, which hurt me even more. I stomped away, unwilling to play any more with him that day. True to the pattern of sibling skirmishes, he enjoyed his trick — until my mom found out what had happened. Then he wasn't smiling.

My brother worked for the Esh family on several occasions, baling hay and harvesting corn. He would come home dirty and sweaty (which I didn't envy) but told of delicious lunches he had enjoyed at their table. I felt a little envious as he described meals that sounded better than any restaurant I'd ever been to. And — wonder of all childhood wonders — they even ate dessert at lunchtime!

Unlike our Amish neighbors, my siblings and I didn't spend

most of our time on chores. Aside from our family garden and Saturday morning housecleaning, we spent much of our time playing. Lots of happy memories were made in Georgetown: fishing with my brother in the stream running through a neighbor's farm (never catching anything but enjoying the adventure), sledding down the Esh field in the winter with my siblings and cousins, roller skating on Furnace Road just down the road from our house, stopping at the bridge to look for fish or ducks in the water below. These moments, while never seeming significant at the time, became a treasure-house of times spent surrounded by subtle beauty.

From spring through summer, the landscape is dotted with roadside stands where Amish families sell the bounty of their harvest: juicy ripe strawberries freshly plucked an hour before, potatoes glistening with the remnants of rich soil, and a still life of crisp and colorful vegetables that could be transformed into a salad no one could refuse — a delight to the eye and tongue. I loved the taste of homemade root beer occasionally available at these roadside stands, far more delicious than conventional sodas, and refreshing on a hot summer afternoon.

But our family's farm-stand favorite was (and is to this day) sweet corn! Sold by the baker's dozen (always thirteen ears, a trademark of this generous culture) and picked within a few hours of being placed on display. As you run your fingers along ribbed husks and fluffy tassels to make your selections, the ears are sometimes still dewy to the touch. And once the corn is boiled, just one bite reveals a milky sweetness that doesn't compare to the corn sold in supermarkets. As a child I even enjoyed husking corn, a chore that turned competitive as I raced my siblings to see who could finish pulling the silk and husk off the most ears.

There were (and still are) two Amish stores in Georgetown. Village Dry Goods sells fabric, books, housewares, hardware, and candy. Visiting was always a pleasure as I was growing up, whether I went to browse, to spend ten cents' worth of hard-earned allowance on gummy fish, or to buy small gifts for my family. The second, King Grocery, is stocked with grocery and bulk items. Consider this: you can buy sugar and flour in 25, 50, and 100-pound sacks, cornmeal, meats and cheeses, herbs and spices, as well as produce fresh from their garden adjacent to the parking lot. You can find enough for a family of four or fourteen or for an entire Amish church meal, wedding dinner, or barn raising. It was the perfect place to pick up any item missing from our pantry when preparing a recipe and brought the convenience of a shopping mall to our small town. The King girls could provide everything we needed and more!

Aside from the post office and two Amish stores, there weren't many landmarks in our town. A small Amish harness shop sat quietly on Furnace Road right near Fisher's Stone Yard. The only other defining feature was Bart Fire Hall. The sound of that fire whistle was unmistakable! Its loud-and-clear call was startling in the middle of the night or if it blared suddenly while we were outside. Once the siren sounded, a flurry of activity followed. Many responders were Amish men from the community who would come running or arrive on scooter (powered by foot, of course). I've never seen anyone as fast on a scooter as those men!

As I grew older, I'd take long bike rides by myself, exploring all the winding country roads but never fearing any danger nor worrying my parents. I was among neighbors everywhere I turned. My grandma and grandpa lived just up the street, so I frequently rode by their home, having no idea that one day my husband, Charlie, and I would build our home on the empty lot next door and build our own little house upon it. The very house where, years later, I would get the call that pierced my heart.

For all the differences, there was one great similarity between our lives and those of our Amish neighbors — the cows never took a day off. They needed to be milked twice a day, every day, with no regard for holidays and vacations. The milk at each farm needed to be picked up every other day, without fail, and there were enough farms to keep all of our family business's trucks busy every day. The local farmers' milk needed to be collected by my dad even on Christmas Eve and Christmas Day and every other holiday. Sundays, at least, broke the routine a bit. Amish don't allow trucks on their farms on Sunday, so every Amish farm's milk must be picked up on Saturday and Monday instead, making Saturdays and Mondays the busiest of all.

Our faith was as natural a part of our lives as eating and sleeping, with prayers at mealtime and bedtime, Bible stories often told, and the language of faith lived out daily by my parents, aunts, uncles, and grandparents. Mom took us to Sunday worship and Sunday school at Georgetown United Methodist, the picturesque little white steepled, stained-glass-windowed church just one house up from my grandparents' home. Vacation Bible school every summer, church gatherings on many occasions, and home Bible studies were all a part of our family schedule.

It was in church that my spirit was first touched by the power of music. The blend of voices singing hymns and praise songs stirred me deeply, transporting me heavenward. I remember as a little girl feeling lifted up, like I was soaring toward the sky on my swing, when the voices would swell in words and melodies of praise. I filled hours playing piano and listening to music, developing an appreciation for classical styles as well as the great hymns of faith I sang on Sundays. When no one in our family was playing music, Mom's classical records filled our home with melody that settled and inspired me.

Looking back now, I clearly see the idyllic quality of the country life of my childhood. But of course, since that was all I'd known, I wouldn't realize for many years how sheltered and unique my childhood was compared to the childhoods of most children born in the 1970s. We watched little television in our home and seldom went to movies. We read instead. When we were young, Mom read to us daily, and as I grew I read voraciously. My school classmates, like me, lived in a spread-out rural community, and though I suppose many of them watched television more than I did, my elementary years were spent largely unaware of the "outside" world of cities and suburbs from which all the tourists came to gawk at our Amish neighbors.

In every way, I was a child born and bred in the Garden Spot of America, as Lancaster County, Pennsylvania, is called. I'd been planted in the middle of everything that would set the stage for who I would become. Until the morning of October 2, 2006, I'd been the milkman's daughter who grew up to be what she always dreamed of being — a wife, a mother, a Christian woman in a Christian family, a woman who loved her husband, her kids, her God, her country, her life.

Yet suddenly, in the space of that one morning in 2006, the warmly glowing pictures of my childhood — of Amish farms, Amish neighbors, Amish children — were torn from the safekeeping of my memories and violently shredded.

Bart Fire Hall, the fire whistle, the scooter-riding Amish first responders, who were wearing straw hats, black pants, and solid-color shirts, were no longer held tenderly as part of my little-girl world in an idyllic country upbringing. After that morning, they screamed an ugly reality to this naive-girl-turned-woman who now bore the weight of being a murderer's wife. The faces in my memory were no longer filled with innocent smiles and neighborly welcome. They were smeared with blood and twisted with terror and horrific grief.

"Oh, God. Dear God. How could this happen? What can I do?" Thoughts like these spun through my mind as I sat in my parents' family room. I gazed out the windows, past their backyard, to horses and goats grazing together in a farmer's field. To the left, I could see one of the storage buildings that sat behind Bart Fire Hall. What was going on at the fire hall this very minute in response to Charlie's actions today?

Charlie. Already that morning I missed him. I hadn't married a murderer! I had married Charlie Roberts, my sweetheart since my teen years.

I was a teenager before I grasped how isolated our lives were from the cultural norms of most of the nation, and that awareness sprang more from my studies than from firsthand knowledge. Although I was shy, quiet, and unsure of my ability to become anyone of significance, I possessed an eagerness to excel. I was a good student, conscientious in my work and respectful of others, but rarely raised my hand in class. I was afraid of giving a wrong answer and exposing my mistake to others — early signs of my shaky self-confidence. I never liked to draw attention to myself.

One event in eighth grade played a profound role in moving me beyond my comfort zone. We had changed churches when I was nine and were now attending High View Church of God. Our church sponsored a weeklong mission trip to a Navajo reservation in New Mexico, and I felt prompted by the Holy Spirit to sign up. The night before we left, I had knots in my stomach. At fourteen years old, I'd never been away from home without my parents before. But my mom soothed me, my dad encouraged me, and I knew I couldn't pull out of the commitment I'd made.

Once there, I felt extraordinary fulfillment in being used by God, and I saw myself in a new light — a bit more capable of speaking up and contributing positively to the lives of others than I'd imagined myself to be. At night, however, I was hit by waves of missing my parents, and more than once that week I was so homesick I wept.

I stepped into high school academically eager but socially reticent, joking at times that if we had labels under our names in the yearbook, mine would read "most likely to be forgotten." I just wanted to blend in, believing it far better to be invisible than to be embarrassed by some awkward words or actions. In my own estimation, I was timid, insignificant, and incapable of meaningful creative expression. There was so much about myself I hadn't yet discovered.

Being a nurturer by nature, I babysat for several families in our neighborhood and provided child care at a local resort that primarily catered to tourists in the summer months. Caring for children came naturally and brought me real joy, so much so that I began to dream of the day I would be a wife and mother. I also began teaching Sunday school. Yet even there I wrestled with feelings of inadequacy, hoping I would not make some mistake or call attention to myself only to disappoint someone by my subpar performance.

There was, however, one place where I felt confident and sure of my abilities — in my father's milk truck. The heavy demands of the Saturday hauling were so significant that my dad and the other company truckers could not handle all the pickups themselves. While my dad had several cousins with the commercial drivers' licenses required to drive the truck, they didn't have the weigher-and-sampler license necessary to load the milk. Plus, they were unfamiliar with the locations of the farms on each route.

Seeing an opportunity to contribute, I studied and took the test for a weigher-and-sampler license to help with the family business. I passed on my first try! Thereafter, I rode along with the cousins — they drove the trucks, and I did the rest. The routine I'd watched as a child from the cab — my dad unloading the hose from the back of the trailer, hooking it up to the farmer's milk tank, measuring and converting the reading into pounds, sampling the milk, then disconnecting the hose, putting it away, and washing down the milk tank — was now my routine. I loved everything about this piece of my heritage; it was exciting to become a vital part of what I had enjoyed watching my dad do when I was a child.

When I turned sixteen, I wanted to buy a car. So I found a job at the Maplehoffe Dairy Store near my school and worked there a few evenings a week. I saved my money and bought a bright yellow used car as old as I was. It wasn't pretty or fancy, but it was mine, and I felt the satisfaction of knowing I'd worked hard for it.

By my junior year of high school, I'd found my comfort zone in my small group of friends at school and moved with ease among my church friends. I sang in the church choir, taught Sunday school, and enjoyed my coworkers at the dairy. And of course, I loved my Saturday job of working in the family business.

Then my comfort zone was unexpectedly invaded in a way that delighted and excited me. A woman from church invited a few others and me to her home for dinner. Seated at the table was her grandson, Charlie Roberts. I'd seen Charlie at church but had never talked to him. It was a casual evening with easy laughter, and I enjoyed getting to know Charlie. He was quiet but friendly and seemed a bit shy, a feeling I fully understood. The limited conversation between us felt comfortable and pleasant.

When dinner was over and I was preparing to leave, Charlie asked, "Mind if I walk you to your car?"

Taken by surprise, I felt myself blush. By this time I had saved up a bit more money and bought a gray Chevrolet S-10 pickup truck. I was relieved that I wouldn't have to explain my old yellow clunker!

"Did you buy it yourself?" he asked, circling it and nodding with approval.

"Yes. It took me awhile to save up." I opened the door but didn't want to climb in and end the chance for conversation.

"It was really nice to meet you tonight, Marie. Would you like to go on a date with me on Saturday night?"

I'm sure my eyes got as big as saucers. My eyes met his. He was smiling shyly. I could hardly believe it. My very first date!

I said yes and drove home with stars in my eyes.

5

the promise

As far back as I can remember I had dreamed of being a wife and mother. Of course, there was that time in kindergarten when I aspired to be an astronaut (stirred, no doubt, by my time swinging toward the heavens on my swing set), but that was short-lived. My heart longed to sow love into children, and I dreamed of the day when my husband and I would have our own. I always assumed that I would meet a good man, fall in love, and get married, all in a seamless journey of sweet love.

That is exactly what I did. Charlie was my first date and my first love. He was an "older man" by four years. I was in eleventh grade at our first meeting across his grandmother's dinner table; he had already graduated and was working at a local home construction company. Though I can't say it was love at first sight, it was a friendship that developed smoothly over time, growing from friendship to love within just a few seasons.

Charlie's early years had been spent in a small neighborhood near Lancaster. He'd moved as a teen to the countryside just south of Strasburg, a ten-minute drive from Georgetown. There his family lived next door to his grandparents, and they became acquainted with the beauty of Amish life. The Robertses had many Amish neighbors, including the girls from the Stoltzfoos farm down the street, who would ring their doorbell selling eggs, fruits, and vegetables during the summer months. Even if you didn't need more asparagus, how could you say no to their sweet faces?

Charlie fit in easily with my family. My dad recognized him as trustworthy, kind, and a hard worker. Although quiet and reserved initially, Charlie was soon comfortable talking with my family, laughing at stories about our family milk-hauling business, easing naturally from suitor to family member as our relationship deepened. He enjoyed evenings together with my family and liked being included when we'd all bake chocolate chip cookies together and play board games.

The son of a policeman, Charlie and his family reflected many of the same deeply held values as my own family. He was respectful, had grown up in a Christian home, loved God, attended church, and valued being a responsible citizen of our community. He had three younger brothers and no sisters, so Charlie related easily to my dad and brother, while also enjoying the tasty treats from all the "girly" baking at our house.

One of the reasons I fell in love with Charlie was the tenderhearted way he treated his cousins. He had a large, close-knit extended family so I often saw him playing with the kids and showing sensitivity toward the ones who lingered on the outside of the group. I admired his encouraging spirit and the way he loved and included outsiders. Watching him connect with children in this way prompted me to imagine how he would be as a dad. What games would he play with our kids? What memories would he make with them?

I think my family first realized how serious we were getting when, the Thanksgiving of my junior year, Charlie went on a hunting trip with his dad. Charlie knew we wouldn't have much communication while he was at the hunting cabin, and the thought of going an entire holiday weekend without talking with one another seemed too much to bear. This was before cell phones, of course. So before heading out of town, Charlie collected tons of change. Each evening, he deposited coins in the pay phone in the lodge at the hunting camp, and we talked for hours, with the operator joining us periodically with instructions to insert more coins. My family teased me mercilessly, claiming that he must have taken wheelbarrows full of nickels. I basked in the glow of feeling so special.

Because of the long hours my dad worked, he often couldn't make it home for dinner, so my mom would fill a plate for him, cover it, and set it in the refrigerator. Soon Charlie was so comfortable in our home that he'd raid the refrigerator and help himself to Dad's plate. Mom didn't mind a bit. She loved making Charlie feel at home, so she would gladly fix another plate for Dad.

One thing, however, was clear to me from the beginning — Charlie lacked self-confidence, a struggle I knew all too well myself. I enjoyed encouraging him to recognize his own talent and potential. The evidence of his growth in confidence through my love had a positive effect on me as well.

Then came a glorious mid-October day for which Charlie had planned a picnic at a park in Lancaster. We met there after work. By this time I had left my job at the dairy store and worked after school as an assistant in the human resources department of a local healthcare company.

"So what's in the basket?" I asked, eager to see how he had

managed in preparing dinner. I don't know that he had ever packed a picnic basket before, but he'd insisted on packing tonight's dinner for some reason.

He neatly spread the picnic blanket, then began unpacking each item. "We have deli sandwiches, fresh fruit salad, deviled eggs, and some delicious chocolate chip cookies." He announced each like a waiter presenting a five-course gourmet dinner. He arranged utensils, napkins, cups, and dessert plates with a flourish.

"You thought of everything!" I said.

"And this surprises you?" he teased. He had me there, but I made up for it by declaring everything I tasted to be delicious.

After dinner we spent hours walking, talking, laughing, and sharing in the beauty of the evening. As the sun began to set, he led me from the path we'd been walking back to our picnic blanket. To my astonishment, he dropped to one knee and gently took my hand.

"Marie, I love you with my whole heart. Will you marry me?"

Hopes and dreams rushed over me, flooding my senses as everything I'd envisioned came one step closer to reality.

"Yes, Charlie, I will," I said in quiet gentleness, certain that our promises would abide forever. Deep in my heart, I was convinced that we would have a wonderful marriage. I wasn't naive enough to believe that troubles would never touch us, but for me, this promise meant that my decisions and responses to life, no matter what the future held, would reflect my devotion to this union first and to my individuality second.

I was still in my senior year of high school. Charlie, ever the gentleman, had asked my dad for permission to marry me, assuring him that we would wait to marry until the fall after I graduated. My parents had seen this day coming and had already talked about it.

"Of course, I said yes," Dad told me later that evening, describing how nervous Charlie had been when he'd asked for my hand in marriage. "But my answer may have been a little slow in coming. After all, I wanted Charlie to squirm a bit." Dad had mischief in his eyes. I enjoyed seeing how much my dad and Charlie liked one another.

We set the date for November 9, 1996, allowing us plenty of time to plan. Charlie had been working hard and saving his money since high school and was eager to buy a house. In the spring of '96, we found the perfect little house in Lititz (about forty-five minutes north of Georgetown). It needed lots of tender loving care, so neither of us moved in. I graduated in June, began working full-time with the healthcare company, and we began spending our summer evenings and weekends fixing up the house — peeling wallpaper, painting, cleaning. It was a magical time. Not only was I preparing for our wedding day, I was also preparing the house that would become our home. As we carefully selected the colors of paint, we envisioned what this masterpiece of our future might look like.

With each step closer to the wedding day, our sense of commitment deepened. I was a girl in love, and the future sparkled with endless possibilities.

We chose two words to be etched inside our wedding bands to stand as a reminder of the choice we had made — *Our Promise.* We embraced the pledge of unity in our home church, High View Church of God, declaring honor and preference to one another, vowing lives led by love regardless of the roads we would travel. My childhood dreams had become reality. I had a wonderful husband who loved me and who shared my devotion to God and vision for life.

We stepped out of our little red-brick church as husband and wife — without a clue of how quickly a shadow would fall over our lives, bringing us back to this very spot with hearts ripped wide open in pain rather than bursting with joy.

A most unexpected change occurred within me in the wake of our wedding vows — a dramatic deepening of my spiritual life. The act of standing before my heavenly Father and declaring a lifelong promise stirred my sense of eternity and my connection to the God who had made me and given me such a gift. Not that my relationship with God hadn't already been important to me; it had been since childhood. But the act of making a covenant with God to be a wife to Charlie for the rest of my life was so profoundly life altering, such a rite of passage, that my eyes were opened to spiritual truths in a richer sense.

My prayer life became more vibrant. Scripture passages took on deeper meaning. The beauty of the world around me spoke to me of the love of God lavished upon our lives. The ring on my finger, a circle without end, became a visible symbol of my unseen covenant, a daily reminder to embrace the choice of selfless love. Only death could part our hearts, and, of course, I assumed that death would not come for many decades.

This choice became the measuring stick by which I judged my life: Was I living in a way that reinforced our oneness? I was learning to be a loving wife rather than a high school student, and I quickly realized how huge a leap I'd made. The desire to honor God and my husband forced me to recognize and lay aside selfish attitudes for the betterment of our marriage. I was discovering something exquisitely beautiful about the selfless love shared between husband and wife. This one-on-one demonstration of preferring another helped me understand the heart of my heavenly Father in a whole new way. The experience of being loved unconditionally, deeply, tangibly, made Jesus more real and deepened my appreciation of God's promise of eternal life in perfect communion with him.

I was full of joyful anticipation! I longed to find out what the future held — never imagining that a hurricane was starting to spin off the shores of our otherwise picturesque horizon.

Within months of saying our wedding vows, my childhood dream for children of my own was deepening. Charlie too was eager to start our family. Around Father's Day in June of 1997, we announced our pregnancy, with a due date in February 1998. Many in our immediate circle — neighbors, family members, friends from church, and coworkers — were also expecting. It seemed to me that everywhere we looked there were precious babies growing! If I thought the beginning of my marriage represented early strokes on the canvas of a masterpiece, there was almost no way to describe the significance of what was growing in my heart now.

Pregnancy was a time of wonder for both of us. Hopes stirred for our child.

"I wonder who he will grow up to be," Charlie said one night, patting my bulging tummy as he crawled into bed.

"Will *she* have my hair and your eyes?" I teasingly countered.

He cupped my chin in his hand and lifted my face toward his. "I hope *she* has your heart," he whispered, catching me by surprise with his tenderness. He kissed me softly.

Everything that my heart beat for was becoming reality. I was living my dream! God was answering my prayers and empowering me to live out my destiny. During this season, I found myself contemplating God and yearning to know him in a whole new way. The Creator of the universe was creating something inside *me*. How miraculous! He was orchestrating this work I could not see, and his love was being deposited into my heart.

While there were many exciting markers along my path toward childbirth, like setting up the nursery and receiving baby clothes, I was especially drawn to the importance of selecting a name. If you look at the Old Testament, you'll see that the meaning of a child's name often ended up reflecting exactly who they turned out to be — for good or bad. So as Charlie and I compared names we liked, I researched their meanings. We decided to give each of our children a middle name from someone in our family, a perfect way to honor our family heritage and carry that legacy into the future.

I felt pretty sure I was carrying a girl, and the ultrasound confirmed it. As we chose to name our unborn child Elise Victoria — Elise meaning "pledged to God" and Victoria after my sister, meaning "victorious" — we felt one step closer to the reality of holding her. Everything was going just as it should. I was healthy; our baby was growing. It felt like perfection.

I soon discovered the special bond among women when it comes to the experience of pregnancy — a knowing nod from a woman who has been there, a shared laugh as we ask questions of one another that we'd never known to ask before our bodies began to change so drastically. I was enjoying sharing every aspect of this journey, not only with my mom, but also with some friends at church. That is when it first occurred to me: Where were Charlie's friends?

When Charlie and I began to date, he, like most men I knew,

didn't have a large group of friends, just a couple of solid relationships with guys he trusted. As our life had shifted toward marriage and his friends remained single, those friendships fell away. The activities they'd previously shared as singles weren't as appealing to Charlie as a newlywed. Now that he was going to be a father, where were the friends with whom he could share this experience?

"Sure, sometimes I miss my old friends," Charlie said when I asked him about it. "Maybe I should give a few of the guys a call one weekend." Though he spoke about rekindling the fading connections, he never actually sought out or replaced those relationships. At the time, it didn't seem like a big deal. But looking back, I can see that his lack of deep, meaningful relationships became detrimental later. He had no "brother" to lean on, no shoulder to cry on, and no one to confide in, aside from me. Only years later would I discover the disastrous consequences of this choice.

At the time, since it wasn't worrying Charlie, I decided it shouldn't worry me. After all, it was common for friendships to come and go throughout the years. Young and living in our idealistic little world, we both assumed that we'd quickly establish new relationships with other couples with children.

I took some comfort in knowing that Charlie greatly enjoyed his construction work and seemed to enjoy the guys on the crew. Though he never socialized with them outside of work, he'd fill me in on the events of his days and the lives of his coworkers.

Charlie also started talking about his interest in becoming a milk hauler like my dad. Secretly, I'd cringe. I would change the subject of conversation. I'd grown up with my dad often working seventy to eighty hours a week, over holidays and weekends. I didn't want the same for my new family.

In late September (right around twenty weeks of pregnancy), life took a frightening turn.

"Charlie!" I called early one morning from the bathroom. "Something's wrong!"

Hearing the panic in my voice, he instantly leaped out of bed and came running. "What's wrong?" he asked, clearly alarmed. "Are you okay?"

"I'm bleeding. Not a lot, but some. Something's wrong." Afraid, I started to cry.

Charlie stayed calm. In a comforting voice, he said, "Marie, you're going to be fine. Don't panic. Let's get you into bed and call the doctor."

We saw our obstetrician that day, who sent me for testing. The tests couldn't determine the cause of the bleeding, so I was put on bed rest until the bleeding stopped or the baby was born. I had to stop working — in fact, I felt I had no connection to the outside world. It was a frightening time for both of us. Although I showed no signs of being in labor, there was a risk that our daughter could be born prematurely. I followed the doctor's recommendation and confined myself to the bed or the couch. Charlie hovered over me when he was home, driven to serve me and make me comfortable.

My desperation for the Lord grew fierce during this time. I needed him to protect our child, to protect me, and to guard our family. I pressed into the Word and into my knowledge of him in a new way. I needed to understand: Why were we going through this terrifying experience? I cried out for healing, desperate for a miracle from Jesus like those mentioned throughout the Gospels. Just one touch could restore me, and I longed for that touch!

With little else to do while confined to my bed for weeks, I read and prayed. Sometimes I felt the Lord still my heart and bring peace to my fears. But that peace would be short-lived, because worry would begin to erode the work he was doing. I'd never been tested by personal crisis. I didn't know how to trust that everything would be okay when appearances told me otherwise. His Word told me to fear not and to cast all my anxiety on him, but I didn't get how it was possible to live out the reality of those Scriptures in my moment of crisis. Was God going to fix this? Not knowing the answer, I did everything in my power to fix it myself, as I always had. I followed the doctor's instructions to the letter, but the bleeding got no better. It came and went and came again, no matter how I prayed.

Charlie was at work from 6:30 in the morning until 5:00 in the afternoon. During those long hours alone, I battled the what-ifs swirling in my mind. What if the baby dies? What if I hemorrhage? What if there's something wrong with my baby? What is wrong with me? Then I'd read Scripture and cry out to God to heal whatever was wrong.

Ever so slowly, God began to show me a new kind of trust. One verse in particular whispered peace into my heart: "I sought the Lord, and he answered me; he delivered me from all my fears. Those who look to him are radiant; their faces are never covered with shame" (Psalm 34:4–5).

By my standards, it didn't feel as if I was getting it right—still, I sensed him tenderly leading my heart and encouraging me to grow in trust *despite* my circumstances. Sometimes it felt like one step forward and two steps back, but I clung to verses of Scripture promising that he was faithful to me even when I lacked faith.

Although the bleeding didn't stop, no other symptoms emerged, so we settled into this new and difficult routine as much as possible, holding on to the hope that Elise would be born at full term.

Charlie and I celebrated our first anniversary on November 9, 1997. Five days later I went into labor three months premature.

I awoke that day feeling sick. I didn't know what labor should feel like, but I was sure this was it. With a feeling of dread, knowing our baby girl wasn't yet developed enough to enter this world, we called our doctor and headed to the hospital in Lancaster at the peak of morning rush hour. We inched along at what felt like a crawl. We tried to reassure ourselves that Elise would not be born that morning. Certainly, we told each other, the doctors could do something to stop this.

At the hospital, they didn't seem to believe me at first when I said I was in labor. But when they finally realized that I knew the truth of what was going on in my body, nurses and doctors started scrambling, and my whole world came crashing down. My daughter was indeed going to be born that morning, and very soon. There was nothing they could do to stop the labor, so they started prepping for delivery and called in the neonatal intensive care unit team. Within minutes Elise Victoria made her appearance — so tiny, so fragile, and so beautiful. She was born at 8:25 a.m., 12¼ inches and 1 lb. 3 oz. The doctors from the NICU immediately went to work trying to place a tube into her lungs, as she was too small to breathe on her own. Each of their attempts proved unsuccessful.

Elise lived for twenty minutes, passing from my arms to the embrace of heaven in mere moments. My brain could not compute that an hour and a half earlier, this whole nightmare was just starting and my daughter was alive within me, her life still a possibility. Now she was gone, my womb was empty, our hearts were broken, and our dreams were shattered.

Our immediate family didn't even know yet that I had gone

into labor. Everything had happened so fast that morning that we hadn't had time to call. Charlie and I were alone. I asked him to call our parents, as I couldn't bear the thought of telling them. I was still holding Elise, knowing that the nurses were going to take her soon. I didn't want to lose one second of precious time with her, because these moments were going to have to hold me until our reunion in heaven. It was going to be a long wait — a whole lifetime.

I can only imagine how difficult that call was for Charlie. As he sat nearby, calling his parents, I could hear his mom sobbing over the phone, her cry piercing the air. Parents have an instinctual desire to love and protect their children, even when those children are adults, and I know our parents grieved to see our pain. As for Charlie and me, to lose Elise made us feel that we had failed to protect our daughter. We knew, logically, that we'd done all we could, but logic couldn't dispel the emotions that flooded us.

Our parents came to the hospital and tried to comfort us. The hospital staff asked about funeral arrangements and other decisions, but I couldn't think. Thankfully, my mom came alongside Charlie, and the two of them took over, deciding to have a private funeral service and burial. I wasn't even twenty years old — what did I know about such things? My progression into adulthood had been jolted in a way I had never anticipated. This beautiful canvas, this masterpiece we'd been creating, was covered in black paint, the beautiful brushstrokes completely hidden by loss and devastation.

We spent one night at the hospital, in the postpartum unit. It was torture. Emanating from the hallway outside my door were the cries of newborn babies and the congratulations of family members filled with exclamations of happiness. But the air in our room was different. It felt devoid of life, dark, and hopeless. The hospital staff kept us at the quiet end of a hallway, but nevertheless we heard it all, and it inflicted agony on a level neither Charlie nor I had ever known before.

We wept openly, trying to comfort one another not with words, but with a tender stroke, the squeeze of a hand, the wiping of a tear. Charlie was so gentle, so vigilant over my care. I could see how badly he wished he could have spared me this grief, yet how helpless he felt to take away my suffering, physical as well as emotional.

There was one moment, however, when a beam of light from heaven broke through my darkness — in the form of my nurse. She was with us that whole day, and during her shift she spent a lot of time in my room. I was touched by her tenderness.

Though not scheduled to work the following day, she came to see me anyway, before I left the hospital. "Marie, I brought something for you," she said, gently handing me a small box. I opened it to find a necklace with a charm: an angel holding a topaz gem. "It's the November birthstone," she explained softly. The gem caught the light and sparkled.

"Elise's birthstone," I whispered, fresh tears spilling over. "It's beautiful. Thank you so much." She fluffed my pillow and tucked the white hospital blanket securely around my legs.

Her small gift spoke volumes of love. It offered me the freedom to celebrate my child, Elise Victoria, in the midst of mourning my loss. It was like a tangible kiss of Jesus, speaking something that I could not articulate. God's light in my darkness.

6

the canvas

It felt like a lifetime since Charlie's desperate call that morning. The afternoon light had faded, and dusk would soon begin to settle in. We had been at my parents' home for about seven hours, huddled together in hiding, trying to absorb the shock of this day.

I got up off the couch, where Bryce had been sitting by my side, and wandered into the kitchen just to stretch my legs and see what Dad was up to. I found him leaning back against the kitchen counter, gazing out the window where I'd stood to watch the Amish men approach a few hours before. He looked like I felt — weary and weighed down.

Typically, we'd be hearing the clippity-clop of an occasional horse and buggy or the droning engine of a car in the early evening, but all I could hear was the unnatural silence. I followed Dad's gaze, wondering if he was thinking what I was: that the buggies were probably all gathered at a few Amish farmhouses filled with grieving families and frightened children coping with the assault on their community this morning at the hand of my husband. My stomach lurched, and for a moment it was hard to breathe, but I forced a few shallow breaths. I moved closer to Dad and laid my head on his shoulder. He put his arm around me.

"How is it possible that just this morning it was a typical Monday, with me leading a Moms In Touch prayer meeting at church, praying, of all things, for the well-being of our children at school?" I wasn't really looking for an answer, just still trying to absorb my new reality. I didn't give voice to the rest of the question rattling in my head: ... *while my own husband was carrying out his plan to murder the children of our neighbors?* I shook my head as if trying to clear it of some horrible nightmare. But this was no dream.

Dad made no attempt to answer the unanswerable. He squeezed my shoulder, then led me through the kitchen door and down the few steps into the ground-level family room on the back of their little one-story house.

My mom was reading a book to my children on the couch. They were snuggled in close and looked tired. I looked at the clock — almost bedtime. I needed to get my children to bed soon. They needed normalcy, or at least as close to it as possible, and a night's sleep would at least put an end to this horrendous day. In spite of the fact that I felt weary to the bone, I couldn't fathom even the possibility of rest.

Earlier in the day, we'd all agreed that the children and I couldn't stay here at Mom and Dad's. Aunt Linda had stepped in and offered the perfect solution. "Marie, Uncle Jim and I would like you, the kids, and your parents to come to our place and stay as long as you need to. You know we have the room. I've been on the phone with our closest neighbors; we've known them for years and completely trust them. They've sworn themselves to secrecy. You'll have peace and rest there. One of our neighbors even offered the use of his garage to keep your car out of sight. Others volunteered to bring meals and treats for the kids. Do you remember the little park down the street? Jim and your dad can take the kids there to play, and no one will know who they are." She'd thought of everything. I was stunned by her generosity and grateful for a hiding place.

The media knew our present location. We couldn't even step outside without the fear of being watched. We knew from friends' calls to my brother, uncles, and aunts on their cell phones that television networks were giving constant live updates, running and rerunning footage of the schoolhouse and the Amish, weeping and praying. Reporters from everywhere were all over our tiny town, in a frenzy to capture the Amish and us on film, phone, or any way they could, with our cooperation or without it. They were canvassing neighborhoods and businesses, asking questions about our family. Bart Fire Hall, literally a few doors away from where we were hiding, had become the impromptu central gathering spot for the live television updates. Our nightmare was their news story. We needed privacy, a safe place somewhere "secret" where we could grieve, breathe, heal, and just be.

I wondered what my Amish neighbors were doing to cope with this media invasion. A surge of guilt jolted through me for thinking of myself when, surely, their pain was much heavier than mine. They lived apart from our society by intention. I could not fathom how violated they must feel to be so hounded at this time of unspeakable grief. The Amish object to having their pictures taken based on their understanding of the second commandment, Exodus 20:4 (KJV): "Thou shalt not make unto thee any graven image, or any likeness of any thing that is in heaven above, or that is in the earth beneath, or that is in the water under the earth." My entire life I'd seen them tolerate tourists who would knowingly disregard this preference just to satisfy their desire for a photo. Now their pictures were being taken incessantly at the most horrific time in their lives. If my family felt like hiding, how much more violated must they be feeling?

Aunt Linda's had been my place of healing from a loss long ago. She and Uncle Jim lived in the town of Lititz, not too far from the first house Charlie and I had bought nearly ten years before. No media. A quiet, secluded neighborhood. Yes, how perfect.

We waited until after sunset to leave my parents' home. I helped Abigail and Bryce into the car while Mom buckled Carson into his car seat. I drove, Dad sat beside me in the passenger seat, Mom followed in her car. That's just me; I didn't want someone to do things for me that I could handle on my own. I was determined to not become paralyzed, to not become a victim. My children had only one parent left, and they needed that parent to be strong and steady, no matter what I felt on the inside.

It felt surreal, sneaking out under cover of darkness. Wasn't this the kind of scene you'd see in a movie? How could this be real? As we passed, Dad nodded to the policeman who'd been parked at the end of our street all afternoon to keep reporters away. Rather than turn right out the drive and onto the main road, we turned left and took back roads through the farmlands to avoid being followed. I checked my rearview mirror for media vans with satellite dishes but saw none.

As we rode in the blackness of night, I felt my fears returning. It felt as if the ground had opened up, revealing an abyss the size of the Grand Canyon. The bold confidence I'd been given by the

Lord this morning seemed to have evaporated. Devastation outside my control had forever changed the landscape of my world. I faced an immense chasm — no bridge could span it, yet there was no way to turn back. I had no choice but to face the other side of my life, a side filled with unfamiliar territory and frightening challenges.

I reached for God in the darkness and offered him my thoughts, asking him to chase out the lies with his truth. A calm began to spread back over me. Never had I experienced such dramatic, instant answers to prayer as I had this day. I felt a flush of supernatural warmth. Even though many things had abruptly changed, some things remained constant, God reminded me. I was still a beloved child of God. I was still dedicated to being the best mom possible. I could still trust the Holy Spirit to help me accomplish what I could not do in my own strength. I would find a way back to "normal," even though our new circumstances were anything but.

As we stepped into Linda and Jim's home, they welcomed us with open arms. The love in their eyes shone like bright lights compared to the darkness I'd just driven through. Memories associated with this place called to me immediately. My great-grandmother at the piano, playing and singing Christmas carols, slumber parties with my cousin, and family picnics in the summer. *This home holds the celebration of life*, I reassured myself. *God has prepared this place for us.*

Everywhere I looked, the love of life looked back. It could be seen in the careful mix of antiques and reproduction art, treasures both gathered and created. Elegance and beauty lifted my heart and encouraged my spirit. Linda lives and breathes with effortless expression. Theorem paintings adorn her walls, marked with her signature. The comforting fragrance of linseed oil, an aroma that speaks of a home well cared for, welcomed me.

In a flash I was flooded with memories of my healing time here after Elise's death nine years before. *Each room holds a story all its own,* I thought. *I stand taller here, walking with a grace inspired by Aunt Linda. She challenges me to think in new ways. She knows herself, displays her style — confidence surrounds me here and penetrates my skin. Yes, God prepared this place for us, for this time. His light is shining here.*

I watched my children absorbing their new surroundings. Abigail's eyes were wide and soulful as she looked at the paintings and antiques. Bryce, still unusually quiet, poured himself into a chair and scanned the room. Carson, however, tried to bury himself in my mom's arms, as if trying to "turtle up" and pull his head into his shell. He was the picture of what I felt I needed at the moment. *God's arms, warm and strong, will hold us securely here,* I thought. *I don't know how long we will stay. I don't need to know. For now, this will be a shelter from the storm.*

Uncle Jim, his usual smile now replaced with compassionate grief, spoke with softness to my children. "How about a glass of milk and a snack?" he offered, leading them into the kitchen. "Some nice neighbors brought cookies just for you."

I remembered how he had encouraged me, at age eight, to play the piano for him when my parents realized that music spoke to my soul and had invested in a piano and lessons. I'd felt too shy to play for Uncle Jim at first, and while it took some coaxing, he didn't give up. He praised and encouraged me until I played with greater confidence. Even as a child I knew that his kindness would last for more than a moment, and Uncle Jim took a special place in my heart. Where Linda brought creativity and new adventures,

Jim added strength and stability. It was a powerful combination that my own children would now enjoy, just when they needed it.

I don't recall much of that evening, but I do remember that I didn't resist when Linda insisted that the children and I take their master bedroom. I followed her up the stairs and into the room. It looked like a spread out of a magazine of a posh hotel. The cherry-wood four-poster king bed sat high off the floor, the mattress thick and inviting. I turned down the plush comforter and ran my hands across sheets that were obviously of a higher quality than anything I'd ever felt before. *Is this what Egyptian cotton feels like?* Downy pillows lined the headboard, at least two for each of us with some left over. They beckoned us to rest, promising softness and comfort after a day bathed in hardship.

"This is just like spending the night in a fancy hotel," I told the kids, trying to ease them into some semblance of their nighttime routine. "Let's skip baths tonight and just change into our jammies and brush our teeth." I pulled their pajamas out of a bag and laid them out on the bed, then found our toothbrushes stuffed into a pocket of one my duffel bags and sent Bryce and Abigail off to the bathroom. I lifted Carson up onto the high bed to get him changed.

"Fluffy!" he declared. Bryce came trotting back into the room and climbed up next to his little brother. Abigail came to my side and just leaned against me, watching her brothers, but no smile on her face.

"Where are you going to sleep, Mommy?" she asked.

"I think we should all sleep together this week. Does that sound good to you?" I stroked her hair as I answered, aching to find some way to soothe her soul. She nodded and pressed herself into me. Her demeanor was so somber and quiet—like mine, I suddenly realized. Given our day, we ought to both be sobbing and wailing inconsolably, showing the external evidence of the sorrow of the day. Instead, we were both very controlled, as if our energy and voices had been dialed back to "low" as we went through the motions of changing for bed.

Abigail crawled onto the bed, and she and Bryce nestled between the layers of crisp sheets and soft blankets. It seemed as if all three of my children were trying to be extra good, looking for ways to bring a sense of peace to our shattered world. Moonlight filtered through the curtains, nature's attempt to diffuse the darkness around us with light. I laid Carson in the portable crib in an alcove under the window. He chewed his pacifier and snuggled with his favorite soft puppy dog. The events of the day did not disturb his ability to find rest—I wished it would be the same for me.

I crawled between Abigail and Bryce, pulling them in close to me, attempting to surround and cover them in love and peace. I prayed aloud over our family and began to sing the songs they loved. Simple lullabies, familiar phrases, ordinary elements in a strange new world. I didn't know if it brought comfort to their hearts, but it settled mine. They drifted off to sleep easily, while I lay awake in ominous silence. I had not expected sleep to be effortless for them. I listened to their rhythmic breathing, first Abigail, then Bryce, and then Carson. The cadence spoke deeply to my weary heart, infusing me with purpose.

I cried out to the God who had met me in my living room, who had promised light beyond this darkness: *You know I don't pray big prayers, Lord. You know that I'd rather do what I can on my own, but I can't do this. I'm desperate for you. There is nothing I can do without you. I know that your Word says you take care of the orphan and the widow, and I know you have seen the deposits of faithfulness we've made throughout past years. I know you will honor them. I'm asking you to do something really big, beyond anything I could imagine, and I am asking you to start right now.*

I lay in silence. When I heard faint sounds of clinking in the kitchen, I imagined cups of tea, warm and comforting, enjoyed in close, loving company. I was not alone. The softness of feet moving up or down the stairs outside our bedroom felt peaceful. Mom and Dad were in the room right next to mine; Linda and Jim were settling into their own guest room. I was not alone. As I lay awake listening to the sounds around me — water running in the bathroom, doors closing, good-night whisperings — my heart smiled. I was not alone. Inside, the voice of God stilled my questions and calmed my fears; outside, my family surrounded me. I was not alone.

The night went on. And on and on and on. I tried not to watch the clock, but it kept drawing my eyes as if taunting me that this night would never end. When it seemed as though evil lurked in the shadows and my solitude in the long, still night was magnified, I prayed for God to fill the minutes with his presence. Though sleep eluded me much of the night, I did find some rest and peace within the arms of Jesus, cradled deeply in a cozy bed, surrounded by the most priceless gifts I'd ever been given — my children.

When morning light first began to dance across the room, I forgot for just one moment where I was and the circumstances surrounding our stay, but as reality dawned on me, I was at least relieved I had survived the long night.

The bedroom was even more beautiful in the daylight. Botanical prints hung on the walls; tasteful decorations and antiques graced the room. My senses took in the stark contrasts of my life—horror threatened me but beauty overtook me. This room gave hope: Did it mean that God saw detailed beauty yet to come, and he was asking me to trust him within the mess and walk with him through the pain?

I didn't want to embrace this day. I wanted to stay in this bedroom, sheltered from the outside world and its threatening presence. In truth, I didn't want to "do" any of this. I didn't want to see the devastation on the faces of those around me. I didn't want to answer a million probing questions from the detectives. And I didn't want to make the decisions for the week's details that loomed over me. This shouldn't have happened, and I didn't want it.

I had spent the first twenty-eight years of my life keenly aware of others' thoughts toward me. I always aimed to please. When clothes were given to me, I wore them, even when I didn't like the color or style, because I didn't want to hurt anyone's feelings. I did my best in school, on the job, and at home because those around me deserved the best I had to offer, and I didn't want to disappoint them. I tried hard to follow all the rules because, to me, correction of any kind was a mark of failure. I didn't raise my hand in class even if I was 99 percent sure I knew the answer, because there was that 1 percent chance I could be wrong. I always erred on the side of perfectionism.

Suddenly the whole world thought things about me that I couldn't do a thing about. Just as suddenly, I realized with a shock, I didn't care!

In one day, my sensitivity to others' opinions had shifted dramatically. The only opinion that mattered now was God's; my Father's voice was the one that counted. I was free from worries of disappointing others and from thoughts of potential failure. And the reasons for this were completely practical: The world would draw its own conclusions no matter what I said or did. I couldn't control what they thought. I could control only the choices I would make for my family. God believed in me enough that he allowed me to be Charlie's wife, even though he knew that these circumstances would arise and threaten to destroy everything I held dear. He allowed me to walk the road that led me here anyway. He was confident that I would make the right choices and find healing, for myself and for my children. What I was feeling now wasn't pressure to perform; just the opposite — it was freedom to simply be myself.

Now, as in my living room the previous morning after I called 911, I felt invaded by a confidence I'd never before experienced: a newfound strength of spirit, mind, and body. In walking through the fire of those first twenty-four hours, something had happened inside of me. Everything that truly didn't matter had been burned away. What remained was stronger because of this refining fire — *I* was stronger! I felt transformed.

I still didn't *want* to handle the meetings I knew lay ahead, to make the decisions, to keep talking about the details with my wounded children. But miraculously, I wasn't *afraid* to do those things. I knew I was capable of walking through all the circumstances awaiting me, but it meant that I must continue to trust God, believing he was infusing me with wisdom, and take one step at a time. I would step out into the day and face whatever needed facing. I was not alone.

When I climb out of this bed, I'll be stepping into a spotlight on center stage, with the whole world watching, I told myself. *God, go before me and beside me.*

I rose quietly so as not to disturb my children, still sleeping, peaceful expressions on their faces. I looked at my face in the bathroom mirror. *So this is what a widow looks like.* I began to get ready, just as I had done every morning before — wash my face, apply makeup, straighten my otherwise curly hair. There were still some private moments, moments for just me. I still retained some control over my life.

With a strong sense of the truly miraculous presence of God, I stepped to the door, stood quietly for a moment, then grabbed the handle and turned — and stepped onto center stage.

Downstairs, I found my aunt in the kitchen. "Want a cup of coffee, Toots?" she greeted me, using the slang term of endearment she often used. A nice beginning. The mug warmed my hands as I stood at her large kitchen island and watched her empty the dishwasher. White cream blended with the amber liquid. It tasted as it always did. Maybe not *everything* had changed. I sat in the familiar high-backed chair in the sun-drenched seating area just off the kitchen, one wall a bank of windows overlooking the garden, the adjacent wall an exquisite arrangement of theorem paintings and original folk art. The physical world around me had not changed. Though my life had been drastically altered, it somehow still fit within a time and space that was as ordinary as last week.

I am with you, my Lord whispered to my soul. *Watch for me. I have you surrounded.*

I was filled with an acute awareness of his presence. The warmth of the mug. The love in Aunt Linda's voice. The beauty of the art. The backyard looked like a pristinely manicured garden from an *Outdoor Living* magazine, flowers still blooming, even butterflies dancing in front of the window on another Indian-summer, October day. Trees ablaze with color declared the ability for life and death to coexist in this moment of time. We belonged to the God who ruled *over* life and death.

"Do you know one of my favorite memories of your place, from my childhood?" I asked Linda. She stopped puttering around the kitchen and took a seat in the wingback chair across from me, her back to the window showcasing her garden. She was literally framed with the life of the garden. All of this was a gift—an extravagant gift given in the midst of losing all I'd ever known.

"Our *Pollyanna* night?" she guessed immediately.

"Yes! How did you know? What was I—maybe seven or eight? And you invited me and a few of Laura's friends to Laura's birthday party." Laura was my cousin, Linda's daughter. "We all watched the movie *Pollyanna* together and you had us act it out. Then you fixed eggplant parmesan, which I had never tasted. I loved it. We laughed all evening as we reenacted our favorite scenes."

Linda beamed at my description. "You girls were nothing but giggles and fun. I loved every minute of it. We made a great memory that night." She paused then, suddenly serious, and said, "Memories feed us in dark times, Marie."

I nodded and sipped my coffee. "I remember clear as day," I said, "when, after the death of Elise, you said to me, 'Marie, you need to paint. Come to my place. We'll paint together.'"

Linda laughed. "Do you remember your answer? 'Aunt Linda, I can't paint. I have no artistic skills at all!'"

"I was afraid I'd make a fool of myself trying to paint. Plus, I think my lack of self-confidence was heightened by my loss of Elise. I was so low. But you did not give up. You coaxed and encouraged until I could not say no."

"Well, of course. It's what you needed. Art heals. You know I believe that."

Aunt Linda's life was proof of that belief. A gifted artist, she is one of my mom's four sisters. She specializes in theorem painting, an early American decorative technique that dates back to the 1800s, and she has work displayed in a number of historic homes and museums. Her home is a testimony of her love of a broad scope of artistic expression, from watercolors and oils on canvas to painted trays, pottery, and glasswork. Linda has a rare passion to reach out to others with the life-giving power of artistic expression. The lower level of her home is an art studio, but not for her alone. She opens it to those who'd like to explore the artist within and find peace.

When I was grieving the loss of Elise, I had accepted Aunt Linda's invitation to come by one afternoon a week. We started with basic mechanics — how to hold the brush and the different types of strokes that created unique effects. Under her tutelage I discovered that my small, uncertain brushstrokes took shape to become a scene upon my canvas. All the while, within I was trying out fresh new brushstrokes on my internal landscape.

Somewhere in the midst of blending colors and creating texture, the emptiness of my life merged into the fullness of hers, and I left feeling less of an ache. She drew out of me the act of creativity, where I found a deep connection with my Creator. As the weeks went by I discovered I could trust that God, the master artist, would paint new scenery into my life in his own time.

Now, years later, I could watch as my children basked in the love of Aunt Linda, who had always been a treasured aunt, filled with such vibrancy that even as a child, whenever I was with her, I'd felt swept into a gurgling, tumbling river teeming with the energy of life. Maybe my children would feel the same.

Suddenly Uncle Jim came bustling into the kitchen. "I'm going to head over to your place now and get those bikes you wanted me to pick up," he said. "I want the kids to have whatever they need to feel at home."

"Be careful of the media," Linda called as he headed toward the garage. "They'll be swarming all over her house. Don't let them follow you home!"

"I won't. Don't worry," he called back, and he was gone.

"What will *you* need today?" Linda asked. "We'll keep the kids entertained, so don't worry about them."

"The detectives will be here before long. I have no idea how much time they'll need, but I'll need some privacy with them."

"Done," Linda declared.

By the time everyone had had breakfast, Uncle Jim returned from his errand with the news that my house had been surrounded by media and guarded by police who'd done their best to shield him from the journalists. Even so, the reporters had shouted questions to him such as *Are you a relative? Where are Marie and the children? Will they be coming back? How are they doing?* I felt nervous at the thought of reporters circling my home, but I was grateful to be miles away.

The doorbell rang, and my heart jumped. I knew it was the detectives. I froze for a moment. Uncle Jim went to greet them at the front door. I heard their polite introductions, so I forced myself to my feet and into the living room despite the sudden wave of nausea that attacked me. I was frustrated with myself for feeling so overwhelmed and intimidated, but I thought that, with my parents by my side, I'd soon calm down. At least it was the same three detectives I'd met yesterday—no one new to get used to. I was struck again with how professional and polite they were.

"Mrs. Roberts, is there a private place we can talk?"

"Yes, you can meet upstairs in the sitting room," Aunt Linda said. She led the way and the rest of us followed. But the last detective in line stopped and said to my mom, "I'm sorry—we need to speak with Marie alone."

My stomach dropped. I hadn't anticipated this. But what could I do? Linda led us into the guest room where she'd already closed the sofa bed she and Jim had slept on, making it a cozy little sitting room. She shut the door behind her as she left.

I was trembling. I felt small. *Just sitting in the same room with three detectives in dark suits is nearly overwhelming to me.* During my high school driver's education class, the instructor made one statement I've never forgotten: "If a police officer follows you for two miles, he can find something to pull you over for." I don't know if that's accurate, but it became the truth to me—to the point that even as an adult, if I noticed a police car behind me, I would turn and go a different way than I had planned. I didn't want to be pulled over! I'm afraid that this attitude of fear of the police heightened my anxiety as we took our seats.

What am I so afraid of? I demanded of myself. But I knew the answer. These men would tell me things I didn't want to hear. They would make the murders real. Also, they would want me to help them understand Charlie's motive; they would be looking for explanations, for clues. The Marie who wanted to help them—Marie the pleaser who wanted to meet their expectations—was clueless. I felt guilty. I had nothing to offer. I felt stupid, because I knew nothing.

"We know this must be terribly difficult, Mrs. Roberts," one of them said. "How are Abigail and Bryce doing?"

"So far, they seem to be handling it well," I answered. "The counselors will be back today and every day this week to help. Carson's too little to understand. How are the Amish families of the girls in the hospitals?" I asked.

"Rosanna King's injuries are extensive. She's still in critical condition," one detective answered. "Rachel and Sarah Ann Stoltzfus, Barbie Fisher, and Esther King have stabilized, but they're still in the hospital."

"And their families?" I asked.

The detectives all seemed to sigh at once. I could feel the weight of grief these men were bearing. "Much in the way you seem to be, Mrs. Roberts. They're surrounded by family and friends. They're worried and grieving but holding on."

I was struck by the compassion in his voice. I sensed that what these three men were doing was far more than "just a job." They hurt for all of us. Tears wetted my cheeks, and as I reached for a tissue I realized that Aunt Linda had placed more than enough boxes of tissues around the room. Another God-sighting of his tender care. But these men were used to tears, so I didn't need to apologize.

"Mrs. Roberts, we know you'll need to be making funeral arrangements. The Amish families are keeping us informed of all of their arrangements. We'll let you know, so you can arrange your service after theirs are all completed."

"Thank you. Yes, of course, we'll want to allow them to make their arrangements first." I hadn't even allowed myself to think about planning Charlie's funeral yet.

The detective continued. "We'll be providing security at each funeral, to ensure that no media or protests infringe on the ceremonies. We'll do the same for yours. The other families are spacing out their services so that they don't overlap, allowing one another's families to attend every service."

"Of course. We can't thank you enough for all you've done to keep the media away." I had wondered if there would be police at Charlie's funeral and was relieved to know that there would be.

"Remember that we are here to protect you, Mrs. Roberts. How are things going with the media? Is anyone harassing you or trespassing?"

I explained that my brother had been taking all media calls, doling out firm "no comments," and declining media interviews on our behalf. Ken, who was imposing not only in person, but in his phone manner too, left no doubt that he meant what he said.

"Just remember," another detective spoke up, "you can tell the media that you do not want them to call you again. And if someone violates that, you just let us know and we will contact them with orders to leave you alone."

"I had no idea. Thank you so much." I made a mental note to tell Ken.

"We have some questions we need to ask about Charlie. But before we start, we would appreciate your permission to enter and search your house again today."

"Of course," I said, picturing an army of police invading our little three-bedroom house.

Then the questioning began. They asked about Charlie's background, work history, and parenting style. Those questions I could answer easily. But then it got harder: they probed deeply into our relationship and our intimacy. I was very uncomfortable and intimidated having to answer questions of such a personal and private nature from these men. Embarrassed, I felt my first surge of anger toward Charlie for leaving me all alone to answer for his actions, subjecting me to such a violation of our privacy. But my anger passed as quickly as it came as I tried to imagine what secret horrors he'd had living in his mind and heart that led him to plan such an act.

As violated and shaken as I felt, I was deeply moved at the kindness of these men. They clearly understood that it was difficult for me, especially as they disclosed more details of events inside the schoolhouse. More than once the detectives asked if I needed a break and expressed genuine sympathy and heartfelt concern for our family.

Then they began to probe about Charlie's plans for the shooting. And I felt utterly useless.

"Charlie had amassed a considerable load of supplies for barricading himself in the schoolhouse. Lumber, tools, ammunition, and the like. Do you know where he stored them?"

"I'm sorry, but I have no idea. You saw that we don't even have a garage, and our house is so small there really is no place to hide anything. I never saw any supplies at all."

That became my refrain throughout this portion of the questioning: "I'm sorry, but I have no idea." And I *was* sorry. I wanted to help. I wanted answers to these questions as much as they did.

"How about in the crawl space under your home. Did he store supplies there?"

"We never used that space for anything that I know of."

"Did Charlie usually stockpile large supplies of ammunition?"

"I don't think so, but it's not something I ever checked to see."

I'm not sure just how long they questioned me. A few hours at least. When at last I escorted them to the front door, they let me know that they'd be back several more times this week. I groaned inwardly but thanked them for all they were doing. I wondered what the rest of their day held. Whatever it was, it couldn't be pleasant.

After the detectives left, I tried to quiet my heart by thinking back to my first awkward strokes of paint on the canvas Aunt Linda had set before me after the loss of Elise. With her patient encouragement, the awkwardness had soon faded, and I'd discovered how to transform my blank canvas into an expression of beauty.

Now Charlie's call had doused my canvas with black again, but in the two days since, God had already begun painting new scenes of startling beauty on the canvas of my life. I envisioned myself painting those scenes. The falling tulip caught and cradled in the hand of God, my uncharacteristically bold self marching through my house, arms uplifted, praying protection over my home aloud, a troop of Amish men embracing my father, Aunt Linda framed by life in her kitchen, and my children sleeping soundly in this home filled with love.

Another scene, this one dark and foreboding, hovered in the corner of my mind, one I did not want to paint, yet knew that soon I must. There was a funeral to plan. I thought of all the shattered hopes and dreams we faced this week, then contemplated God's generous provision for our every need, above and beyond what I ever would have dreamed. God would see us through the funeral. His light would shine through his gentle brushstrokes on our lives, creating a masterpiece of love. The funeral would be no exception.

I had no idea how, but of this I was certain.

7

mosaic

I was nervous about asking the question and afraid to hear the response. How exactly do you ask a funeral home if they are *willing* to bury your husband?

Ours was a small community. I would understand if they declined. Would a funeral home want to risk alienating future clients by agreeing to bury Charles Roberts IV? My husband hadn't simply died. He'd committed suicide after barricading himself inside an Amish schoolhouse, terrorizing innocent girls, and taking the lives of five beautiful children.

The combination of those realities made it very hard for me to breathe.

A haunting memory made it even harder.

I will never forget the scene of Charlie carrying Elise's small casket out of the church when her funeral service was over. The smooth oak box that held our tiny daughter weighed so little that it was easily carried by only my husband, but over the years his grief would prove too heavy a burden to be borne by this young father alone.

And now, nine years later, I was preparing for the funeral of Elise's father.

I had put if off long enough. I dialed the phone and tried to steady my voice. "Hello, this is Marie Roberts."

Thankfully, I didn't need to ask my question. A man speaking in soft tones immediately spoke up and saved me the embarrassment. "Hello, Mrs. Roberts. I am so sorry for your loss. I've been wondering if you might call. I remember your family from the burial of your daughter some years back. Are you calling to make arrangements for your husband?"

"I was hoping you might be willing to serve us," I began nervously.

"This must be such a difficult time for you and your family," the funeral director said kindly. "I've already given this some careful thought. At first, I thought I might not yet be able to say yes, but my mother always taught me that every man deserves a proper burial. Yes, we'll be happy to serve you."

How does a wife bear the weight of such shame? I would not have been able to — but for the grace of God. After making an appointment for the following day, I hung up with a wave of relief.

I was exhausted when it came time to finally put the children to bed for our second night at Aunt Linda's safe haven. When we pulled down the sheets, we all got the most delightful surprise.

"Look, Mommy. Smiley-face stickers!" Abigail called out.

"They're everywhere," Bryce laughed, as he pulled the top sheet down farther and looked under the pillows. Sure enough, Aunt Linda had secretly come into our room and planted her surprise to bring smiles to our hearts at bedtime. The children counted them as they carefully pulled them off, one by one, and each placed their own stack on the nightstand for safekeeping.

Another reminder, through Linda's loving hands, that God was smiling on us. We were not alone.

As I lay awake between Abigail and Bryce, the minutes turned to hours, yet still I could not sleep. The questions asked by the detectives kept replaying incessantly, as if my mind insisted on trying to find answers where there were none. Charlie's letter clearly identified his grief over Elise as the source of his anger toward God. While none of us — the detectives, my family, myself — could make sense of a choice to kill little girls as a response to that grief, clearly in Charlie's broken mind, there was a connection. I found myself sleepless in bed, reliving that time of grief through new eyes, in search of whatever clues I could find.

In the wake of Elise's funeral, grief swallowed us both. Only twelve months and one week before, we had exchanged our wedding vows in that very same church, a bride still in her teens and a boyish groom, twenty-two, both filled with dreams and anticipation. The abrupt way our world changed from beauty to ashes brought shock waves to our frail human hearts, jolting us to the core. *If I could change one thing about the way this fallen world works,* I cried out to God at the time, *I would see to it that no parent would ever have to endure the grief of burying a child.*

How grateful I am now, looking back, that my future was hidden from me. At the time, the loss of our baby daughter seemed more than I could bear. How could I have survived the knowledge that the loss of our daughter would one day trigger the unspeakable murders of five little girls?

Our family rallied to support us, helping to arrange details and cover costs, a huge gift as we weren't financially prepared or emotionally capable. The presence of Charlie's parents, filled with compassion, spoke volumes of love. My mom joined Charlie in managing the planning and the countless details. Dad sat with me in silent alliance, held me tightly in strong arms of love as I mourned, and willed strength into his little girl. Charlie and I wept together and alone. I remember looking into his eyes and seeing the same depth of pain I felt. In the earliest days no words were needed between us; we were united in our grief.

Charlie went back to work within a few days, but I did not. There was no way I could attempt jumping back into "real life," and since we had been planning for me to be a stay-at-home mom, I embarked on that lifestyle without my child.

Had Charlie needed more time than he'd taken?

To say that this season of life was hard for Charlie and me would not really be saying anything at all. Everywhere we looked—church, stores, extended family gatherings—we seemed to be surrounded by couples expecting children of their own, a continual reminder of our loss. Those pregnant bellies shouted *Life!* in a way that our lives could no longer echo. We were trying to find healing and wholeness in circumstances that weren't "fixable."

The follow-up appointment with my doctor was scheduled on, of all days, my twentieth birthday, December 5. We celebrated Charlie's twenty-fourth birthday only two days later. The six weeks between Elise's death and the end of the year were packed full of intensity—Thanksgiving, our birthdays, Christmas. I had to focus deliberately on the most basic tasks of self-care each day. That was about all I could do—just breathe and keep going. Charlie, on the other hand, seemed more able to resume his daily life. I admired his strength and questioned my weakness.

"Marie, have you and Charlie put up your tree yet?" Mom asked over the phone.

I replied, "No, Mom, I don't think we're going to bother with it this year." Actually, Charlie and I had avoided talk of holiday celebrations. It felt as if we had nothing to celebrate.

But my mom knew that Christmas was a treasured holiday for me, and she had decided to do for us what we were incapable of doing on our own. "I thought you might say that. You must have a Christmas tree. Your dad, Vicki, and I will bring you one this Saturday. We'll help you and Charlie decorate it, and we can order pizza to be delivered for dinner. Sound good? This will be good for you."

I knew there was no sense in arguing with her. I had secretly wanted a tree, but it seemed like too much trouble. I wanted it to magically appear. Mom to the rescue.

Mom, Dad, and my sister, Vicki, arrived late afternoon on Saturday, tree in hand. Dad and Charlie set the tree in the corner, and without slowing down, Dad headed to the basement and started bringing up boxes of Christmas decorations. The hustle and bustle and cheerful dispositions of my parents and sister lightened the heavy air in our house, and before long the five of us were trimming the tree and laughing at the old family stories Mom and Dad told of my siblings and me at Christmas in years gone by. The intervention of my parents warmed our chilled hearts that day.

"Don't let yourself get depressed," a well-meaning friend advised me over the holiday season. I wondered how it was possible not to. I was still supposed to be pregnant, celebrating and enjoying these holidays and special moments leading up to February, when Elise should have been born. I wished I could erase all those hopes and plans that had taken root in my heart and mind.

Discontent and struggling to find meaning, I soon longed for another baby to fill the gaping hole left by Elise, for an outlet to release this love Charlie and I had stockpiled in anticipation. Charlie agreed.

Several months went by without a positive pregnancy test. What happened so easily the first time proved elusive now. Watching those around us bring home their long-awaited infants made our unfulfilled yearning more consuming. I battled with God, not understanding the pain and brokenness that lingered, nor why God would allow it.

One cold winter morning, while praying, I heard him speak to my heart, asking me to demonstrate that I was content with exactly what I had before he gave me anything else. I was sitting Indian-style on the log-cabin quilt on our bed. I thought back over the months I had worked quilting it with ladies in our family and other friends before the wedding. I remembered how we'd gathered at my mom's house and the hopes and dreams I'd stitched into it and the laughter we had all exchanged, imagining the years to come and the love that would be shared in my own home. Those dreams included children of my own, but now there were none. I felt the frustration of unfulfilled longings.

"Are you crazy?" I cried to God. "How can I be content with *exactly* what I have, when I have nothing?"

The silence cried back to me.

Nothing? My conscience reeled. Had I really just said that? How could I look at my life and say I had nothing? I knew better. I had a tender husband, loving parents, childhood memories filled with life and beauty, a warm home, food on my table, a church family.

Humbled, I bowed my head. "God, I yield myself to you in this process of grief. I know you've given me much. But losing Elise shattered my heart." I let the tears come once again. How many tears had I shed these past months?

"Lord, take these broken shards of my heart. I know I am impatient, but even so I will wait for you to glue them back together."

This time of hurting and healing and hurting some more was grueling. Many times I pouted, telling God I wanted out of the pain. Grasping for things to feel good about, I focused on losing weight, and we purchased a new car (not the best idea). Such diversions didn't work. Nothing we contrived could help me feel better.

As one who leans toward perfectionism, I was not enjoying my up-and-down journey of self-discovery. I wanted to heal right the first time, arriving at my destination via the most direct route. I found it hard to give myself grace to not perform well, and to celebrate instead small steps of growth, even so small as simply acknowledging when things went "better than last week."

Being still didn't come naturally to me; I liked to "fix" things. But I sensed Jesus asking me to lay aside my Martha disposition in order to choose "the better part" like Mary and sit at his feet (Luke 10:41–42).

"Worship me, Marie," his Word called to me. "Just worship." At first it was hard to worship through pain, but slowly I began to come, sit, and worship *from* my place of broken dreams, my place of doubt and despair. Sometimes I sang out loud, sometimes I sat quietly, focusing my heart on recounting his goodness and allowing it to spill over with gratitude, despite my grief. The voice that "spoke" within me provided guidance in the fertile ground of my surrender, and I felt a new heart-connection with my God like I had never known.

Winter gave way to spring.

That summer I spent a lot of time mowing my grandfather's acreage — a large green canvas upon which I could paint my thoughts. Charlie and I were still living in our first house in Lititz at the time, and the mowing took me back to my hometown of Georgetown, about forty-five minutes south. Returning to the scenery of my childhood brought a fresh whisper of peace. The hours spent bumping along on Grandpa's lawn tractor proved a perfect setting for worship. The roar of the 48-inch-deck mower provided anonymity for me to sing aloud with abandon. I nearly wore out a Vineyard CD as I listened over and over again to Mark Miller's lyrics: "I delight in you, Lord; you make my heart jump." Sometimes I could feel my heart jumping. God was stirring me, lifting settled dreams, bringing them back to the surface.

I had no inkling that I was mowing the very ground that would one day become my new home with Charlie, a home filled with the laughter of three precious children yet to come; no idea that on that very spot there would one day be a porch where I would watch helicopters rushing to the horrific scene of Charlie's grief and rage unleashed.

As I write, I am moved beyond words that God chose to make that a place of healing for my first broken heart. He had me cover that very soil with prayers for his presence and peace, with songs of praise, with whispers of his words from Scripture, all falling on that unbroken turf.

One particular day, as I sang aloud while mowing Grandpa's acreage, I heard the Lord whisper a name to me: "Abigail."

I was so jolted by this strong sensation of hearing God's voice that I stopped the mower, pulled off my CD headphones, and sat still, bolt upright, straining to listen.

"Abigail." It wasn't an audible voice from the heavens. It was more like an intimate whisper to my soul, and with it this time came instructions. "Look up the meaning in your baby name book."

I felt goose bumps from head to toe. Knowing I couldn't leave the mowing uncompleted, I zoomed over the remaining grass and drove home. I was positive I was *not* pregnant, yet I felt a sense of holy expectation to discover what God was going to reveal. When I pulled up to our house, I dashed inside, grabbed my Bible and baby name book, sat on the floor of our still partially finished nursery, and turned to the A's in the baby name book.

My heart leaped. Abigail was defined as "source of delight." The book included a reference to Psalm 37:4. My fingers flew through the pages of my Bible to the verse, and I read aloud: "Take delight in the LORD, and he will give you the desires of your heart." God was giving me a glimpse of his plan, and I absolutely believed I was going to have another baby, a girl named Abigail.

A rainstorm pelted the roof while I was having this conversation with the Father, and once the rain stopped I rose to gaze out the window. With equal parts disbelief and delight, I beheld a rainbow painted in the sky above. God's palette stretched vibrantly, declaring that he was, indeed, painting the story of my life. Just as the Lord had covenanted with Noah to preserve life on this earth, he was confirming his promise of new life to me. I took lots of pictures of this affirmation from heaven, eager to document the event for Charlie and to keep them as a reminder of God's promise for any difficult days ahead. I couldn't wait for Charlie to get home!

When Charlie arrived home that night, I had dinner waiting. Hard as it was, I held my surprise until we both sat down and began to eat.

"Charlie, something happened to me today. Something strange and wonderful."

He looked at me with curiosity. "What happened? What do you mean strange?"

"And wonderful," I added, not wanting to alarm him. "I hope you won't think I sound crazy." I suddenly felt concerned that he'd think I'd lost touch with reality.

"Marie, you're the sanest person I know. Now tell me what happened." He'd put his fork down now and leaned toward me, returning my beaming smile.

I told him everything, step by step, and stopped when I described the rain pelting the windows. "So I got up off the floor of the nursery" — I reached for my camera and held it up — "and there in the sky I saw a gorgeous rainbow! I took pictures so I can show you. I'll get them developed right away."

Charlie stared at me for a moment, a mix of bewilderment, surprise, and caution on his face. "Wow, Marie. I don't know what to say." He paused. "Do you really think God was *talking* to you, telling you we will have a girl named Abigail?"

"I do, Charlie."

He took my hand in his and squeezed it to reassure me he wasn't discounting my experience. The caution in his eyes remained.

"I *really* do," I repeated.

Charlie's eyes bored into mine as if he were trying to see what I'd seen. His face now looked hopeful yet guarded, and I understood completely. All afternoon I had been praying that God would give Charlie a similar encounter, one that would validate God's message to me. I'd thought about the way Mary encountered God, when the angel told her that she would give birth to Jesus. And how, afterward, Joseph had his own encounter, and that had settled his heart. I knew that I had met God that day, and I wanted Charlie to meet him too in a similar way. I felt that my healing from grief had advanced significantly because of this promise, because of *knowing* that God had seen me and had heard every cry and every word of worship that left my lips as I mowed the grass. During all those months of crying out, I'd needed to know God heard my heart. And now I knew. Looking into his gentle eyes, I ached for Charlie to believe in the promise as much as I did.

"I hope so. I truly hope so." He placed the fingers of his right hand under my chin tenderly and guided my lips toward his. "I love you, you know," he said softly, and he kissed me.

I glowed in the warmth of his kiss, and thought to myself, *Kissed by God today and kissed by Charlie.*

The rainbow was a turning point for me. Dawn was breaking.

I began enjoying life again and finding the purpose and contentment I'd been seeking. Peace settled on me like a thick blanket. I started a part-time job as an administrative assistant for a local manufacturer and stopped "trying" to get pregnant. I had not given up on my dream to have a daughter; I just gave up trying to make it happen. I had my promise from God, and I trusted that he didn't need help to fulfill it.

And apparently he didn't. A few months went by, bringing us to just over a year since we'd conceived Elise. Beginning to suspect that I was pregnant, I secretly bought a pregnancy test. The following Saturday morning, when we woke up, I surprised Charlie by setting a test stick on his pillow.

His face lit up. "Really?" His eyes searched mine. "Have you taken the test yet?"

"Not yet," I said. "Let's do it right now." I ran to the bathroom and returned a few moments later, stick in hand, and we sat together, holding our breath, and watched it. Like magic, it revealed the answer for which we'd prayed.

"This is too good to be true," Charlie said, and he gave me a hug that nearly squeezed the breath out of me. We were both crying, too thrilled to speak for a few moments.

Over breakfast, we agreed that I'd see the doctor right away, and that we'd tell our parents now, knowing we would need their support on this new journey. We would wait to tell others until we had passed the twelve-week mark.

As the next few days passed, Charlie and I were joyful yet guarded, trying not to focus on the loss of Elise but telling ourselves that regardless of all else, we needed to trust God. Each morning I awoke filled with delight over the life growing inside me again, only to contend with moments of fear of losing this baby.

As we crawled into bed one night, I cuddled up to Charlie, laid my head on his chest, and said, "Charlie, I'm struggling with worry. I know God gave me the promise of Abigail, but I can't help but worry that I might lose this baby like I lost Elise."

"You too?" he asked. "Every time I get excited, I tell myself not to get my hopes up. I don't want us to go through that pain again."

I was relieved to hear him talking about his feelings.

"Whatever we face, we'll face it together, okay?" I asked. "God will be with us."

"You have such strong faith, Marie," he said. Only later did it occur to me that maybe in that comment he was implying that his own faith was faltering. It didn't seem so to me at the time. I thought he was just affirming me.

Within two weeks of discovering our pregnancy, I started having pain on my right side — something like cramping but much more intense. And I felt sick, as if I had a stomach bug. I made an immediate appointment with my family doctor. He thought it was just a virus and sent me home.

At work the next afternoon, I felt a piercing pain and almost passed out. I went home and climbed in bed, knowing something was wrong. Because there was no bleeding, I remained hopeful that my symptoms weren't related to my pregnancy.

Over the next couple of days the pain came and went. My family doctor continued to advise that I should rest and stay hydrated.

Two days later, I started bleeding. My hopes sank. Was this the beginning of the end? I called my ob-gyn. When I described the symptoms I'd had earlier that week, this doctor felt certain that the baby was growing inside one of my fallopian tubes. She ordered some tests.

"I'm so sorry," the doctor began, when the test results were in. I was sitting on the examination table with Charlie standing by my side. He squeezed my hand, but our eyes were on the doctor.

"You have an ectopic pregnancy," she explained. "Your baby is growing in one of your fallopian tubes instead of the uterus. It can't survive there. You're starting to lose the baby. You also have a cyst on one ovary, and another cyst that has already ruptured, which probably caused the intense pain you experienced a few days ago. We'll need to watch you closely over the next few weeks to see if you'll require surgery."

I started to cry. As Charlie turned to me, I saw on his face fear, worry for me, and his disappointment over losing our second child, all reflecting my own thoughts and feelings. The weight of his grief added to my own, and I could see that the same was true for Charlie. How hard it is to comfort one another when the pain we see in the other's eyes increases the burden for both.

"Is Marie in any danger?" Charlie asked the doctor. I sensed his anxiety.

"We'll keep a close eye and repeat ultrasounds and blood work frequently. If you suffer any sudden pain, dizziness, or fainting, don't hesitate to call. But right now I'm not seeing signs of danger."

Charlie didn't look reassured.

We drove home in silence and tears. What was left to say? The next day we chose to name our precious unborn child Isabella, meaning "consecrated to God." She was in his arms now, having never passed through ours.

Part of me was frustrated with myself. Why had I once again allowed the joy and excitement of new life to take hold, only to be faced with the pall of death all over again? Charlie was mostly quiet, except for his frequent inquiries of how I was feeling. But when I would voice my own feelings, he confessed he felt the same.

But as I prayed over the next few days, I found myself increasingly thankful that I had spent every possible moment rejoicing and believing in the promise my Father had given concerning Abigail. I realized I *still* believed that promise would be fulfilled.

When I told Charlie what I was thinking, he shook his head. "I don't understand your confidence in that, Marie. Maybe it's just wishful thinking."

Though Charlie seemed mystified by my confidence in God's promise, my hope was not dimmed. And I could see that Charlie's worry for me was overshadowing his other emotions.

The next couple of weeks were a blur of doctor visits, blood work, and ultrasounds. Even though my baby had died, it was still lodged within my fallopian tube. We prayed for a miraculous touch from God.

With one more day and one more test before being scheduled for surgery, we returned to the office. "I've got some good news for you this time," the doctor reported. "Everything is unexpectedly clear. Your body has cleared the fallopian tube as I'd hoped. You won't need surgery."

Charlie beamed, relief obviously washing over him. He leaned over and gave me a kiss on the cheek.

While it was indeed great news that I wouldn't need surgery, I could not escape the sadness that all traces of my second child were now gone.

I revised my identity: mother of two babies in heaven ... wife of Charlie on earth ... and mother of Abigail yet to come.

My doctor explained that with the scar tissue inside one of my fallopian tubes, it would be more difficult or maybe impossible for an egg to pass through that tube, reducing my ability to conceive to only half that of a normal person. While I respected the doctor's opinion, it didn't shake my confidence in God's promise. I knew I was going to hold Abigail in my arms one day.

"I'm afraid to hope for that," was Charlie's reply.

For me, the intensity of my second loss was not as overwhelming as it had been with Elise ten months earlier. The searching and struggling I had come through in the past year had increased my capacity for faith and trust. "Now faith is confidence in what we hope for and assurance about what we do not see" (Hebrews 11:1). I was determined not to lose forward motion in my healing journey. I had learned I could walk through grief and find God with me. I had discovered that even in darkness I could praise. I had seen God take the shards of my shattered heart and begin to craft a mosaic out of them, a new heart that incorporated the broken pieces, using each one, none gone to waste.

With every ounce of my being, I clung to God's promise of a daughter named Abigail — a promise sealed with a rainbow.

In the weeks that followed, Charlie and I celebrated our second anniversary, Elise's first birthday, Thanksgiving, and then our birthdays in early December. The fall and winter holidays, time traditionally set aside to gather with family and celebrate the goodness of the year, were now marred by substantial loss. Still, I was thankful for the brilliance of God's love expressed in tangible ways, in the form of our love for one another and our loving parents and family.

"Charlie," I said one night over dinner, "on my last trip to the doctor's office they gave me this list of local support groups for parents who've lost children through miscarriage and stillbirth. I was thinking it might be helpful. Would you like to go with me?"

He didn't look up at first. He sipped his tea, clearly thinking, but he seemed uncomfortable. "I don't think so. Why don't you go without me."

"I just thought it might help both of us. I've got my mom and Aunt Linda to talk to. And you know how I talk to God all the time and feel like he's really healing me. But you don't have anyone to talk to."

"I don't need to talk about it," he answered matter-of-factly, though not unkindly. "I know you do, but that's not my way. It is what it is. A group isn't for me."

"Okay. Well, I'll check it out." I was disappointed. I wanted to draw closer as we healed. But even I had to admit that it was hard to picture Charlie feeling comfortable with a group of strangers discussing feelings. Maybe it *wasn't* for him.

While I was still standing in faith and believing for a daughter named Abigail, I also still had resurgences of emotional pain and perplexity, but as I worshiped through my pain and recalled God's promise, the screams of doubt would be silenced. And so I embraced the occasional sadness, knowing that as I was open and honest with God, he would somehow reach down and continue to heal my wounded heart. Over time, his love would infiltrate my emptiness, and his life would saturate my barrenness.

I was beginning to accept God's decisions over my life without fighting, and in this way I found joy again. Charlie, on the other hand, continued to be reserved about his feelings toward our losses, although he seemed to be reaching for the hope I was feeling.

I assumed that over time he would track with me — an assumption that could not have been more wrong.

"Mommy, come see what the neighbors brought!" Abigail called as she climbed the stairs at Aunt Linda's to get me. It was midmorning on Wednesday, I was upstairs. After folding the laundry I'd decided to read my Bible. It had been a quiet morning so far, but I was soon to discover it would be another day of ups and downs and ups again, not unlike the emotional journey I'd been remembering last night.

Abigail looked a little brighter this morning. Not quite cheerful, but with more expression on her face and in her voice. I'd heard the doorbell awhile back, but since no one had come to get me, I'd assumed that whoever it was didn't need me. Now I realized from Abigail's exclamation that it had been one of Linda's neighbors.

"Okay, I'll follow you," I said. "Where are your brothers?" I put aside my Bible and stood.

"They're already playing with the new stuff."

"What new stuff?"

"You'll see, Mommy."

Downstairs in the living room, I saw Bryce and my dad sitting on the floor, spreading out the pieces of a brand-new puzzle with large pieces perfect for my five-year-old son. Mom and Carson were hitting a big red balloon around the living room.

"Whatcha working on, Bryce?" I asked.

"Some of Aunt Linda's neighbors brought a bunch of cool stuff. This puzzle, balloons, coloring books. It's in that box over there." He pointed to the corner.

"And sidewalk chalk too," Abigail announced brightly. "Aunt Linda said she'd draw with me out front when she finishes putting all the food away."

"What food?" I asked.

"Brownies!" squealed Carson. Leaving the red balloon to fall where it may, he took my hand and led me to the kitchen.

"What's all this?" I asked of no one in particular. Linda and Jim had the refrigerator open and seemed to have it half emptied out, with Tupperware, covered dishes, and containers filled with food covering her considerable stretch of kitchen counter.

"This," Linda answered, her head in the fridge, "is the abundance of good friends and neighbors. I'm just trying to find a place to fit it all in until lunchtime." Linda's neighbors, still keeping our whereabouts a secret, had dropped off two platters of meats and cheeses for lunch, a bowl of fruit, brownies, and covered dishes of a mystery dinner. As the week progressed, they and other friends and family would quietly slip in and out, bringing a steady stream of breads, cheeses, meats, desserts, fruits, and beverages.

"One thing's for sure," Uncle Jim said, just before popping a brownie in his mouth. "We'll have plenty to share with everyone who drops in this week."

"No brownies before lunch, Jim," Linda chided him, too late.

"Can I have a brownie?" Bryce and Abigail asked in unison, having followed us into the kitchen.

"Me too!" Carson cried.

Linda looked pointedly at Jim with her "now see what you've done" look.

Jim looked at me for approval, and I gave a slight nod. "One small brownie for each of you," Uncle Jim said. "Then nothing else until lunch. Go sit at the table, and I'll bring them out to you."

The kids raced for the dining room. I smiled for what may have been the first time in two days.

Then the doorbell rang.

"Don't any of you answer it," Linda said. "It may be a reporter."

She was right.

"Good morning, ma'am. I understand you're related in some way to the Roberts family?" I could just barely hear the man's voice from the kitchen because Linda had barely cracked open the door so he couldn't see in. Still, she told us later, he was craning his neck, trying to see around her.

"Who would you be?" Linda asked firmly.

"I'm just trying to reach the Roberts family." He avoided her question.

Linda would have none of that. "Are you a reporter?" she demanded. I had no trouble hearing *her* voice.

"Yes, ma'am, just trying to — " But he didn't get to finish his sentence.

"I have no comment. Kindly do not return." I heard the door firmly close. Aunt Linda, I could see, was as strong a guard as my big brother, Ken.

Shortly before lunch, a representative from a local bank came to visit us, bringing with her the softest stuffed animals I'd ever touched and a stack of cards from the bank staff and customers, containing messages of compassion and hope that warmed my heart. She'd called ahead and Dad had agreed to an appointment with me. We sat in the lovely seating area adjacent to the kitchen.

"Mrs. Roberts, I have something else for you."

I wondered what it could be. I was already moved by the gifts and cards she'd brought.

"A trust fund has been established for your children at our bank. All the funds have been donated. Nothing is required of you but a signature on a few forms, and there's no rush on that. It can wait until you find the time. We just wanted to let you know, hoping that it would relieve any financial fears you might be feeling for their futures."

Her words stunned me. I was speechless. A wave of awe washed over me. I had nothing to offer except two very small, inadequate words: "Thank you."

I could trust God to act above and beyond my imagination. Our lives would no longer be the solid piece of glass we'd known. He was already picking up each broken piece and reassembling the fragments into a beautiful mosaic. This gift was his deposit for our mosaic, a precious gemstone.

After she left, I went back up to the sitting room and closed the door. There, I wept. The floodgates opened once again, and for a few minutes I couldn't stop crying. I cried for God's goodness and I cried because I wanted to go running to Charlie to tell him what the Lord had just done for our kids. I cried for the memories of God's healing in the wake of losing Elise and Isabella, and I cried because Charlie hadn't felt God's healing as I had. I cried for my children, for the ways God was providing them shelter and love through family and friends, and for the milestones ahead of them where the absence of their father would leave an open wound. I cried for the dread of the afternoon ahead of me at the funeral home.

Every tear I cried, those of sadness and those of gratitude, I offered up to God, confident that he was catching each one. He would save them all. They were needed. Because mosaics are made not only with broken bits of tile and gems, precious metals and broken glass. Until there is a moist bed of clay in which to set the many pieces, the artist cannot create his masterpiece.

With my tears, the Artist was making the clay for his masterpiece.

8
the holy exchange

Charlie's dad, Chuck, pulled up in front of my aunt's house shortly after lunch on Wednesday. He'd offered to drive me to the funeral home, where we would meet Terri, Charlie's mom. My dad and mom talked to him quietly in the living room while I hugged my children goodbye.

"I'll only be gone a few hours," I told them in the midst of lingering hugs that neither they nor I seemed to want to let go of. This would be the first time we'd been separated since the shooting, and my "hovering" instinct was in high gear.

The forty-minute drive to the funeral home felt surreal. We'd spoken on the phone earlier in the week, but now that I was seeing Chuck for the first time since the day of the shooting, the heaviness of grief on his face sent new waves of sorrow through my heart.

I tried to control my feelings of nausea at the thought of the funeral home. At the thought of what I was going to do in the next few hours, my mind screamed, *Run away! Run away!* Yet we were inching closer and closer to the unavoidable.

"A call came from a local pastor yesterday that left me speechless," I told Chuck, thankful that I had some good news to share with him during the ride. "He wanted me to know that their congregation is praying for us and felt moved by God to show their support in some tangible way."

I paused to maintain emotional control, afraid that if I lost it now I'd be unable to regain my composure before we arrived at the funeral home, and I desperately wanted to keep under control there.

I continued. "They've offered to cover the full costs of the funeral, Dad. They encouraged me to make whatever arrangements we'd like, and the pastor has already called the funeral home to arrange for the billing. Do you believe it?"

I could see how overwhelmed he felt.

The call from the church had shocked me. Had they not given me such an unimaginable blessing, my reality would have been bleak. In addition to the horrific circumstances of Charlie's death, I would have faced the struggle to afford the cost of surrendering his body to the earth — a cost I could not pay. First the trust fund for my children, now this. God had touched human hearts, and they had responded, giving me his mercy and his provision. I will be eternally grateful.

Other than my forays into Linda's backyard, I had been inside for two days, so I tried to enjoy the familiar countryside of rolling hills dotted with red barns and white silos, but the windmills that marked Amish farms brought fresh waves of grief. Between our long silences, we talked about the amazing outpouring of love and support from the community. He and Terri were experiencing it as well. As we neared the funeral home, I silently prayed for the Lord to replace my anxiety with the awe I'd felt when I heard of the trust fund and the covering of the funeral costs. I longed to exchange all that was negative for all that was good.

As we stepped into the funeral home, I took a few deep breaths to calm my queasiness. Terri arrived just a few moments later. The avalanche of emotion felt crushing.

We agreed to a closed-casket funeral service to be held on Saturday, which would allow enough time for the families of the victims to have their services first. The burial would be held at the small cemetery behind Georgetown United Methodist, directly adjacent to my grandpa's property—a part of the landscape of my life since the day I'd been born. After choosing the casket and discussing the service, the director offered us the opportunity to view the body, but I declined. I wanted to remember Charlie as he'd lived, rather than have my mind seared by the image of him in death.

For the closing music I chose a song that had been the melody of heaven for me ever since the day of the tragedy: "All I Want" by Jeff Deyo. Music had been my lifeline since childhood, a place of reflection and worship, my secret place with Jesus, the atmosphere where I felt his Spirit speak to mine. I'd sung this song over and over in the last two days in my mind and sometimes out loud in a solitary moment. It spoke to me of complete restoration.

I come, with a heart that is desperate
And I cry, wanting just to be heard by You
And I pray, that You won't remain silent
That You'll stand here beside me
That my heart won't call out in vain

'Cause all I want is just to see You, Jesus
And I long, just to hear Your voice
And I need, just to be near You
'Cause Your presence is all I want

Each time I'd sung it this week, as I asked Jesus answered, and as I cried he comforted. Considering how much I dreaded the funeral, I knew that I would need to *rest* in that song at its end. It would be my anthem, my light at the end of the tunnel. Jesus would be there to strengthen me in the end.

"One last thing before you go," the funeral director said. "Wait here — I'll be right back." He stepped away for a few moments, then returned with a small box. "Since you've decided to have a closed casket," he said, holding it out, "I thought you might like to take this with you now."

He pressed the small box ever so gently into the palm of my hand. I lifted the lid.

Charlie's wedding band.

Tears sprang to my eyes. I lifted the ring and looked inside for the inscription. *Our Promise.* I slid his ring onto my finger and we left.

Back at Aunt Linda's home, the warmth of family greeted me. The aroma of dinner in the oven came wafting through the living room, carrying peace right to my core. It was as though the difficulties of the previous hours were forbidden to enter the graciousness of the home. The windows were open, and I tuned in to the sounds of life — my children playing in the backyard, neighbors chatting, the faint hum of a lawn mower in the distance. The neighbors were succeeding at keeping us well fed; a variety of delectable choices graced the table, the most difficult decision being, once again, how to fit all the leftovers into the refrigerator!

I still can't imagine how Aunt Linda and Uncle Jim pulled it off, but in spite of all the comings and goings with the overflowing plenty of food, supplies, and gifts, the house remained calm and peaceful. No television, no radio, no newspapers or magazines entered my line of vision all week. My dad and uncle took the kids to the park just down the street at least once a day — with no one there aware of who these kids were — and played with them in the sanctuary of the shrub-screened backyard. Watching my children being loved on by the men in our family in the absence of their father was a stunning visual assurance to me of God's protective care. We were cocooned in his love.

After dinner I played in the backyard with the children. We tossed a new ball, yet another gift from a neighbor.

Exhausted by the emotion of the day, I had my eye on Linda's garden bench. "You guys keep playing," I said. "I'll be right over here on the bench."

I tried to drink in the colors. The grief of the funeral home exchanged for the peace of this shelter — the contrast was startling. I twirled Charlie's wedding band on my finger. *Our Promise. Our broken promise*, I thought with a burst of pain.

Lord, the color of my life has been drained. I'm empty. How quickly our hearts can plummet from moments of grace to deep despair. I felt stripped bare, like a young tree once full of tender shoots but now dismantled, branches and bark torn away. Only the ravaged trunk remained, struggling to remain upright. The image of my nakedness and seeping wounds brought to the surface an ache I'd kept repressed all afternoon. *Quench my thirst*, I prayed. *The heat of this day has left me parched, and my heart is dry and cracked with crevices I cannot mend. I have nothing left to give, and yet I must be prepared to do it all again tomorrow. Help me, Father. I can't do this alone.*

He whispered back, *Trust, open, yield, surrender to a new*

depth, give me more of you. You know only limitations—I am limitless.

Sleep, once again, did not come easily that night. By now I'd barely slept in days. My trip to the funeral home had stirred up memories of losing Elise, a time when my hopes and dreams were completely swallowed up. After we lost our daughter, during long sleepless nights I would place my hand where she should be, only to find the emptiness of loss all over again. Now, years later, my mind lingered in the past, calling me to grieve anew for a loss I'd thought was healed.

Had Charlie struggled with such thoughts yet, in an attempt to spare me, kept them to himself? I didn't know.

In the wee hours of the morning, my thoughts turned to the Amish families. In their sleepless moments between twilight and dawn, how were they coping? Surely, like me, they faced the crushing reality of loss all over again as they grieved that the daughters they had embraced Monday morning were now beyond their reach. I had no idea how God would accomplish their healing. Yet no one but God was orchestrating the generosity coming our way, as people around us stepped in and stepped up, not shrinking back, but rising to the challenge. Our community—friends and strangers—had crawled into the chasm with us to help us with the long climb out. I hoped the world was responding to the suffering of the Amish families in even greater ways.

What I didn't know that sleepless night—due to my seclusion from the media—was that the generous grace that the Amish had extended to us, Charlie's family, had caught the attention of the world. As I dozed and tossed and turned, their act of grace was rippling around the nation and throughout the globe, bearing witness to the God who is, himself, grace.

~

Thursday morning dawned foggy and dreary, and I missed the cheerful morning light of yesterday. Finally tearing myself away from the comfort of the bed, I headed downstairs to have breakfast with my parents before they left the house.

"Please tell the families that I continue to pray for them," I told my mom as she and my dad prepared to leave. Two Amish families had invited my parents to the funerals of their daughters, both held that day. My parents knew these families from years of visits picking up milk from their farms.

"You know we will," Mom said. "And don't worry about the meetings at school. We'll get everything worked out."

My parents had an appointment that day at my children's school, in my place, to prepare the way for Abigail and Bryce to return the following week. I was grateful. I didn't have the emotional energy for a meeting with school staff.

The house seemed quiet in their absence. It was the first time they'd both been gone at the same time since we'd arrived. Their absence made me realize how much their presence had been giving me comfort and strength all week. I heard Carson calling for me upstairs and silently prayed as I climbed the stairs, *Help me — I'm a single mom now. Be their daddy, Lord. They won't have their father to lean on like I've still got mine.*

~

Later that day, the doorbell rang, and once more I ushered the detectives upstairs to what had become our usual spot.

"So the service will be at High View Church of God, followed by a drive to the cemetery behind Georgetown United Methodist. Is that correct?" a detective asked.

I nodded.

"Rest assured, we will block off all road access to the church in Ronks, and to the entire town of Georgetown for the graveside ceremony, since that town is so small. That way we can avoid having the church and cemetery overrun by media vans and satellite dishes. We'll set up police checkpoints, and any non-Amish will have to show their ID before being allowed to pass."

I was grateful but a little rattled at the extremes they were going to for security. How bad were they expecting this to be? A sense of nauseating dread washed over me. Was the world angry with me or resentful that Charlie's children were alive while Amish children were dead? Were the police concerned about protests? Retaliation?

The detectives must have seen the worry on my face. "Mrs. Roberts, I'm not sure you've heard how fascinated the world is with the story of forgiveness in the wake of this shooting."

What? No, I didn't realize it. How could I, secluded from all media? Were they saying that it was the miracle of forgiveness that was drawing the media frenzy?

After the detectives left, I allowed myself to revisit favorite memories of Charlie. If, before this week, I'd heard of such a shooting, I would have thought that only a monster could do such a thing. Somehow I had to reconcile that with what I knew of Charlie: that the man I'd spent my life with was no monster. Revisiting good memories not only helped me, they were necessary for my children. I wanted Abigail and Bryce to remember their daddy building sand castles and splashing through the waves as he chased them on the beach during a family vacation, and I wanted Carson to learn through such stories what his daddy had been like.

Our extended family had always enjoyed making memories together, celebrating birthdays, holidays, and everything in between. In the summer months, and guaranteed on Independence Day, my dad would make his special, hand-cranked ice cream. My mom mixed the cream, milk, and flavorings, and my dad did the rest. He preferred his old-fashioned freezer to anything electric. He would sit on the driveway for over an hour, sweatband collecting beads of perspiration upon his forehead. Slow and steady, he would turn the crank arm, adding ice and sprinkling salt as needed. Charlie would jump in, taking his turn and giving my dad a break. As we ate the fruit of their labor, Charlie would entertain us with fireworks. He loved lighting them as the children cheered.

My family loved Charlie. He'd been part of the fabric of our lives for thirteen years. We all simply "did life" together — parents, siblings, aunts and uncles, cousins, and grandparents. Charlie was quick to offer help anytime and loved the banter of family conversations and playing with the kids. Whether it was tackling a household chore with the kids or helping my dad with a construction project, Charlie was a patient teacher or handy sidekick, knowing just how to match himself to someone's personality. He had a quiet way of reaching into another's circumstances and being just what they needed in that moment.

The man who'd committed the shooting was not the man we knew, loved, and trusted. At the funeral on Saturday, we would celebrate the man we all remembered.

“I was thinking today about some of my favorite memories of Daddy,” I told the kids later that day. “Do you know what I remembered?”

I was sitting Indian-style on the living room floor, helping Carson build a tower with blocks. Abigail and Bryce were stretched out on the floor next to me, coloring in the brand-new coloring books that had arrived in a basket of goodies from a friend that day.

“What?” Abigail said.

“Well, when Daddy and I were dating, and I was still living with Grandma and Grandpa Welk, we had a big German shepherd named Jake. Jake loved our family and was the world’s best watchdog. Anytime someone came to our door, Jake’s deep growl would start, and he’d run to the door and bark and bark like he was going to eat them alive. People would step back, afraid, and Jake would bark even louder.”

“Like Dale!” Bryce said, referring to our yellow lab who’d been staying at my sister’s home all week.

“Oh, he sounded much meaner than Dale does,” I said. “Dale’s barks are almost friendly, and he wags his tail because he likes meeting new people. Not Jake. Jake was ferocious to strangers who came to the door.”

“Grrr,” Carson growled.

“So the very first time your daddy came to visit me at my house, Jake ran to the door, barking and howling. Do you know what your daddy did?”

“What?” they asked in unison.

“He stepped toward Jake instead of away, and he said, ‘Hey

there, boy. You're a big fella,' and within minutes he was scratching Jake behind the ears and tossing him his favorite chew toy."

"He wasn't afraid?" asked Abigail.

"Not even a little bit," I said. "Your dad loved dogs and dogs loved him."

"From that day on, when Jake heard your dad at the door, Jake was so excited to see him that he'd leap over the couch and bound to the door, his tail wagging, his tongue hanging out. He couldn't wait to play with your dad."

"Yeah," Bryce said, "dogs love our daddy."

"And we loved Daddy too, and he loved us. Bryce, what's one of your favorite memories with Daddy?"

Bryce didn't hesitate. "Wrestling together! And it always turned into tickling time. Daddy had a funny laugh."

Abigail and Carson nodded. Then Abigail spoke up. "My favorite memory is shopping with Daddy at the Amish store. He always let me pick out a candy. And he'd take me to the book rack near the register and let me look at books."

"Daddy always loved to take you shopping. He loved all of us very much. I'm really sad that Daddy's gone, but it helps to remember special times, doesn't it?"

I stood, thinking I'd spent enough time on the topic for now. The counselors had recommended brief, natural conversations, then moving on to something fun. "Who wants to play ball with me out back?" I said.

"Me, me, me!" my kids called as they followed me to the back door.

But pleasant memories of Daddy weren't the only topic of conversation with the kids that painful week. I also had, in quiet moments with each of the children, conversations that I did not want to have — about the way their father died, the girls who were shot, and the wrong decisions he'd made because of a deep hurt in his heart. I assured each of them that their daddy's act in no way had any connection with anything they'd ever said or done. I bathed each exchange in prayer, explored their understanding, answered their questions, and reassured them of their safety. I needed to help them understand that God's love did not mean he would keep us from walking through painful times. It meant that he would walk *with* us through painful times. I explained that it was okay to be sad and that slowly, over time, God would exchange our sadness for joy.

And while I reassured them, God reassured me.

After the kids were sound asleep, I went downstairs. Linda and Jim were with my parents in the kitchen, getting a bit of dessert and chatting. After years of quiet evenings while Charlie ran his night route, I wasn't used to company in the evening, so I loved this time.

"Dad and I had to drive through three police checkpoints today on our way to the funerals," Mom said. They had been back to Nickel Mines and Georgetown and had seen firsthand what I could only imagine: our obscure town had come under a national spotlight.

"The detectives told me it will be the same for Charlie's funeral," I said. "Were there a lot of reporters around Georgetown today?"

Linda said, "Yes, but it's different than you might think, Marie. Instead of focusing mainly on Charlie's actions and motives and the grief of the community, the world has been captivated by the Amish people and their immediate forgiveness of Charlie, and the way they've reached out to his parents and your family. *That's* what people are talking about — TV and radio talk shows, newspapers, online."

Mom's eyes were soft as she began to speak. "God is doing something. And not just here — it's touching people all over. This response from the Amish challenges people. It challenges me, all of us, to extend forgiveness to one another. People are amazed. They're asking how the Amish have been able to forgive. What an opportunity for the gospel to be in the spotlight. God is moving."

I sat quietly, trying to absorb that the world was being stopped in its tracks by the grace-filled response of the Amish community. The ones whose daughters had been taken by death were beaming radiant life not just to our family, not just to the community, but across the globe. My spirit lifted.

"Oh, I wanted to tell you all what happened to us this morning," Mom said. "You know that dense gray mist hovering here when we left this morning? Just as we reached the highway, the clouds suddenly parted and these incredibly radiant sunbeams pierced right through the clouds with a brilliant light. The landscape around us had been completely hidden, but when the light beams appeared through the lingering mist everything glistened. Marie, you should have seen it! It took our breath away."

"That sounds so beautiful, Mom. I wish I'd seen it," I said, picturing the scene.

"I said to your dad, 'I can't wait until God does something grand in this situation, just as he lit up this sky and burned away that bleak fog.'"

When I heard the expectancy in Mom's voice, it occurred to me that my own expectations for the week had been bleak. I just wanted the entire ordeal to be over. I hadn't been looking forward to the new things God was going to do. I'd just been in survival mode, groping for God's help to cope, rather than living in expectancy of what great things he might do.

Mom's words rang in my ears: "I can't wait ..." Her encounter with the sunbeams reminded me of my encounter with the rainbow years ago, and of how my anticipation of God fulfilling his promise of Abigail had filled me with joy and sustained me through the loss of Isabella. Maybe I was missing an opportunity to worship God in a spirit of *expectancy* this week.

When I finally crawled into bed that night, though I had no *emotion* of anticipation, I closed my eyes, willing to yield myself to this Holy Exchange — my nothing for his everything. All God required of me was to trust.

"Father of Light, stir my faith with expectancy of great things from you, even in this utter darkness."

I don't know exactly how it happened — not all in a moment that can be identified — but as I look back now I see that as I kept reaching, so did my Lord. As I reached up to the Lord, he reached way down deep inside of me, and bit by bit exchanged my despair for faithful expectation.

This swap, completely unmerited by me, revealed to me God's nature as my loving Father. Even when I was wounded and unable to see who he truly is, his goodness was not confined by my limitations. Even when I was blinded by the darkness of grief, his light still shone.

We so seldom see the present in light of the future. Thankfully, our Creator does. He is constantly creating us with the future in mind. I would never that day have dared to dream a dream as big as what God had in store for me yet that week. God is so much bigger than our dreams.

9

the wait

My memories of much of that week are a blur, and over the final couple of days, I remember little of the daylight hours. It's the nights I remember — the interminable nights of lying sleeplessly in bed as my mind ranged far and wide and the hands of the clock refused to move. During those silent, timeless nights, my sleeping children breathing peacefully at my side, I did the only things I could do. I thought. I prayed. I remembered.

I waited.

In the silence of Friday's early morning hours, I crept out of bed and down to the kitchen. It was only 2:00 a.m., at least four hours before the sun would rise, but I'd tossed and turned long enough waiting for dawn. I'd been thinking about the first responders and felt something stirring in my heart.

Aunt Linda had created a gift basket of some items she'd thought I might need this week, among them some lovely stationery and pens. I fixed myself a hot herbal tea, a fruity blend, and arranged myself at the large kitchen island.

I began my letter to the firefighters who'd worked heroically to save the lives of the innocent girls and so tenderly cared for the bodies of the girls already lost. I wrote how sorry I was for what they had seen, and though I couldn't imagine what they'd experienced that day, I told them I was sorry for the difficulty they must be facing in putting those images out of their minds. I told them they were heroes with servants' hearts. I signed the letter and began my next, this one to some neighbors who had reached out to meet our needs.

I realized that I was writing for my own benefit as much as for others', because I had no way to repay them for their sacrifice. I ached to do *something* for what Charlie had done, and I prayed with expectancy that God would work in each life of those who'd served with such kindness. This seemed a much more productive way to pass the minutes and felt far more useful than endlessly waiting for dawn to come.

After a few letters, I stood to stretch and felt drawn to the door leading down to Linda's art studio in their lower level. My children had told me that while I'd been with the detectives yesterday, Aunt Linda had given them "art lessons." As I went down the steep staircase, the scents of the art studio — paint and paper and linseed oil — rose to greet me, carrying with them pleasant memories of my healing days here after Elise.

Linda had tacked their artwork up for display on the wall, and I easily imagined the words of praise she'd found for each. I brushed my fingers over the watercolor "masterpieces" my children had painted under the inspiring tutelage of their aunt Linda. Who knew what seeds of creativity had been planted?

The memories of my studio days while healing from the loss of Elise turned my thoughts to Charlie. I so wished he had found an outlet for his pain.

One day, years ago, I'd tried again to help him purge his feelings. It had been the week of Easter, which I remembered because each Easter season the loss of our two girls always seemed to resurface for him.

That Easter Sunday as we watched Abigail and all the other little girls walking into church, he said to me, "There's just something so beautiful and innocent about little girls in new spring dresses, with barrettes in their hair and shiny new shoes." He squeezed my hand and I sensed, though I wasn't sure, he was thinking about Elise and Isabella.

The following Sunday afternoon, while Abigail, then age two and a half, and eight-month-old Bryce were taking a nap, I took a glass of iced tea to Charlie on the porch, where he sat reading a hunting magazine. He smiled and took the glass. I came back a moment later with my own glass and sat beside him. I waited a few moments to make it seem as if I were bringing this up casually, even though I was sure he could see through me.

"Charlie," I said, "I've been thinking a lot about Elise lately, about how life goes on after a tragedy like that. Even though it's been nearly five years, I know it's still hard for me. It must be hard for you too — but you don't talk much about it."

He kept his gaze on the magazine and sipped his iced tea, as if I hadn't spoken.

"If you don't want to talk about it with me," I said, "is there someone else, a friend, or our pastor, that you could talk to about it?"

He looked up from his magazine and gazed beyond the fields across the road. I waited, because Charlie had never been in a hurry to put his thoughts into words. "I don't know what difference it would make," he said at last. "I don't find it that helpful to talk about my feelings. It doesn't change anything."

I longed to ask him whether he was talking with God about it, as I was, but since Elise's death Charlie had seemed very uncomfortable talking about his relationship with God. Even before her death he'd been reserved about his feelings — since then, he'd been even more remote. "But is there someone you could talk to if you wanted to?"

He looked at me briefly, then away. "No men I know ever talk to me about their pain or their feelings — why would I think they would want me to talk to them about mine?"

This memory saddened me. I'd prayed, I'd shared, I'd hoped, but as far as I knew, after the loss of Elise, Charlie never seemed to find a connection with God intimate enough to allow him to release the pain and find a measure of peace.

Back in the present, in Aunt Linda's kitchen, the dishwasher suddenly came on, the timer having been set by Linda so its noise wouldn't interfere with the peacefulness she maintained during our days. I found the swishing rhythm a nice break from the silence of the bedroom where I'd lain awake so long.

When my fatigue made it too tiring to sit up anymore, I headed back to bed, snuggled between Abigail and Bryce again, and let my mind wander.

There was much to be done before the funeral. I decided to do my best to view the several visits still ahead of me through the new lens of expectancy I'd prayed for last night, and see these visitors as God's agents, playing a role that I needed, whether or not I felt I had the emotional energy to deal with them. It occurred to me that every choice I made this week would model for my children how to handle the weights and worries of this world. I needed to help them expect to see God at work as a shining light every day, even when all we see is fog and all we feel is pain.

It was easy to look forward to the visit of the two counselors later that day. They were great with the kids and were helping us find the words to talk about the events of the week and Charlie's choices.

"All three of your children," one counselor had assured me, "are responding in healthy, normal ways to this very unhealthy, abnormal situation. You and your family are doing just what they need. Keep up the great work."

Listening to the quiet breathing of the children in sleep, I clung to those reassuring words. I also appreciated how the counselors offered me a safe place to explore my thoughts and feelings. My mom and dad, when comforting me, were themselves grieving a horrible loss, and I often tried to hold my grief in check so as not to increase their pain.

There was something more I yearned to discuss with the counselors, though I realized it would take far more than one conversation. I wanted their insights on depression and what might have been going on inside Charlie that had led to this violent act. There would never be, of course, any logical explanation for his actions, as his unconscionable acts defied logic and reason. But I needed help understanding how such darkness could have been gnawing at Charlie without leaking out to those of us who loved him most. With sadness I realized that I would likely need to wait a lifetime before I could ever truly understand. Some mysteries are held for us until heaven.

While it was easy to wait in expectancy for the counselors, I wasn't nearly so positive about the day's upcoming session with the detectives. How could I apply my lesson of expectancy to them? I appreciated their kindness and the importance of their work but was filled with anxiety for them. They had carried an enormous burden since Monday morning, returning many times to the bullet-ridden, blood-spattered schoolhouse and visiting the families of all the children. Were they able to sleep at night? Did they see images of the dead and dying girls when they closed their eyes? Did they still hear the cries of the wounded and the grief-stricken wails of parents and grandparents who'd rushed to the schoolhouse in terror? When they chose this work — to serve, protect, and save the lives of those around them — they couldn't have envisioned that it would look like this. How would they recover? Would they be able to go back to work?

I did the only thing I could for them. I prayed and believed God for his healing in their lives and his provision for their families in even greater ways than he was already doing for me.

Four a.m. The clock on Aunt Linda's dresser stared me down in the wee hours of the morning. Would this waiting never end?

The funeral would be Saturday. Still more than twenty-four hours away. Though I was dreading it, I had reached the point where I wanted it behind me. All I had to do was make it through today, if today would ever dawn.

The children were longing for home, though home without Charlie was impossible for me to imagine. Mom and Dad too must be eager to get back to their own beds. Surely Aunt Linda must be ready for a break, though I'd never caught as much as a whisper of complaint. She'd been a woman on a mission of mercy, and all of us had been on the receiving end.

Four days. Is that really all it has been? I felt as if since Monday morning, when Charlie had called me, we'd been trapped in limbo — a bizarre existence of intense emotions, from the heights of burning-bush moments on holy ground to the depths of desperately black chasms of grief. Yet on every one of those days, God made himself known in unmistakable ways.

I had two more hours till dawn, and clearly sleep was not coming. I turned on my side to study Abigail's sleeping face and thought back to the rainbow God had given me to seal his promise that Charlie and I would have our Abigail.

"We have the most wonderful New Year's Day surprise for you," I announced to my parents with Charlie, glowing, by my side on the couch. We were in my parents' family room, enjoying the warmth of their woodstove, along with my brother, Ken, and sister, Vicki. All eyes turned toward us.

"We have a card for you," Charlie said as he handed them the handmade card I'd created. My mom and dad opened the card and read it before passing it on to my brother and sister.

Happy New Year's Day!

This year holds a promise and whispers of a dream come true. With great excitement we invite you to join us on this adventure as we prepare for a new baby to enter our world in early September.

Everyone leaped to their feet for hugs with tears of joy. Somehow, even from the first moment of knowing I was pregnant, Charlie and I had both believed that this pregnancy was different. Though we were anxious about reaching forty weeks, our outlook was predominantly hope-filled, believing that the baby growing in me was our Abigail.

Each of the many medical tests I underwent confirmed that hope — everything was progressing perfectly.

"What do you think you're going to have?" a friend at church asked me when word got around. I always answered the same way:

"A girl, because God told us so." I would then tell the story of mowing that summer day and the exchange that followed between the Lord and me, including his choice for her name, Abigail, and the rainbow that sealed his promise. Some people lit up with interest in my God-encounter. Some looked at me askance or smiled condescendingly at what they perceived to be my naiveté. Their responses didn't matter. I loved sharing my story.

Being pregnant with Abigail demonstrated how the trials of losing Elise and Isabella had deepened my trust. Had I given in to anger and bitterness at their loss, I would not have enjoyed expectantly watching to see what God would do. Instead, I had gone to God in prayer, immersed myself in his Word, sung his praises, and returned to my Father over and over again during the wait. Would God have given me my Abigail even if I had not done those things? I believe he would have, because I did not *earn* her through those actions. She was not my prize for a job well done; she was an expression of God's goodness and grace. But the joy and confidence of my faith would not have been so overflowing had I not waited expectantly, arms outstretched, watching for his good gifts.

I thought of the day when God spoke her name to me and sealed his promise with the rainbow — up to that point, my most powerful experience of hearing God's voice. But as I lay wide awake in bed, watching Abigail's eyelids flutter in sleep, I looked back on the several times this week since Charlie's call that I had heard God's voice. Back in 1998 and again this week, I could have dismissed the experience as the desperate delusions of a grief-stricken woman, her imagination running amok — but I didn't. I had been given the faith to believe his words about my future.

I would need that faith and expectation over the next few days, especially Saturday, the day of the funeral — no matter how overpowering the grief over losing Charlie.

I looked across the room at the clock. Finally! 6:00 a.m. Friday morning. I had things to accomplish and dawn had come.

Counselors. Calls from a few close friends. Conversations with the detectives reviewing a few final security details, and a conversation with the funeral home refining a few details of the service. The day was a blur. But there was one thing I couldn't neglect to do: prepare the children for every step of tomorrow.

"Hey, kids, let's go outside and color with sidewalk chalk," I said. Three eager kids were out the door before I was.

"Tomorrow is an important day." I tried my best to sound casual as we colored. "We will have a special service at our church — a funeral for Daddy — with our closest friends and family. Then we'll ride to the cemetery together where his body will be buried." And so we talked. I did my best to prepare them for what was to come and to answer their questions. They were somber but didn't appear to be worried or frightened. Maybe they were more prepared than I.

One final task lay ahead. The children and I needed suitable clothes and shoes to wear to the funeral. I'd brought nothing appropriate to Aunt Linda's house, and I wasn't yet ready to go back to my house. Besides, we'd been advised to stay away until after the funeral. So my sister and a close friend offered to take me shopping.

Vicki and Kristin arrived, filled with the gentleness that only a sister and a good friend could offer.

"You ready?" Vicki asked.

"I'm nervous about going out in public!" I said. "What if we run into someone I know? What if a stranger recognizes my face or the name on my debit card? I don't feel up to conversation."

"We'll make a quick job of this," Kristin tried to reassure me.

But a long list of fears circled in my mind for the entire twenty-minute drive to the mall. Would I overhear people talking about the shooting? How did people feel about me? What reactions would I have to endure? Since Monday morning, whenever feelings of personal guilt for Charlie's actions began to creep in, God had stepped in to quell those feelings. But a sense of shame still clung — the sense that somehow I should have known what was coming. The time I'd spent with the detectives had convinced me that there had been no clues to his plans that I could have seen. And it was clear in my conversations with the counselors and my family that none of us had seen this coming. Did people outside my family believe my innocence of any knowledge of Charlie's intentions, or were they skeptical and judgmental? I suspected the latter.

Once we parked, Vicki was ready to jump out of the car and get started, but I hesitated. "Okay, let's keep a low profile and slip in and out in a hurry," she said.

Easy for her to say. Since I was significantly taller than my fashion entourage, there was no hope of them providing cover! Still, however he might do it, I knew that God was capable of sheltering me. He had to, because I was simply incapable on my own.

I got out of the car, filled with misgivings, and we did our shopping. I tried not to look at newspapers or magazines in the mall, for the same reason we hadn't listened to the car radio on the drive over.

When we arrived home, Mom was eager to hear how it went.

"God sheltered me," I said. "I didn't encounter a single reporter, and though I saw a few people I know from a distance, they didn't notice me." I was tremendously thankful.

When at last I crawled into bed Friday night, I hoped I'd finally be able to get some deep sleep. I replayed a few favorite worship songs in my mind and meditated on verses of praise. After a long time in prayer, thanking God for all he'd done this week, I decided that tonight, the night before we would place Charlie's body in the ground, I would dwell on happy memories of Charlie.

Charlie. I could still see his face ...

"Charlie, quick — she's kicking!" I'd been sitting on the couch, and Charlie seemed to leap from the kitchen in a single bound, not wanting to miss a second of it. Feeling her every hiccup and even her kicking my ribs was delightfully fun. Our years of waiting were almost done. We couldn't wait to hold her! My dreams of motherhood were finally going to be fulfilled.

During those same months, maybe because our long-awaited dream was coming true, Charlie was allowing himself another dream: From the time he was a child, he had dreamed of having his own trucking company. At play as children, he and his best friend had pretended to be truck drivers. Now, one morning over breakfast, those dreams lit his eyes as he said with a shy but eager smile, "I know you're not crazy about the idea, but I still think about getting my commercial driver's license so I can drive a tractor-trailer. If your dad would take the time to teach me, I know I could do the same job — I know I could! Sure, I'd have a learning curve, but ..."

And on he went, getting more excited by the moment. And

suddenly my eyes were opened to a truth about myself that I didn't like — but couldn't deny. Through the years of our marriage, I had been discouraging Charlie from his dream.

"Charlie," I said, when he stopped to take a breath, "I see a brightness in your eyes as you talk about this. And it's made me realize something: I need to ask for your forgiveness. I've been wrong, and I've been unfair to you."

He looked confused. "You? No, never. You've always been the ideal wife." He squeezed my hand.

"Have I?" I said. "There's a job you would love to have — and I've told you over and over that I don't want you to have it. I've been so blind, Charlie — so selfish. I've been standing in the way of you pursuing your lifelong dream. I've always wanted to be your encourager, your confidence-builder — and I thought that's what I was doing. And yet my own family is the doorway to your accomplishing your dream, and I've been blocking it."

Charlie granted forgiveness freely, touched by my admission of remorse. I talked to my grandfather to open the door; Charlie took it from there, and soon he was spending his Saturdays off sitting beside my dad in his truck. Continuing to work full-time at his regular job Monday through Friday, Charlie trained over the weekends and whenever he could squeeze in some extra time. This was part of what I loved about Charlie — he was a hard worker who took seriously his commitment to provide for our family.

Charlie would come home talking excitedly about his progress, describing new skills he'd learned with the gears and in maneuvering the truck around the barns and lanes of his customers. He would recount scenes of the Amish families that I had so enjoyed as a child. I loved seeing him so excited.

After only a few months of training, he took the CDL (commercial driver's license) test. His first attempt was successful, and he was ready to embark on a new career!

"I can't wait to get up in the morning," Charlie said more than once. He was enjoying a role he'd been designed to fill, and he was great at it too. He could back an eighteen-wheeler down farm lanes and around buildings, making it look easy. And he enjoyed talking with the farmers and other truck drivers at the dairy. He would tell me about his conversations with his favorites when his workday finished. I wonder if those men ever realized that they had become his treasured friends. He enjoyed their friendly banter and laughter, and he cared about their lives. Once, when the owner of another truck company lost his son, Charlie filled in for him on his routes for a while, visited the family, and tried to find ways to bring some comfort to those grieving.

While Charlie was still learning to drive the truck, we moved from Lititz back to my hometown of Georgetown, wanting to be closer to our families — and knowing that Charlie would start driving for my grandfather when he had his CDL license. My grandparents had offered to let us put a home on the lot adjacent to their property, the very place I had mowed while healing from the grief of losing Elise. We decided that once Abigail was born, we'd buy a modular house to be placed on the property, and in the meantime, just before Abigail's due date, we moved into a small makeshift apartment above my grandfather's truck garage, across the parking lot from Grandpa's house.

God's story for our lives had seemingly been reversed! What had seemed months before to be a tragic story of loss, we now saw as the love story of a family. Not only was I going to be a mother and Charlie a dad, but Charlie was now a driver, and I had gone from milkman's daughter to milkman's wife. And my daughter too would be the daughter of the milkman!

Then came the scare. The pregnancy went well until midsummer, when I started experiencing preterm labor. With my history, the doctors weren't taking any chances, so they put me on medication to stop the contractions and gave strict orders for bed rest from then on. Charlie and I were both frightened, but this time I had a deeper awareness of God's presence. I sensed him reassuring me to be at peace, all would be well. I kept returning to God's promise: I was going to have my Abigail and hold her in my arms.

The medication they prescribed worked. I had no further issues with preterm labor, though I was still confined to bed rest for the duration of the pregnancy. We were showered with frequent visits and love by our family, something that would not have been possible when we lived farther away in Lititz.

September 2, 1999, Abigail's due date: Right on schedule, Abigail began pushing herself into the world that had been waiting for her so long. At 7:30 a.m., Charlie gently walked me to our Ford Explorer and buckled my seat belt for me. If he could have, I think he would have backed the car right into the bedroom so I wouldn't have to walk. Giddy, we made the thirty-minute drive, laughing and celebrating that we'd made it full term.

Once we arrived at the hospital and were safely in the birthing room with our midwife, Charlie encouraged me to have an epidural. "I just don't want you to be in any pain," he said.

"Charlie, I've waited forever to give birth to our little girl. I don't want to miss a moment of it. I'd much rather feel her entering this world than have a needle in my spine!"

What could he say? As most dads have learned — never argue with a wife in labor. So he gave me sips of water and held my hand until she arrived a few hours later.

The midwife, as agreed, handed him the scissors to cut the

umbilical cord. Charlie looked at Abigail, then me, then nervously at the midwife. "I'm not going to hurt her, am I?" he said.

"She won't feel a thing," said the midwife.

In a flash, the deed was done.

As I held my baby girl in my arms, I experienced a completely new kind of love, along with heavenly contentment. I breathed deep, savoring the moment I'd waited so long to enjoy.

Charlie gently took Abigail into his arms, and I was filled with the sweetness of love shared between Charlie and me for this precious gift of life God had given. We marveled at her beautiful pale skin, like a porcelain doll, her vibrant blue eyes and feathery lashes, her delicate fingers and tiny toes. I wondered if she might play the piano. Would those sweet hands dance across ivory keys?

There was completeness to our family now, wholeness. The pain we'd experienced in the delivery room nearly two years before with Elise was overcome by a surge of rich joy. Having Abigail, I thought, would never fill the void left by Elise, but it brought love unimaginable so that loss was now overshadowed by anticipation of a future together and God's merciful redemption.

Our son Bryce was born twenty-two months later. He came tumbling into our world filled with laughter and energy, an inquisitive mind, and enough noise to fill every corner of our house. Abigail was fascinated with her little brother — maybe almost as much as her dad and I. Charlie loved being a father and beamed with pride when we'd take the children to church or to visit family.

Carson eased into our lives in April 2005, laid-back and happy. His sister was now five and a half years old, his brother four, and he seemed to know instinctively that his role was to make them laugh. Our home was a place of giggles and tickles, stories and songs, tumbles and spills, and everything else that a young couple and three young children bring with them.

Yet why did those pleasant memories now make me squirm with discomfort? Our prayers had been answered not only with Abigail, but then with Bryce and Carson. Charlie's dream job had been just what he'd hoped — he'd loved it. Why, so many years after the loss of Elise and Isabella, good years in which we'd lived our dreams, did Charlie's hidden grief boil over into a murderous rampage? I couldn't imagine what secret pain had so twisted his heart. I only knew that, to me, it made no sense!

Careful not to wake Abigail or Bryce, I wiggled my way to a sitting position and propped myself up with a few of Linda's fluffy down pillows, my arms crossed, my brow furrowed, my frustration intense.

Our lives had felt beautiful. By October 2006, I had been married almost ten years and loved my role as a wife to Charlie and mom to our three precious children, by then ages seven, five, and eighteen months. Charlie loved and enjoyed our kids and loved his job. Though life wasn't always easy, we were living our dream.

Then came the morning of October 2, 2006.

A call came that shattered that dream into a million fragments.

The police came with facts too gruesome to speak.

Questions came without answers.

But now you must hear the rest: how God came with me into my darkness and lit it with brilliance beyond comprehension.

After all, this is a love story.

10

wall of grace

The morning of the funeral dawned peacefully. There was a stillness in the neighborhood, as if nature itself was holding back, not wanting to touch the reality of this day. I rose early, knowing that the knot in my stomach would remain a tangled mess until it was all over and we returned, as a family of four, to the sanctuary of my aunt's home for one last night.

Even time seemed to stand still. I glanced at the clock often, willing the hands to move faster. It stared back at me in stubborn defiance. My aunt's home held a flurry of inactivity. We were all trying to find something to do to fill the dragging seconds before leaving for the 10:00 a.m. service. My heart could scarcely hold the truth of this morning. *I am going back to the church where we were married almost ten years ago for the funeral ceremony for the only man I ever loved. My children will look upon the casket containing the empty body of their father. How will we endure the next few hours?*

I lifted my heart heavenward, thirsty for the sense of expectancy I'd found on Thursday night and Friday. It did not come that morning. I felt only numbing emptiness.

We were adorned in our new funeral clothes — outfits that would only be worn this day, then never see the light of day again. They would be buried in the back of a closet somewhere, unworn because of the emotion irrevocably tied to them. All three of the children were quiet and solemn, taking their cues from the unnatural heaviness that seemed to fill the house.

I slid Charlie's wedding band upon my finger behind my own rings so it wouldn't slip off. The phrase *Our Promise* etched inside now rang hollow. This ring symbolized bonds of love. At our wedding ceremony, we had proclaimed they could never be broken. The idealistic, romantic girl I used to be had thought this to be true. My circumstances now told me otherwise.

My car had been parked in a neighbor's garage all week, protecting the secret of my whereabouts. Strange — it was now Saturday, and I hadn't driven myself anywhere since arriving Monday night.

I remembered listening to the radio on my way to and from my Bible study on Monday morning. I'd been a naive twenty-eight-year-old Christian wife and mom whose entire sheltered life had been lived in idyllic Amish country. Would I ever feel like that again? Ordinary? Normal? So much of my life before last Monday morning had been spent assuming that the blessings surrounding us, the gifts placed within our lives, would continue for my lifetime. If we truly realized the treasure we behold each morning as the sun kisses a new day, our lives would be lived differently. *I must live differently from this day forward*, I promised myself.

Finally, the time came to leave for the church. I shivered in the cool, breezy air; the clear blue skies of a few days ago were now partly obscured by clouds. I buckled the kids into their car seats and climbed behind the steering wheel. Dad once again took his place of support next to me. How do you thank a father for simply knowing what you need? I asked him if he was going to put on his seat belt. At least some things never change! It felt good to feel a tiny smile tug at the corners of my mouth for an instant.

As we neared the church, I realized that the trip there had taken less time than I'd expected, and being early didn't seem like a good idea. I decided to go through the car wash. That would've made Charlie happy. He made it a priority to take good care of his belongings. Our cars and his eighteen-wheeler were always spotless.

An odd thought occurred to me: I had no idea what widows were supposed to do *after* the day of the funeral. *Should I wear black for a while? What do I do with all of his stuff?* Those questions and others swirled through my head as foam and spray pelted us in the car wash.

We pulled into the parking lot at High View Church of God, a place full of memories. I was relieved to see no media trucks. As I approached the glass double doors with Abigail clinging tightly to my right hand and Carson on my left hip, I was hit by the image of Charlie carrying Elise's tiny coffin out those same front doors. In about an hour, it would be Charlie's coffin crossing that threshold. Dad's presence by my side holding Bryce's hand kept me steady.

I searched for a happy memory to cling to as I stepped inside. In this building, for six years, I had sung words of praise, helped in the nursery, taught Sunday school, worshiped with Charlie, and pledged the vows of marriage. In more recent years, since becoming part of this church's launch of Living Faith Church of God, we had returned here with our children for Easter egg hunts and vacation Bible school programs. But those wonderful family memories served only to emphasize the stark reality of the devastation of the Amish families ... and my own.

Many family members and friends had already arrived. My children and I took our seats in the front row, directly in front of Charlie's closed casket, my parents by our side. My brother and sister sat directly behind us, and Charlie's parents sat in the front row across the aisle from us. The seating arrangements seemed much like our wedding — Charlie's family on one side of the aisle, mine on the other. I felt the eyes of the congregation on me but sensed no judgment — only love, compassion, and the reassuring knowledge that their prayers were covering me. I was safe here. My children, their bodies pressed against me, were still and silent, their eyes, like mine, on the coffin.

More than a third of my twenty-eight years of life had been spent as Charlie's wife. Yet only now was I able to see something I'd never realized before — not in the aftermath of the shooting, not while talking with my parents, the detectives, or even the counselors: In all honesty, the emotional health of our marriage had been dying for several years. As Charlie had increasingly kept to himself his thoughts and feelings about God and about his sorrow over Elise and Isabella, he had also withdrawn from expressing his heart to me. I realized that I had actually been grieving the loss of emotional closeness for some time. It wasn't that he had stopped loving me — I never felt that — but in retrospect I could see how the pain within Charlie had overshadowed everything else. He must have fought that battle every day and poured the love he could express upon our children. That was fitting; I would always have wanted them to be the ones who got the most. They deserved it.

What was said at the brief funeral ceremony eludes my memory. Though I was present in body, my mind was elsewhere. The sounds of Scripture verses being read, music being played, and

Pastor Dwight speaking became nothing more than a distant backdrop for the memories of the past twelve years that flooded my mind during the service. Our first date, the day he taught me how to drive a stick shift, long walks together, his picnic proposal, our engagement party, planning for our wedding, pregnancies lost, newborn babies, the joy of children, playing in the sand at the beach on summer vacations. A video of a million memories played back in minutes. How could love and commitment be sown and this tragedy reaped? How could this be my life? Where was the surety of promises made over our children?

Our youngest sat on my lap and the other two children on either side. I covered them with my arms and embraced them with my heart. I was now all they had — two reduced to one. My efforts would now have to be concentrated and multiplied to fill the hole within their lives. *God help me!*

My mind jolted back to the present as the song "All I Want" started playing — my anthem of the past week, a proclamation over our future. My hands lifted as my tears fell. I didn't try to wipe them; there were too many. I felt God near me; I felt him hold my hands — he was reaching down as I reached up. I succumbed to the compassion and tenderness of Christ and let it wash over me. Gone was the numb emptiness of the morning. In poured the warm presence of the Lord. But I couldn't allow myself to totally collapse into his arms. I wanted to, but I held in check the urge to let all my emotions surface and flow. I didn't know what would happen if I did that. I needed the *perception* of being in control, or my emotions would take over, something I did not want to let happen. My children needed a steady mother, and I needed to retain my composure so that I could greet those who'd come to the service and endure the graveside ceremony.

The service ended, and we filed out into the church lobby where those in attendance expressed their heartfelt sympathy and concern for our family. Warm embraces reassured me and the children, and tears flowed freely, but I found myself at a loss for words in response. The number of loved ones surrounding us overwhelmed me. Though I knew everyone there cared for us, I felt an impulse that made me feel ashamed: I wanted to gather my children and run from the building. But I couldn't — there was no way out. So while I appeared calm and collected, a vision of strength and endurance, everything within me quaked.

We moved to the parking lot in preparation for the fifteen-minute drive to the cemetery. Charlie was to be buried at the little church cemetery in Georgetown, just three houses up the street from our home. Our daughter was also buried there. Charlie would lie next to Elise.

I wanted to ride in my car to the burial as I had that morning, but I met fierce opposition. My dad and our pastor's wife, Heather, tried to convince me to ride in the back of a car provided by the funeral home, which would lead the processional. If I rode in the funeral home's car, I would be riding separately from my kids, and I didn't want anything to do with that. I finally gave in when I saw that my dad wouldn't take no for an answer.

Heather rode with me in the funeral home's sedan, just behind the hearse. My parents drove my car with my children just behind us, and Charlie's family followed them. The partly cloudy skies had now clouded over completely; it was dark, cold, and windy. We didn't take the most direct route to the graveyard, and as we meandered back roads I wondered if this route had been chosen to keep a low profile.

As we topped the small rise in the road, I expected to see the little white church and cemetery on our right. Instead, I gasped in horror and instantly understood all the steps taken to protect me. Along the grass on our left, across the street from the cemetery, crowded a group of reporters and photographers who held cameras that looked like telescopes. I was mortified. All week my family had been explaining that the media had invaded our town, but I'd not fully grasped what they meant until this moment. The detectives had told me that the police would block off the road, so I hadn't expected any media here. But I could see now that the reporters and cameramen had parked their trucks beyond the security checkpoint and walked some distance to this spot on the roadside from which they could view the cemetery. Every camera was focused on us. How thankful I was for those dark tinted windows.

But how would we stay out of the spotlight at the graveside? For the entire week, I'd worked so hard to keep our faces from being strewn across newspaper front pages and television reports. I'd declined interviews and hidden my family from public view. But now what could we do? We had no way to take cover. How would I shield my children?

I was devastated. Here I was on one of the hardest days of my life, and this intrusion into our privacy only added to the agony. I didn't want the world to see my heart breaking all over again. I wanted to shout, *Let my children weep by the grave of their father in private!*

Slowly our procession turned right into the narrow driveway alongside the church and inched our way toward the small stone parking lot and cemetery tucked behind the church.

Straight ahead as far as the eye could see were rolling fields of cornstalk stubble dotted with white silos. To our right was the small square cemetery, no more than five car lengths across in either direction. To our left, on my grandfather's acreage, stood his long green truck garage, easily twice as long as the cemetery.

Behind us were the reporters, their telephoto lenses fully extended and their cameras clicking. I could almost feel them boring into the back of my head.

While we were still on the driveway, before we'd even pulled into the little parking lot, a movement caught my eye ahead on the left, behind the corner of my grandfather's garage. A quick blur of black and blue. I focused on the spot, afraid that some photographers had snuck onto my grandfather's property to get even closer shots.

I spotted the rim of a black hat first, clearly Amish. He'd been hidden behind the garage, undoubtedly to avoid being within view of the cameras.

The Amish man looked directly at our procession for a second or two, then stepped out from behind the garage and moved slowly in our direction. He was followed by another, then a woman, her long black cape flapping in the wind, her black bonnet shielding her face. One after another, the line of Amish men and women grew to about three dozen, walking in our direction. The hearse moved forward to the grave site, but our car stopped and waited.

I watched unbelieving, tears streaming down my face, as that line of Amish formed a crescent wall in front of us, hiding the grave site from our view—and from the view of the reporters and photographers.

Our car began to inch forward again, and as it did the wall of Amish parted in the middle, allowing my car and the car with my children and parents to pass through. The moment our cars were inside the crescent, those good people closed the gap behind us.

They were shielding us! The Amish were shielding the family of Charlie Roberts.

The cameras of the world could see only one thing — the backs of the Amish people.

From inside the crescent, I could see only one thing — faces of grace. We were shielded by love, by sacrifice, by unmerited favor. God was protecting us with a wall of grace.

You must understand — the Amish *do not have their pictures taken*. To do so violates their belief that picture-taking creates a graven image. This act was a true sacrifice, unconditional love poured out upon the wife and children of the man who had taken their daughters from them. That they would choose to give such a gift to us was beyond comprehension.

I stepped out of the car, joined hands with my children, and walked the few dozen steps past gravestones old and new, some worn by more than two hundred years of winds and weather, some of polished stone still gleaming. A white canopy stood over Charlie's coffin, already placed beside his open grave. To the right, in pink granite, stood the heart-shaped stone that bore the engraved epitaph:

Elise Victoria Roberts
pledged to God
dau. of
Charles & Marie
born & died
Nov. 14, 1997

As I looked through my tears at the fresh-turned earth, I thought about the five other funerals that had taken place that week. The Miller family had buried two daughters. The Ebersol,

Fisher, and Stoltzfus families had each buried a daughter as well. Their worlds were broken, turned upside down like the dirt lying before me. Treasures lost, now buried; hopes ended and dreams destroyed. Yet poured into those chasms of loss was not bitterness nor anger, not hatred nor revenge, but love poured out to overflowing.

My eyes looked beyond the cemetery to scan the landscape I'd known all my life. I'd biked those roads, visited those farms, been welcomed into those barns, bounced down their lanes in milk tankers and sampled and weighed the milk from those cows. My great-grandfather and grandfather had done the same before me, as had my dad beside me, and my Charlie.

Our pastor lifted his voice in prayer. My children and I picked a flower from the bouquet atop the casket, one last remembrance of this day. And then the wall of grace became a receiving line of shared grief, hands extended, arms encircling, tears mingling with our own. It was at once excruciatingly painful and profoundly healing to grieve the loss of Charlie in the embrace of the Amish community.

As we were greeting each other around the grave site, my mother approached with a lovely Amish woman. "Marie," she said, "this is Mrs. Miller, the mother of two daughters lost that day."

I was standing face-to-face with the mother of Lena, age seven, and Mary, age eight, who'd died at Charlie's hand. I was amazed—one of the families who lost daughters at the schoolhouse had come?

"I'm so sorry," I choked out as we stepped into one another's arms, weeping freely.

"And I am so sorry for your loss as well," she said. She moved back to include the man standing behind her. "This is my husband."

Then, one by one, every Amish family greeted me with words of comfort and compassion. To my utter disbelief, *all* the parents of the girls lost at the schoolhouse had come to grieve with me — to be certain that I knew I was not alone.

I've never been so emptied. I've never been so filled.

God's strength flowed into me within the arms of that wall. I was forever changed.

On that day, at the graveside of my husband, I could not see the darkness of our loss. All I could see was the light of God surrounding my family. And it was a light so bright I felt I'd just been given a tiny glimpse of what awaits us when we stand face-to-face with God Almighty in paradise.

Years have passed since that day. Yet as I write these words, my heart still races and my mind still spins as I ponder and treasure the tenderness I was shown. The wall of grace that day told a love story.

part three

Dawn's Light

11

home fires

Pastor Dwight stood before an unusually large crowd Sunday morning, every seat filled, and welcomed the many visitors who had come to show their support for my family. We loved worshiping here every Sunday alongside my parents, Charlie's parents and grandparents, and other extended family. The outpouring of love and prayers from this congregation had covered us all this past week. Even so, my children and I had waited until the last minute before entering, unprepared to socialize on this first day after the funeral. Eager as I was to be here, my emotions were too raw for condolences and shared tears.

We'd made the right decision to have Charlie's funeral at our old church, High View, the church of my past, a place of memories. Today I was back in the church of my present, Living Faith Church of God, which had been planted by High View. I was grateful that I wouldn't have the image of Charlie's coffin in my mind every Sunday as I worshiped here.

Abigail, Bryce, and Carson had awakened with excitement from their final night's sleep at Aunt Linda's. Today they were going home! Before leaving for church, we had scurried around packing up the belongings we'd brought to Linda's place. The kids had chattered the whole time about how good it would be to sleep in their own beds and play with our dog, Dale. They were adorable as they discussed how glad Dale would be to come home as well, after his week with my sister and brother-in-law. It was fun to hear the anticipation in their voices, as if we were getting back to normal.

Normal. I had no idea what that might mean for us now. A *new* normal, I supposed. What would it feel like to be home? Charlie was everywhere and nowhere. Did I even want to go back? The knowledge of what lay ahead brought thoughts I was not prepared to deal with, so I pushed them aside, knowing their time would come soon enough.

I was relieved when we pulled into the church lot and saw no signs of media vans. When my pastor, Dwight, and I had talked a few days before, I'd told him I wanted to address the congregation today to share a bit of my journey over the past week with our church family. They needed to know we were okay. We'd been a part of this close-knit group of believers for nine years. I wanted to assure them that their prayers had brought strength. I wasn't hiding under a bed somewhere, I wasn't panic stricken, and I wasn't a basket case, because God was doing something astounding in the midst of this tragedy.

Pastor Dwight shared briefly with the congregation about the events of the past week and the mending he saw God doing in the midst of great brokenness. Quite a startling concept — God's ability to put the pieces back together in the midst of such great loss. Then Dwight called me forward, and as I walked toward the front I heard gasps and saw looks of surprise on many faces. The response didn't bother me, and surprisingly, I wasn't concerned with what they were thinking. The evidence of God's bountiful love surrounded me, and despite the wrecking ball that had splintered my world, I knew my foundation was secure.

Standing before the sea of faces, I recognized the look of hunger for good news. Mine hadn't been the only life shaken six days ago. My entire community was in pain, crying out to God with grief, grappling to understand how a friend in their midst could do such a thing. *Where was God? How could he allow this to happen to us, our church, and our town?* These questions were haunting my friends and neighbors. I had to tell them what they had *not* seen: how God showed up, infused me with his strength, surrounded my family with his love, met our every need.

The Marie who stood before them now was not the same Marie of last Sunday. I wonder to this day if they could *see* the change I felt. The timid, shy, stay-at-home-wife-of-the-milkman who'd always shunned the spotlight, always placed herself in the middle of the crowd — never at the front — now stood before them burning to bear witness of how God's deep mercy, his incalculable strength, had invaded her this past week. The old Marie would have been trembling to stand before them. Today's Marie could hardly wait to open her mouth. And so I did.

"I have some things to share this morning that will surprise you," I began. "If I were you, I'd have assumed that Marie was hiding under a bed somewhere, afraid to go out into the world. And I admit — it isn't easy to come out of the covering we've had this past week. But I am not afraid. God's strength is made perfect in our weakness, and his strength has been much in evidence this week.

"First, I want to thank you. You have poured out your prayers and love over us, and God is answering those prayers."

I went on to tell them how God had responded in huge ways to my cries for help. "I don't know what to expect of the future, but I do know God is bringing healing in deep ways. I feel like I've been given two years of healing in one week.

"Among the many things I understand more deeply now than I did a week ago," I said, "is the role of God as my Redeemer. To redeem means to exchange one thing for another, to buy back, to recover the value of something by exchanging it for another. Over these past few days, God has been replacing my weakness with his strength, the ugliness of sin with the beauty of forgiveness, the blackest darkness with his brilliant light. As impossible as it may seem, I am walking in confidence in God's ability to repair each broken place in our lives and to restore our lives so that they are once again characterized by hope and joy.

"Please continue to pray for me and my entire family. Pray for the Amish families. Pray for the first responders and the burden they bear. Rejoice with me that God is working in all our lives through this."

The congregation clung to my words. They had needed to know that God was with us all. I'd been given a glimpse of a depth of faith I'd never known, and as I shared it, I felt it multiply.

~

On the twenty-minute drive home from church, I noticed an unfamiliar car following me. It had exited the church parking lot right after me and stayed with me through several turns, even as I'd left the highway behind and headed down country roads. A reporter, perhaps, hoping to steal some pictures of my children's return to their home? Maybe not. It might have simply been a neighbor on his way home from church, like me. But I didn't want to take the chance. I attempted to lose him by taking a roundabout route on rural back roads. Glancing frequently in my rearview mirror, I felt as if I were in a scene from some TV show or movie. I vacillated between feeling foolish and feeling dumbfounded, but the longer the car followed, the more my anxiety grew. I couldn't believe this was happening the very first time I drove the car without another adult with me since Charlie died! The few times I'd been behind the wheel since last Monday, my dad had been by my side.

As I made my way south through Strasburg and toward Georgetown, I did my best to chat with the kids as normal. They didn't need to know we were being followed. *If only Charlie were here, I wouldn't be afraid.* A stupid thought, I told myself. If Charlie were here, none of this would be happening. God and God alone was my protector now. Without their father, it was now my job to make my kids feel safe. That's why I decided not to call anyone on my cell phone — I didn't want to alarm my happy kids.

Eventually, I outmaneuvered the car on my tail. There is a distinct advantage to growing up in the country and knowing all the shortcuts. As I neared my house, I left the main road and cut right across the back end of my grandpa's property, bouncing over the grass. I did my best to make it seem like a fun adventure by telling the kids that I could four-wheel just like Daddy could. They laughed and thought it was a delightful way to make our grand return home. Little did they know how rattled I was, how vulnerable and abandoned I felt.

Relief eased my grip on the steering wheel as I parked my car in my grandparents' garage. No need to announce my return to the media. Let them wonder. I herded the kids across my grandpa's driveway toward the house, eager to get inside and out of sight as quickly as possible. The kids had no idea of my anxiety, and since they were happy to get back to their own house, they didn't resist.

Then, short of the door, we all came to a sudden stop, happy to see "Old Grandpa" waiting for us. Warm hugs and bright smiles all around.

We were home.

Within ten minutes, our house was filled with family members wanting to show their support. Some had stopped at a local sandwich shop to pick up lunch items. As the food was laid out, others scurried around my house cleaning, rearranging, and trying to find something to do. Though well meant, the flurry of activity was too much for me to handle. I didn't particularly *want* my kitchen rearranged and didn't mind that there was dust in my living room after a full week away. Those things were unimportant at the moment. I just wanted to sit in my home and surrender myself to the reality of the future. So much had happened since the last time I'd awakened in my own house. It was hard to take it all in, and being back within our own walls brought a nearly crippling intensity of emotion.

With so much going on around me, so much noise, I lost sight of Abigail. I had *not* wanted to do that. What was my seven-year-old thinking and feeling?

I found her in her room and sat next to her on her bed. We sat quietly, looking out the window. A tear escaped and slid silently down my cheek, followed by more. What was to become of us?

Bryce and Carson came walking through the doorway. "Mommy, let's look at the photo albums," Bryce said. I could see it in his eyes: he missed his daddy.

My son, I'm sure, was looking for a way to make us all feel better and our hearts grow stronger.

We would make it through this together.

Minutes later, the four of us were huddled together on the couch, slowly turning pages of our family albums. Though surrounded by family milling around and talking to one another, we were our own island of four. As we looked at photographs of past joys we had celebrated together, my eyes could not contain the collection of sorrows spilling from my heart. Tears and more tears kept falling. Bryce's eyes searched my face, looking for reassurance that I was going to be all right. My children seemed unsure about my display of emotion. "It's okay to cry," I explained. "When we feel sad or when we're hurt, we need to express those feelings, and one way we do that is by crying." I wanted them to be comfortable enough to cry too. Charlie had been unable to express the depth of his emotion — but that need not become true of their little lives.

Day slipped into evening as one by one our family members left. I was alone with my children for the first time in a week. As strange as it seemed, I felt a deep sense of peace. I was not afraid to be on my own. Doing my best to keep the evening routine fairly "normal," I bathed each of them and put them into bed. We read stories and prayed together. This had been our routine for their whole lives — Daddy worked at night and Mommy put them to bed. Normal.

But what will happen in the morning?

I pushed the nagging question back where it had come from. I would deal with tomorrow in its own time.

To my surprise, they each fell asleep without difficulty. I'd been worried that the evening would be emotionally hard on all of us. I gave thanks to God and felt my trust grow that he would fill in the gaps of our lives and pick up the pieces I missed.

Yes, there was undoubtedly much I was missing. I walked

through the house — all but my bedroom — and let my eyes linger over the home Charlie and I had built together. The police had obviously gone through my house more than once in search of anything that might be considered evidence. I did notice a few things gone. But one thing stood out among all the others, and it was irreplaceable. Charlie was missing.

I went into the kitchen and opened the pantry doors. Clearly the police had as well — my organized shelves were now in total disarray. At least my supply of imperishables was adequate for several days, and thanks to friends and family, my refrigerator was now as overflowing as Aunt Linda's.

But running my fingers along the pantry shelves of my heart yielded nothing. No bits of treasure left, not one morsel hidden. I saw myself on tiptoe, reaching, searching, but empty-handed. I felt empty and desperate.

I'd put it off long enough. With a deep breath, I stepped into my bedroom for the first time since I'd been home. Clothes were strewn everywhere, evidence of the search by police. It unnerved me that they had touched everything I owned and every article I wore. I started sorting piles of laundry. I would wash each item before I placed it on my body again. I gathered the pile of dirty clothes from the hamper in our bathroom but separated out Charlie's things before throwing the clothes into the washer. I couldn't bring myself to wash any of Charlie's clothes. I'd leave them in a basket for a while. In some strange way, it afforded me the chance to momentarily escape the harsh reality of my life.

If his things are here in our room, then life is normal and none of this is real.

I spent the next few hours doing every load of laundry and putting my ransacked belongings back where they belonged. By the wee hours of the morning, everything was neat and tidy and my children were sound asleep. And then I didn't know what to do. I'd read no books for this, knew no one who'd faced such a time as this. I wasn't a typical young widow, if there is such a thing. My husband wasn't just dead. He'd *taken* himself from me and from my children, and he'd taken far more than that from this world — innocence and life.

I recalled a conversation with one of my mom's friends on the day of the shooting. I'd been sitting at my parents' kitchen table, trying to figure out the next steps for my children and me.

"What am I supposed to do?" I'd asked her.

"Marie," she'd answered with reassuring confidence, "this has never been done before. Whatever you choose will be the right choice."

I threw myself onto Charlie's side of the bed and wept. As I clutched the sheets and pressed my face into the pillow, I could smell him. The essence of his being still permeated this place. Part of me wanted it to stay there forever, and part of me wanted it gone right away. The struggle between, on one hand, my grief at forever losing him and, on the other, the nightmare surrounding his death ripped at me, pulling my heart in opposite directions.

I don't know how long I lay there. I do know that slowly the suffocating weight of grief lifted just enough to allow me to pull myself up, prepare for bed, and turn on my CD player. Back in bed, I let the melodies of worship wash over me. I needed to reach for something beyond these circumstances and my ability to reason them out. I thought of all the ways my Lord had shown up since last Monday. He had come in strength from the very first moment, and I had been confident of his presence and his power all week long. I had never before felt him so tangibly. It was as though he really was right next to me, in physical form. My senses were acutely aware of his nearness. Learning about God and truly knowing his heart are two vastly different experiences. I had spent my whole life knowing *about* him. In the past week, I truly *knew* him to a depth I'd never imagined possible.

And as I lay in bed that night, he was there in the room with me. I knew he saw my longing for him, and in a beautiful way that drew my heart toward his even more. It wasn't that he delighted in my circumstances, but rather that my desire to turn completely toward him and surrender the little that I had left was all he wanted. An awareness of his presence and of his desire to be ingrained in my every movement washed over me.

While I couldn't in this moment imagine good things springing forth in front of me, God could. He was writing a new story: mine and my children's.

With God anything was possible. Had I not seen God's vision of me as a tulip petal falling, caught by the hand of God?

Had I not been filled with a supernatural zeal to pray his Word over my home even before the police came to tell me what had become of Charlie?

Had I not seen my weeping father embraced by a man whose family had lost a child at the hand of my husband?

Had I not been cocooned in the shelter of his wings at Aunt Linda's? Watched as gifts for my children arrived on the doorstep? Been fed by the kindness of strangers? Heard the whispers of God invite me to a Holy Exchange?

Had I not stood shielded by the wall of grace?

I opened my Bible and turned to John 1:1–5 (NASB).

> In the beginning was the Word, and the Word was with God, and the Word was God. He was in the beginning

> with God. All things came into being through Him, and apart from Him nothing came into being that has come into being. In Him was life, and the life was the Light of men. The Light shines in the darkness, and the darkness did not comprehend it.

Christ is the Word. He is with God, and he *is* God. I left my Bible open on the bed next to me. Since he is the Word, then Jesus was lying right next to me.

I slept in peace until the light of morning.

12

tapestry

How does a family move forward when the fabric of their lives has been ripped apart?

One thread, one stitch at a time. There was no other way.

On the one hand, I found great solace in knowing that the Master Craftsman was weaving a grand tapestry of our lives. Every scene — the frightening, scary scenes as well as those wondrous, light-bathed ones — would somehow fit together to show the story of God's intervention in the lives of this mother and her three little ones.

On the other hand, in my current state, not only could I not see the tapestry in its entirety, there were many moments when all I could see was a mass of tangled string snarled around my hands, twisted around my feet, knotted around my heart.

As much as I longed to know where God was taking us, it was not within my reach to see the whole — only this part. My job was to trust that every stitch he made was in his complete control and to simply live the scene of the day.

God, in his infinite wisdom, knew better than to show me the woven masterpiece of my future. I would have laughed at the seeming absurdity of what he had in mind. He knew I needed time before he unveiled the secrets of my future.

I awoke early Monday morning, grateful to have slept four hours. This was the first day back to school for the kids. I wasn't worried, but I was unsettled. Were they ready? Was I?

The foundation had been laid with great care. Abigail, Bryce, and I had spent a lot of time talking throughout the past week at Linda's. I'd shared the details of the schoolhouse shooting with each of them. How their little hearts could possibly hold such information, I did not know, but it appeared that they had absorbed the knowledge of the events without crumbling and, to my relief, looked forward to this new day. The school, my parents, and I had worked through a plan together, and I was thankful for the presence of counselors and personnel trained in helping children and educators through crisis and trauma. The teachers had been prepared to help the students and to offer suggestions for appropriate word choices in conversations with my children.

I could see some anxiety in Abigail as I got her ready for school; she wondered what her second-grade friends might say or ask. Bryce, in morning kindergarten, just didn't want to be in the spotlight. *That* sounded familiar. We agreed that we all just wanted to feel normal and blend in, but, I emphasized, it might take some time before we felt that way. We'd have to be patient and trust God to help us get through any uncomfortable moments.

My plan was to drive them to and from school for the first month or so, as an extra precaution against any unwelcome conversations that might happen on the bus. Teachers, I'd reasoned, could keep an eye on things in the classroom, but a bus driver couldn't possibly be aware of conversations on the bus. I felt like a tigress determined to protect my cubs.

We'd decided to ease back into the school routine, attending for a few hours each day, building up to a full day by the end of the week. After I dropped them off, Carson and I headed home for our first alone time in our new life.

Eleven a.m. arrived. It had been one week ago, this very minute, when Charlie had called me for the final time. Eleven a.m. passed. I was still breathing. Another stitch in the tapestry.

Carson was building a tower with his favorite blocks. Had he really understood the words I'd spoken about his daddy? What would happen at noon? That was the time Carson usually woke Charlie, who had worked overnight and arrived home to go to bed at around 4:00 a.m. Would my toddler go looking for him? I didn't think my heart could bear to see him running into our room with that big smile, only to be disappointed when he didn't find his daddy there. Did he understand that Charlie was gone?

I was relieved when noon came and went without incident. Maybe Carson understood more than I suspected. In fact, the entire day went smoothly. A gift. A few more stitches.

It's easy to take everyday life for granted, and a shame to recognize precious moments only once they've passed. In my new reality, I welcomed a sink full of dirty dishes, laundry awaiting a spin through the washing machine, and scraggly grass in need of the lawn mower. The pain of my grief still throbbed behind every thought, but the idea of normal life held a quality of profound beauty now that soothed me.

It was with that celebration of normalcy that, on Monday

afternoon after school, the kids and I walked to the post office, just a few doors down from our house. We strolled past the neighbor's house and crossed the street to the post office, directly across from the Village Dry Goods, an Amish store where Charlie had often taken Abigail for a shopping treat. Everywhere I looked I saw the memories of my childhood, my adolescence, my married life. Good memories.

I'd had my mail held all last week in a locked post office box. As I walked in, key in hand to unlock it, the postman gave a friendly laugh. "It wouldn't all fit," he said.

"What do you mean?" I asked, opening the little brass door. I saw just a few letters.

"I've got the rest back here in a crate. I'll go get it."

I'm sure my jaw dropped when he came back holding a white corrugated mail crate filled to the brim with letters and oversized envelopes. "You can take this crate home with you and just bring it back for refills," he said. "I expect there'll be more to follow."

I was stunned. I suppose I'd been so protected from the media that in spite of explanations from my family and the detectives, I hadn't comprehended the global impact of this horrific event. I was soon to find out.

"Whoa! Is all that mail for us?" Bryce said, eyes wide.

Abigail helped carry the crate back home, since I was carrying Carson on my left hip. We all wondered the same things: Who were the letters from? How did they get our address?

When we got home, I placed the letters a handful at a time on our living room floor. To my surprise, our complete address didn't appear on most envelopes. Apparently, address lines like "Shooter's Wife" or "Marie Roberts, Bart, PA" were enough to get the mail to my little brass box from many other states and, to my total shock, from countries around the world. The kids sat with me, and we stared at the piles, trying to decide what to open first.

I picked up an envelope and held it, nervous. What if some of these letters were filled with hate and accusations? I peeled back a corner and slid my finger along the top.

But when I read the words carefully written inside, a wave of relief, love, and compassion flooded me.

> *I don't know how to help you, but I want you to know you and your children are in my prayers. This was not your fault, you must bear no guilt. Try to eat and have fun with your kids. Take all the help that's offered to you. I hope this small gift will help sustain you and your family.*

How did she seem to know exactly what I was thinking and feeling? I was touched by the tangible expression of her concern in a small check.

I opened another card.

> *I am thinking of you as you cry through your own pain and grief. I hope the loving support of family and friends lightens your load.*

Also in the envelope was a picture drawn by a child for my children.

Words of life poured over me, washing away fears and heaviness. I was lifted and comforted with each message.

A woman in Scotland wrote:

> *Life contains some terrible mysteries, which at the end of the day we have to leave in God's hands. I know that the Lord Jesus is strong enough to get you through this.*

These cards were evidence of the many people around the world who were praying and encouraging my family through this tragedy.

"I pray you will feel the Heavenly Father's arms wrapped around you, holding you close," one letter read. Through these tangible expressions of love, I most certainly did.

One of the letters I received that day was from a woman named Dara. She'd grown up in a small town just a couple of miles from where I lived. She too knew the pain of sudden loss. Her words went straight to my heart:

> *Dear Marie — my first husband was killed in a traffic accident when I was twenty-eight, leaving me with four young children ... You have had to endure more pain than most people can ever fathom ... God knows your heart and it makes him smile ... and when it comes down to it, that's all that matters.*

She included her email address, and I emailed her back the same day. Her life had gone on after her loss — a message I needed to hear. In the years since her husband's death, I learned, she had met and married a missionary and now they lived in Guatemala with their blended family. We developed a friendship that endures to this day — an unexpected gift on this journey.

Until I read those letters, I'd seen the media as the enemy — a great intrusion upon our lives and our town, a hungry force seeking to devour my children's privacy and my family's peace to feed its insatiable appetite for ratings. All true, I suppose, from one perspective. I'd listened as my family had tried to convey how fascinated people were by the forgiveness of the Amish, but without seeing or hearing it for myself. But reading these deeply personal letters, my eyes were opened to this truth: *God* was using the media to broadcast the power of his forgiveness, and he was stirring mercy and kindness in the hearts of good people stamped with his image all over the world. Light from darkness.

As the week went on, there were a few nervous moments for my children at school, but I was only a phone call away and could have been at school in less than ten minutes. No such phone call ever came. Since Bryce was in morning kindergarten, we had the afternoons to spend together while Carson napped. I was often nervous in the afternoon when we went to pick up Abigail, because it meant waiting with other parents for our children to come streaming out. I realized how strong an urge I felt to hide. *Do they know who I am? What are they thinking about me?* Sometimes other moms chatted with me, but none of them asked about the crime or its aftermath. We talked about homework, class activities, and funny moments with our kids. I was thankful for "normal" conversations — I didn't want to stand out any more than my kids did!

When Friday came, we were all amazed that we hadn't experienced anything troubling or hurtful at school. It seemed miraculous. Abigail's and Bryce's friends had been caring and thoughtful, as had their parents, and many had reached out in tangible acts of kindness — new videos to watch, fun snacks to eat, notes of encouragement. We felt loved on all sides — evidence of God's love for us. I saw this as an unexpected gift.

When we hear a story on the news or read something captivating in the newspaper, we experience a general curiosity: a part of us wants to know more, and we wonder how we'd face the same ourselves. I felt true repentance for any judgment I'd ever made against someone else based simply on what I'd heard or read about them — a mistake I was determined to never make again. And I felt true gratitude for our school community and the kindness we'd been shown.

Another few stitches.

While I rejoiced that school life quickly felt normal, little else did. My phone rang constantly, as did my doorbell. My close friends and family called my cell phone, and while many calls on my home phone were touching calls from neighbors and friends, most calls on my home phone — all of which I let go to voicemail — were from producers inviting me to be a part of their show. These were quickly and easily deleted and forgotten. Calls filled my answering machine so quickly that it was not unusual to see the words "Mailbox Full" flashing on the screen by early afternoon after emptying the mailbox the night before.

One message was unique. The calm male voice began by saying, "Your aunt gave me your number." I missed the rest of his message as my mind went off in its own direction. *Someone I know gave someone I don't know my phone number?* I wasn't happy. Then I relaxed. After all, my aunt was trustworthy.

I rewound and replayed the message.

"Hi, Marie, this is Dan Monville. Your aunt gave me your number. My coworkers and friends at church have been praying for you. They know that I have a distant connection to your extended family, and they gave me some things to give to you. Give me a call so I can drop them off sometime."

I vaguely knew Dan Monville. When I was thirteen years old, I'd gone to his wedding when he married my dad's younger cousin.

In the years since, I had heard my Aunt Shirley and Uncle Barry speak highly of Dan, most often to my grandparents who lived next door. I knew he had two children, a daughter several years older than Abigail and a son close to Abigail's age. He and his wife had been divorced for several years, but even so I knew that he was highly regarded by his in-laws, my aunt and uncle and grandparents. This seemed unusual, since so often families tend to side with each other regardless of reason and truth.

He must be a decent man, I thought, but I wasn't interested in meeting with someone I didn't know well. His eyes would undoubtedly hold questions and looks of pity. The eyes convey much, announcing the heart's intent before one word is spoken.

I deleted the message. He would have to figure out another way to deliver whatever he had.

Requests continued to pour in from news and media outlets across the globe, asking me to come to them to be questioned — or at least that was how I perceived it. They called them "invitations," but rightly or wrongly, I imagined that they were more likely to be interrogations, with only one goal — to increase their ratings. Since they weren't police, they held no authority over me, and I had no desire for any further inquisition. I'd had enough in one week to last a lifetime.

I was desperate to keep my family out of the spotlight, to protect my brood like a mother hen sheltering them beneath her wings. I felt a fierce determination that no matter what it took, we were going to be normal — maybe not now, but someday. While the schoolhouse tragedy was an inescapable part of our life, I was determined not to allow it to define our destiny or prevent us from living healthy, normal lives. We were not going to be paraded around by the media. My resolve was rock solid.

One day an evening-news journalist called Charlie's family with a request for someone to come on the show; he promised to put the information for the trust fund on the bottom of the screen during the interview. Some thought it sounded like he was trying to do us a favor. But I was angry. I would not be bought — and God certainly didn't need to rely on this man to provide for our family. I declined the request. This wasn't just a story; this was my life.

Another afternoon, the doorbell rang. I looked out the window and saw that it was a floral delivery. When I opened the door, the entire upper half of the delivery woman's body was obscured by the largest bouquet of long-stemmed white roses I had ever seen.

"You won't believe who these are from," the voice behind the roses said.

"Try me," I said, laughing.

She lowered the flowers so she could see me over the top and spoke the name of a well-known talk-show star. "There's a card," she said, clearly suggesting that I read it right then so she could hear. Instead, I thanked her, said goodbye, shut the door, and then opened the card. It spoke of concern for my children and me and offered deep sympathy. I was touched but skeptical. Still, at least it had come with no request for me to call and no strings attached.

Less than five minutes later, the phone rang. My guard down for the moment, I answered.

"Hello, Mrs. Roberts?"

"Yes, who's — "

"Do you like the roses we sent?" she interrupted. Then, without waiting for an answer, she launched rapid-fire into what sounded like a script. "I'm the producer of ..." She mentioned the well-known daytime talk show hosted by the one who'd sent the roses. "We are *so* concerned for you and your children and wanted to extend the opportunity to appear exclusively on — "

This time, she was the one who didn't have time to complete her sentence. "No thank you," I said, "and please do not call again." I hung up feeling manipulated and used. I hadn't sensed concern for us at all — only a desire for a hot story.

Their card didn't make it into the keepsake box with the many others. It went out with the trash.

I had no doubt that God was using the media in a powerful way, and I understood the public's interest in discovering the story behind the story. But my first priority was to nurture and protect my children and provide a healing home for all of us. When and if God called me to step into the public eye, I felt certain he'd let me know.

While I was still at Aunt Linda's, a local counselor who had been helping many in the community in the aftermath of the shooting, including some of the Amish families, had called to set up a meeting between the Amish community and my parents, Charlie's parents, and me. He offered to be the moderator for the meeting and suggested that we gather at the Bart Fire Hall.

In our little community, this building had long been the home of quilt auctions, fundraising meals, craft and antique shows, and receptions. So it had naturally become the hub of all the activity surrounding the shooting — the staging area for the media, as well as the drop-off location for gifts and supplies for the Amish community and for us. Most of the on-air reports, I was told, took place with the fire hall as the backdrop.

The day for the meeting came a few weeks after we returned

home. I was nervous as I walked with my parents just a few doors down the street from their home to the fire hall. My memory paints this as a cloudy, gray day. Puddles lingered on the ground from rain in previous days, and the air felt chill and raw. The natural surroundings echoed the feelings in my heart.

The closer we got, the more anxious I became. I was afraid I'd be unable to keep my composure in a room filled with so much grief brought on by my husband. But remembering my new commitment to living with expectancy of what God would do, I forced myself to keep walking forward.

Inside the hall was a circle of chairs several rows deep. I sat with my parents and Charlie's parents on one side of the circle. Our pastor, the counselors who had been working with our family, and a few close friends joined us as well. Directly opposite us were the families from the Amish schoolhouse. In the second and deeper rows sat other Amish family members, as well as many police and other first responders.

The moderator began with a prayer. Inside I was crying out for God to sustain me. Seeing the faces of the families all together brought home to me in a new way the severity of the loss. It wasn't that I hadn't understood the scope of the tragedy. Still, seeing all the families face-to-face made my heart hurt. *Charlie, why did you do this? How could you do this?* I sent a plea heavenward. *God, comfort us all.*

The Amish families were invited to share their thoughts or ask questions. The room was etched in silence, as if everyone held his or her breath, waiting for the first word to be spoken.

An Amish man began, saying the same thing I'd thought that first day a few weeks ago: "We didn't know how we would get through this." He and his wife shared that they had been leaning upon each other and God for the strength necessary to walk through each day. His grace, they told us, sustained them. I sat beside my parents, absorbing the weight of the words spoken, trying, unsuccessfully, to hold back tears. Each shared a heartache that pierced the core of our being. It was a tender exchange of truth, grace, and mercy. It was painful, but within the pain was a healing balm.

Then it was our turn. My parents and Charlie's nodded for me to go first. What did I have to say of value? What could I possibly offer? The families facing us had suffered unspeakable loss, yet had reached toward me, extending forgiveness and mercy to all of us for what Charlie had done.

I don't recall my precise words, but I spoke from my heart.

"I am so terribly sorry for your loss. I cannot find words powerful enough to express my gratitude toward each of you and your entire community. God is using your forgiveness of Charlie and your grace toward our family in our healing."

Then I addressed the first responders with great sorrow for what they had witnessed and immense appreciation for how they had served us all so selflessly. Emotion choked me, and my words felt inadequate to touch the nightmare of pain in the room. Charlie's actions had wounded so many.

Finally, I told them of the sustaining power of Christ we were experiencing in our home. I described the healing that God was doing in my own heart and those of my children. I was totally unprepared for the visceral response in the room as soon as I mentioned my children. Many leaned forward, others tilted their heads, and all eyes focused on me as I said, "I've been so worried for them at school, afraid that other children or parents might say cruel things and inflict wounds that could last a lifetime. But God has protected them. To my amazement, not one unkind word has been spoken to them at school. Not one."

I saw relief wash over the Amish faces, relief that reached straight into a most tender place inside me. Several of the men and women responded, saying that they too had been concerned about my children and were praying for them. Words failed me. They had been praying for the children of the man who'd murdered their own children.

Charlie's parents and my own then offered their contribution to the circle, for which I was grateful. They too were suffering deeply, and I prayed for God's healing and release as they spoke.

Of the many expressions of compassion and genuine love exchanged around the circle that day, there is one I will never forget. An Amish father, one who had lost a daughter, began to speak, directing his words toward me. As he spoke, my heart melted, and I felt embraced not just by his words, but also by the arms of God.

He stood as he spoke. "We think about you and pray, because when the day is over and the night is quiet and we feel our grief close in on us, my wife and I have each other. We can cry together and be held in one another's arms. But we feel compassion for you because you are alone."

To know that in the midst of their grief, they were capable of seeing the truth of my life, and the sorrow I knew in private places, penetrated my heart with radiant, heavenly light.

Their hurt went deep, but not so deep as to drown out the ability to see into the life of another suffering human.

We spent about an hour exchanging thoughts and feelings around the circle. Then we were all told that gifts and packages had been accumulating for both my family and the Amish families at the fire hall, and they'd been sorted out for us. I wish I could find the words to convey my amazement when we were ushered to a table with groceries, cards, and gifts for my children and me. One Amish family had brought a handcrafted doll bed labeled for my Abigail — who, of course, was the same age as several of the girls whose lives had been lost. I wept freely.

I had come to this meeting with dread, afraid I would fail to find the words, fearful that I could not endure the depth of pain that hall would hold. I came away enriched and full and deeply bonded to all in our circle of shared grief. I left with a heart that, while broken, experienced great mending at the hands of those who knew the pain and empty places left by Charlie's choices. The darkness of our tragedy had been redeemed, exchanged, replaced with beauty and light unimaginable.

The glow of that light was planted deep within my heart. It glows still. I am certain that in the tapestry God is weaving of our lives, this scene is woven in golden threads.

13

breakthrough

I heard a knock at the door and jumped. Chiding myself for being so edgy, I left the kids eating breakfast in the kitchen and looked out the French doors. A woman a few years older than I was, wearing casual clothes, stood on the deck. She didn't look like a reporter. I opened the door halfway.

"Are you Marie Roberts?" the woman demanded.

No courteous greeting. I was a bit taken aback. "Yes," I said.

"I just needed to come see for myself if what they say is true — that you really knew *nothing* about your husband's plans to murder those girls."

She'd said it — exactly what I'd been fearing the general public must be thinking about me. *A liar, covering up her failure to act, or an idiot, blind to the obvious.* Until now, no one had confronted me with it directly.

I stepped out onto the deck and closed the door behind me, hoping this would not be a lengthy conversation. I was getting the kids ready for school and didn't have much time to chat.

"I didn't know." I felt like a girl called to the principal's office to explain a cheating scam she knew nothing of. "I had no idea at all."

"How is that *possible*?" Her voice, which up till now had sounded like she was conducting an interrogation, now took on a pleading tone, not so much a demand as a desperation to understand what seemed unfathomable. "There must have been *some* clue!"

"I'm so sorry," I said. "Charlie had never been violent a day in his life. No rage, no threats. I knew nothing until I got his call from the schoolhouse that morning. I'm sorry."

She stared into my eyes as if trying to see into my soul. I could see her anguish, trying to comprehend the incomprehensible. I knew the feeling. I'd seen the same look in the mirror.

"Okay, then," she said abruptly. "That's what I needed to know." She turned, walked down the steps, got into her car, and drove away. I never learned her name and never saw her again. But I didn't need to. She was, for me, the skeptical public that I feared lurked in every store, gas station, bank, and schoolyard, throwing accusing glances and whispered disdain in my direction. She was the reason I wanted to hide.

Several days later, I returned home after picking the kids up from school and found a second message from Dan Monville among the many on my answering machine. He gave much of the same information as before. This time he said that he'd told my aunt that I hadn't called him back. He had asked her if she couldn't just drop the stuff he was trying to get to me off at my house, since she visits her brother (my grandfather next door) frequently. But, as he explained in the voicemail, she had declined, saying that I was probably just busy and he should call me again.

This time I rolled my eyes as I deleted the message. Yes, I *was* busy, and no, I still didn't want to have "visitors" over. The only people I trusted in my world now were those who'd already been in it before the shooting. I didn't need the stress of anything new right now. I felt guilty and rude for not answering, but I simply didn't have the energy for things like this.

~

The process of trying to find "normal" again was giving me whiplash.

Healing takes time and energy. The damage Charlie had done in a span of minutes was going to take me, and everyone else touched by that violence, a very long time to sort through.

I did what I knew to do—I sought God's comfort, asked his protection against the lies of the enemy, recited what God had done for me so far, and sang words of praise that I didn't *feel* yet knew were true.

Then one morning, my open Bible in hand, I realized that what I was feeling was dread, almost resignation, for all that lay before me.

Yearning for peace, I immersed myself in the Psalms before tackling the challenges of the day. In the verses I read there, God asked me to take a leap.

> Praise be to the LORD,
> for he has heard my cry for mercy.

God, I prayed, *I know that you alone have heard every cry.*

> The LORD is my strength and my shield;
> my heart trusts in him, and he helps me.

My heart leaps for joy,
and with my song I praise him.

The Lord is the strength of his people,
a fortress of salvation for his anointed one.
Save your people and bless your inheritance;
be their shepherd and carry them forever.
(Psalm 28:6–9)

I'd *been* doing this. I'd been trusting in him, believing he was my strength and shield. I'd had tremendous moments of miraculous joy—God was keeping his word! But as God knew, that peace would also evaporate at times, leaving me weary. *Lead me like a shepherd, Lord. Carry me forever in your arms.*

You turned my wailing into dancing;
you removed my sackcloth and clothed me with joy,
that my heart may sing your praises and not be silent.
Lord my God, I will praise you forever.
(Psalm 30:11–12)

I didn't know how there could be anything so beautiful as what I felt him promise in those verses—to take away my clothes of mourning and clothe me with joy.

I felt God gently encouraging me to focus—no, to refocus—to embrace every part of my life as being clothed with promised joy instead of weighty dread. It wasn't failure when I recognized the heaviness as it resurfaced, but I knew that to move beyond it, I would have to allow him to transform the elements of my life into the very promises I read in the Word. As I surrendered to his prompting, the heaviness would lift — God's peace and joy would come.

I thought over the details of my life: I had three beautiful children on earth and two more walking glorious streets above. And a husband lost. Horrible things really do happen. Tragedy strikes midsentence. Yet in the midst of it, there is still joy.

He wasn't simply asking me to forget that harsh realities existed, but instead he asked me to embrace life and love *all* of it!

You want me to love this? I asked — in awe, not arrogance. Shocking as it may seem, he said simply, *Yes.* As I considered his words, my perspective shifted: *He is a good Father who gives good gifts to his children. He is, somehow and unbelievably, purposing to give me goodness. My heart cannot contain the mystery nor comprehend what it includes or requires, but I want it desperately. Help me love this existence, all of it.*

He was not asking me to love the circumstances, the tragedy, the loss and devastation — those things broke his heart. He didn't love them. But he challenged me to look *through* them and love each day, each hour, each minute of my future.

This would require an act of wholly devoted sacrifice. I grabbed his hand that morning. I closed my eyes and leaped toward him — not wanting to see what I was jumping over, nor even wanting to know if I was going to make it. I knew I must cross over to the other side if my perspective was to change.

I want to love my life. Will you show me how?

The kids seemed to be adjusting well. No nightmares or acting out, both things that the counselors had said to expect. I knew that didn't mean their grief was over, and I wanted to do all I could to keep positive memories of their father alive.

Bryce had always enjoyed tagging along with his daddy, working together on projects of any kind and playing together in the yard whenever the weather was nice. They spent many afternoons playing soccer, Bryce charging down the yard attempting to kick the ball around his dad and scoring a goal on the other side. Charlie, like any good father, often pretended to be completely overpowered by Bryce's furious pace. Bryce and Charlie would high-five after a successful shot and then switch positions, with Bryce then set to block Charlie's shot. Almost every time Charlie came running toward him, Bryce's skill routed Charlie's kick. His confidence soared, and his enthusiasm for the game deepened. He couldn't wait for the next opportunity to take on his daddy.

I wasn't Charlie. I wasn't a soccer player! But I did my best to kick the ball around with Bryce in the yard many afternoons. And I realized that I didn't need to be what I wasn't. God had provided my brother and my dad, who made it a point to roughhouse and play ball with my boys.

Carson's vibrant personality and snuggly disposition had always delighted Charlie and me. Charlie, in fact, had been the more likely of the two of us to launch into spontaneous play with the kids; I was usually more focused on household responsibilities.

One morning while his siblings were at school, I snagged Carson as he was running by and tossed him onto my bed for tickles. "Guess what I remembered this morning?" I said to my wiggly little boy. "Sometimes, if your daddy and I wanted to talk, just the two of us, Daddy and I would sneak in here and sit right on this spot of our bed." Our master bedroom, just off our family room, gave Charlie and me the opportunity to sit on our bed and chat while the children played — we could see them but also have a bit of privacy.

"But *you*"—I gave him another tickle—"always loved to close doors. I remember that if you saw us sitting here you would come running toward us, grab the door, and pull it shut. Daddy and I would laugh and open it again, and you would squeal and do it again and again. One day, after you closed it, Daddy laid down on the floor like this." I demonstrated by shutting the door and pressing my face to the carpet to peer under the door, spying on my young son.

"I 'member," Carson said. I'd known he would because this had been a favorite for Charlie and Carson.

"Daddy tapped his fingers on the bottom of the closed door like this," I said, tapping, "and you would sneak up on the other side of the door to find out what that sound was, and Daddy would suddenly stick his fingers out under the door. And then what did you do?" I said.

"Grab Daddy's fingers!" he said.

"Let's see if you can grab mine," I said. With the door closed between us, we played the finger-grabbing game. Carson laughed on his side of the door. I was glad he couldn't see my tears.

I continued to have occasional sessions with the counselors.

I didn't want to carry unanswerable questions about Charlie with me for the rest of my life. I needed to address them as best I could, bury them as we had Charlie, and then move on.

So what *did* I know?

I knew that Charlie didn't know how to communicate his deep feelings. I knew that he didn't understand the necessity of releasing the pain he felt. He thought that he could keep it all bottled up inside and deal with it on his own.

Even though our lives were beautiful and full with three children he deeply loved, there was a gaping wound in Charlie's heart. He did his best to deal with it, but it was there even when we couldn't see it. He wasn't able to understand how a God of love had allowed us to walk through such heartbreaking circumstances. His note on the day of the shooting had said that he felt he was "getting back at God" for taking our daughter away. How could his reasoning have become so severely compromised? I needed to surrender that question to the God of mercy and leave it in his hands.

For nine years Charlie had lived through the pain of loss. It was a cancer that ate away at everything inside of him. I was thankful that he wasn't dealing with the pain anymore, but I was aghast at the pain he'd inflicted upon so many.

Though I loved my husband, I hated what he had done to those children, their families and ours, and the community. And I hated the way he'd left me to deal with the aftermath. It was beyond my comprehension that he would choose to leave our kids like this and take the lives of other children, creating in their families the very pain that had plagued him for so long. I honestly wasn't angry with *him* — his brokenness pierced me far too deeply to evoke my wrath — but I had no vocabulary sufficient for how grieved I was by his choices.

What I knew about loss and difficulty so far was this: our circumstances do not prove or disprove God's love for us. His love is not measured by our circumstances. It is meted out instead in terms of his sacrifice, his grace, and his redemption. We live in a fallen world. Everyone has the ability to make behavioral choices, and those choices ultimately have consequences, positive and negative, in our own lives and those around us.

Charlie made a choice that ravaged the Amish community,

our family, and many others. In ending his own suffering, he had inflicted far greater suffering on the people he left behind. I would never understand all the reasons why — as if there could be rational reasons for a decision like that — but I did recall signs of his struggle. For instance, as I'd told the detectives, from time to time over the years, I'd been able to see that Charlie continued to struggle with the loss of our daughters. He wanted concrete answers but there were none.

For my part, the joy I found through Abigail, Bryce, and Carson diminished my ache for those joys we'd lost. Once when Abigail was in first grade, Charlie and I had spent an hour or two at school during parent visitation week. Afterward I had said to Charlie, "You saw the way Abigail loves jumping rope on the playground with the other girls at recess." I smiled. "Singing their rope-skipping songs, trying to work their way up to double Dutch ... I was thinking today that Elise would have been two years older than she is. I wonder how they would have gotten along."

Charlie thought for a minute, then said, "Abigail seems to get along with everybody, like her mama." He threw me a sly smile. "I think they would have loved being together. I wish Elise were here."

"I do too, Charlie. As much as I don't understand losing her, I cling to Romans 8:28, that all things work together for good for those who love God. Somehow God still brings good out of loss," I said, hoping to start a discussion.

But he remained silent.

It's odd, the things that can trigger sadness. Often in a moment you never expected, your breath is completely taken away. Words, a smell, a picture — seemingly insignificant — bring back profound memories and thoughts. *What would it be like if she were here now? How would her laugh sound? Would her hair be curly like mine?* Charlie wasn't the only one who missed our little girl. But for some reason, while I healed over time, his pain must have become silently toxic.

Charlie's "bouts of depression" rarely lasted more than a few days and never interfered with his ability to keep in step with daily tasks and work. During those times, which seemed to happen a few times each year, Charlie would withdraw — so I countered by trying to do everything within my ability to keep life enjoyable and moving forward, hoping that I could encourage his healing. I knew that he would feel better if he would just talk about his pain, but he wouldn't. The more I pushed him to talk to someone, the more he withdrew. I wanted our marriage to include a sharing of burdens with a transparency that left us mutually vulnerable as well as mutually loved. Instead, Charlie slowly built a wall of silence I was not welcome to cross.

I was disappointed; this was not what we had promised each other — to love and to cherish, to go through life *together*. His silences weakened the vibrancy of our marriage, and over time, I mourned the loss of what we'd once shared.

In turn, I stopped sharing with him much that I was going through.

Looking back, I could see that I began to keep my problems of everyday life between myself and God. I lost the habit of including Charlie in my spiritual journey.

Of course, Charlie's periods of apparent depression were only occasional. And though our deepest thoughts were not often shared with one another, our family time was still filled with joy. My husband loved his family, and he was a tender father who enjoyed each moment with his children. He took our daughter shopping, taught our son to build things, and changed the diapers of our youngest without hesitation. I have many happy memories of the years we spent together and the variety of ways he gave his love and provided for our family.

Charlie and I, like most young couples, were simply living life as it came.

Yes, my husband was a quiet man, especially when it came to his feelings. Many men are. True, Charlie had bouts of lingering sadness, but they always passed.

And although my husband seemed to lack deep, meaningful relationships with other men that went beyond work, weather, and sports, how many wives would say the same of their husbands?

I, like many wives, had my prayer list for Charlie. My heart had cried out for what I knew God wanted for him. My desire was to see a close relationship with God rise up within my husband. How many hundreds of thousands of Christian wives would say the same? In the weeks before his death, I had cried out to the Lord, "Do something powerful with his life."

Regardless of what we were missing, I loved what we had. After all, we were young. We would have other seasons of life to reignite the emotional closeness. We had a lifetime ahead of us.

Only we didn't.

"Marie, you're so strong." I heard those words, and words like them, at church, at the grocery store, even in the lobby while I waited for Abigail at dance class. It wasn't true. It wasn't my strength they were seeing, but God's.

I marveled at it myself. This woman so infused with strength was not the girl I had known myself to be. I had always been the one who ran from the spotlight, avoided confrontation, the middle-child-peacemaker-problem-solver, always self-conscious about others' perceptions of me, trying to tweak my every thought or action to total perfection before taking a step or uttering a word. Anticipating, planning, organizing the next action or need, always attempting to stay one step ahead, *never* asking for help lest I burden others. All those traits had been to compensate for and cover my weaknesses.

I was strong now not because of some innate characteristic, but because I was acutely aware of how, in all aspects, I fell so far short of the mark, and therefore I was crying out to God for help in a multitude of ways. And he was answering! I had leaned into his whispers, longing for peace, and he'd replied with a shout that redefined me.

Jesus was removing my old worn garments of self-perception and showing me instead who *he* says I am — his daughter, recipient of grace sufficient for every moment, focus of his eyes ablaze with love unconditional and truth unavoidable.

The result was not at all what I expected. Never in a million years would I have expected this breaking of myself to result in a fresh outpouring of self-confidence! In the midst of suffering, loss, and questions, I was finding episodes of irrepressible joy and unstoppable hope. I became fully convinced that not only could God do anything — but he *would* do everything needed.

By November our new family routines had been established. Daily I worked to treasure normal moments, trying to enjoy each single day without regard to what lay ahead. The calendar, however, showed a heartbreaking concentration of milestones over the next few weeks. November 9 marked what would have been my tenth wedding anniversary. November 14 was Elise's ninth birthday, then Thanksgiving. December held my birthday and Charlie's, then Christmas. I didn't want to think about even one of these dates without Charlie; the accumulation of them was overwhelming. To top it off, everyone around me was also suffering, dealing in his or her own way with loss and inner turmoil from Charlie's actions and his death. As those dates came nearer, I felt myself slipping into gray, a deepening sadness coming over me, in spite of the newfound strength God had been giving me.

The life of a single mom isn't glamorous. My days were long and intense. I rose early, feeling like the sole player in a symphony, racing from one instrument to another, trying to play each one perfectly according to the score set before me.

Wake up, get ready, feed the dog, wake the children. Invest myself in meaningful conversations on an elementary-school level before it was time to jump into the car and drive to school. Come home and breathe for five minutes before laundry, house cleaning, and phone calls. (*Message deletions* might be more accurate, thanks to the still-relentless producers.) Play with my baby and connect with his heart, inspire curiosity and creativity. Run out the door and back to school by the end of morning kindergarten. Then back home to feed my hungry little bears, read stories, play together, and put the baby to bed for a nap. Deposit coins of love into my son's account, sweet moments carved out and shared between mother and son. Wake the baby, drive back to school, wait in the lobby until my eldest was dismissed. Then back home, my three treasures playing together while I made dinner, then homework, baths, and bed.

In my solitary, dusk-kissed moments after their bedtime, I

spent the last of my energy for physical exercise on my elliptical trainer to strengthen my body. While I did, I meditated on Scripture. I knew God loved to exchange my stale air for the very breath of heaven, and I was desperate for it.

One day would bring the confidence necessary to propel my little family through the next twenty-four hours. The following day would suck the air right out of me, and I would find myself weeping repeatedly. On top of all that, continued assaults from the media wanting interviews exhausted and annoyed me. When would they give up? But even on the airless days, I set aside my doubts and searched for God's wisdom and truth, inviting it to penetrate deep, to the very center of my being.

My newfound peace answered many of my questions about the process of grief. With the quieting of those questions, however, an ever-so-gentle whisper made itself heard. From the time I was a little girl, I'd known that as God knit me together in my mother's womb, he meticulously sewed into my heart the desire to be a wife and a mother. Yet as an adult, these most prominent desires of my heart had been defined by loss and devastation — the deaths of Elise, Isabella, and now Charlie.

Why did you make me this way? I asked the Lord. *Why must I seek to satisfy my longing for a family only to see it consumed by the fire of loss?*

I thought of all the prayers I'd prayed for my marriage. I'd desired greater growth for Charlie, enabling us to walk our road together, arms linked, conversations about the Lord easy, giving and receiving who we were, empowering each other to new heights along the way. Had those prayers been in vain?

As I searched for God's good things in the midst of that question, I found myself praying surprising words: *I've always wanted to be a wife—but, Jesus, if it's just you and me, forever, I'm okay with that. You are my husband. You will protect, provide, refresh, encourage—you embody all a man should be. If there isn't a man on the face of the earth capable of sharing my life as it is now, I am disappointed—but I understand.*

I sensed the Lord replying that no prayers were in vain, and he encouraged my heart to believe that there still might be a future husband for me and that I should continue praying those same things I'd prayed for Charlie for the new husband he would bring.

But I had no desire to meet a man anytime soon. With my first dream freshly broken, still cleaning up shards left along Charlie's path of destruction, I wasn't ready to contemplate a new relationship.

And I had one request: *If there is a husband in my distant future, please—just bring me one guy, Lord. I'm not going to date.*

I closed the subject. God had shown that he knew my heart, and that was enough for me.

One day I received a call that encouraged me to keep my heart focused and my priorities in all the right places. An Amish neighbor called me. He was very close friends with the King family, whose six-year-old daughter, Rosanna, had sustained a severe brain injury in the shooting and had been in Hershey Medical Center ever since. The Amish gentleman wondered if I could drive his family the thirty miles to Hershey to visit with the King family at Rosanna's bedside. He told me that he sensed that the visit would offer an opportunity for connection, given their grief and my own.

I was in awe of his invitation. I saw God at work, agreed without hesitation, and arranged for my kids to stay with my parents.

I was nervous as I drove to the Amish farm a few days later, up hills and down, across bumpy roads. The jolting ride seemed to match my emotions. Fog clung heavily to the earth that morning, and I could see only what was immediately before me. Surprisingly, that brought my heart and mind into clearer focus. I didn't have to figure everything out in advance, I realized. It was okay to simply take the day as it came, embracing the moment but not necessarily preparing for it. I found that outlook of simplicity freeing — especially given the too-demanding expectations I was constantly placing on myself.

Once I'd picked up my guests, I chatted easily with the Amish family — husband, wife, and three children — during the forty-minute drive. When my Amish friend and I entered the elevator at Hershey Medical Center, another couple stepped in as well. The man clutched *People* magazine, details from the shooting blazed across the cover.

"Tragic, isn't it?" he said, holding up the magazine cover for all to see. "Too awful for words."

He clearly had no idea we were directly involved.

"Yes," I said, keeping my anonymity. "No one can fathom the toll of such a loss." The door opened, we stepped out, and when the door closed behind us we all looked at each other. In one glance, our eyes conveyed a heartrending exchange at a depth our mouths could not utter. My spirit felt dark and frozen. But I called on the Lord to bring my eyes back to the good he was doing in the midst of the tragedy.

Love the moment. Love my life. Expect to see God at work. I practiced as best I could, and God enabled me to put one foot in front of the other toward Rosanna's hospital room.

As I stepped into the room, Rosanna's parents rose to greet me. I exchanged embraces with Mr. and Mrs. King and was moved to tears as the two Amish dads, clearly dear friends, embraced, joy mingled with sorrow.

Then an awkward silence settled over us for a moment, and I wrestled back the anxiety rising inside me. I focused on a thermos full of coffee, books on the window ledge, food brought to share between friends. These typical comforts of home settled the quaking inside me, reminding me that love and gentleness could exist in a place otherwise scarred by violence and cruelty.

Rosanna's mother accompanied me to her daughter's bedside. I wasn't sure whether she was unconscious or sleeping. Monitors were beeping quietly and a bag of medication was dripping silently in an IV.

We shared life in the face of death. They spoke of Rosanna's injuries. *Injuries sustained at the hand of my husband*, I thought. Wounds on her body, wounds in our hearts. Raw trauma in their lives and mine as well.

"Tell us, how are your children?" Rosanna's father asked me, turning the conversation.

"They're sleeping well and are glad to be back in school. They both rejoined their soccer teams." I paused.

"That's good to hear," Rosanna's mother said. "We've been praying for them." I was struck by the relief on their faces.

"Tell us how you are," Rosanna's father said, while her mother looked into my eyes with such tenderness. It was clear that they wanted the sincere truth.

In this room I needed no pretext of strength. None of us did.

"It's hard to know how to be a mom right now," I said. With the words came tears. "I want to be everything they need, but I know I can't be. I'm reaching for God's strength, but I'm so aware of my limits."

They nodded and we all looked at Rosanna. It was clear I had just spoken their hearts as well, and their tears joined mine. I felt accepted in grace and tenderness, not in judgment.

Then came the gentlest sentence, spoken by Rosanna's father: "At the end of the day, we each have someone to hold, someone to cry with. We have each other. And we think about you. You don't have anyone." This same sentiment was spoken at Bart Fire Hall by another Amish family. The concern these families showed for me was beyond my comprehension.

I felt so unworthy. I still carried shame for Charlie's actions — shame that did not belong to me, that God did not want me to bear. This family's tenderness toward me and my children was the picture of the heart of God for us. No guilt. No shame. Just grace, poured out to overflowing — and a gentle call to heal in his truth.

I couldn't stop the tears.

Who am I, I asked, *what right do I have to be a part of this indescribably grace-filled exchange? I have nothing to offer that's of value to them, yet they give me a beauty beyond description.*

What happened to me within that hospital room was a mystery too sacred to adequately express. Grace is a seed planted, and it sprouted inside me there at Rosanna's bedside.

Their love was abundant; it was selfless; it was extraordinary. It was as if a host of angels was gathered there, pouring out rivers of grace from heavenly vessels. My heart was showered, washed clean of Satan's clinging stench, then doused with holy oil. Heaven was almost in my view. And when I do finally arrive there in God's perfect timing, it will not be foreign to me, for I glimpsed that holy realm from Rosanna's hospital room.

14

the giving tree

"Can I go over to Old Grandpa's house for a visit?" Bryce said one afternoon after school. I knew what he was up to; he was probably looking for a snack.

"Of course!" I said. "You go ahead. I'll be over in a few minutes. Why don't you let Dale out on the deck when you go?" I heard him call our yellow lab, open the door — and a thought struck me. "And, Bryce, ask Grandpa about the time he pretended to walk to school but hid under the porch the whole day." I knew Bryce would love to hear a Grandpa story.

"Okay, Mom," he said as the door closed behind him.

I was more grateful than ever, since losing Charlie, to have my grandparents next door. We'd moved into this house within a few months of Abigail's birth. Immediately, I'd felt that living next to my grandparents with my husband and new daughter was one of the most wonderful gifts I'd ever received. Being back in Georgetown after our few years in Lititz meant that my dad stopped in every day to see the baby, or we walked up to the truck garage to see him when his truck rolled in the driveway. Mom loved spending time helping to care for Abigail too.

I enjoyed chatting with my grandparents every day, learning gardening tips, hearing the stories of their childhood. They loved watching my kids play in the yard and invited them over for Popsicles on hot days and for soda anytime. They said watching the kids kept them young! My grandfather often teased my grandmother that she was the "ol' seed." When Abigail was two years old, she picked up on his antics and began calling them Old Grandma and Old Grandpa. They loved it, and the names stuck.

Shortly after Charlie and I had moved in, I was reminded of how I used to watch Amish families gardening together. The inspiration of my grandparents prompted me to begin gardening, even though I hadn't enjoyed it as a child. I relished the feel of rich brown soil beneath my feet and under my fingernails, and living next to Grandpa meant that we often worked together. Grandma scolded him for working too hard and planting too much, but he winked at me and paid no attention to her comments. His garden was about the size of a football field, filled with rows of sweet corn, peas, potatoes, lima beans, tomatoes, and onions.

I soaked up the tips he shared, such as when to harvest rhubarb (in months spelled with three and four letters) and proper methods for stringing beans (tying string to poles in various formations). Grandpa didn't like cherry tomatoes, so I always tried to sneak a few from my plants into his baskets of plum or beefsteak tomatoes. When he found them, he would laugh and throw them at me.

Charlie and I worked on flower beds in front of our house, and he gave me several rosebushes as gifts; we cared for them together. I often snipped a few fragrant blooms as a centerpiece for the dinner table.

I forced my mind back to today — a late October afternoon. I wondered if my busy life as a single mom would allow me to join my grandfather in the garden later. I finished up the cleaning, put away the vacuum, and decided to check messages before heading next door for a chat.

There was yet another message from Dan Monville. His third. Couldn't he figure out that if I hadn't called him back, then I didn't want to? Why wasn't he going away?

I called my mom. "Hey, it's me. You and Dad know Dan Monville, right?"

She did and reminded me that I had gone to his wedding with my grandparents when I was thirteen. "Why do you ask?" she said.

"Because Aunt Shirley gave him my number shortly after the shooting. People at his office knew we were distantly related and asked him to drop off a box of gifts they'd collected. He's called a few times, but I've just deleted his messages."

"I think he works on the north end of town. He's in insurance, I think. He must be about thirty-nine or forty by now. Two kids. We haven't seen him in a long time, but he's a good man. Your dad's folks think highly of him. They know him better than we do. Why don't you just let him drop the gifts off one day, Marie?"

It was a reasonable question, but … "Mom, I just don't have the energy for small talk with someone I don't know. I don't think I've ever seen him other than that one time when I was a teenager. I'm sure he's nice, but it just sounds awkward. Would you mind very much if we arranged for him to drop them off at your place one evening? I'll bring the kids over so there'll be a bunch of us. That way I won't feel on the spot for small talk."

And so the plans were made. Relieved, I hung up and headed next door to see Grandpa.

Dale bounded up to me when I stepped out the door, so I let

him come along. Tail wagging, he ran a few circles around me. *Poor thing. He must be missing Charlie.* He'd always been Charlie's dog. Charlie had always been a dog lover, having grown up with dogs in his home. Dale was his constant companion in the house and yard. If Charlie was outside, Dale stayed right with him, never wandering off. (I had no such luck. Dale seemed to enjoy running away from me when I called, as if he was God's reminder to me of what I couldn't control!) Many afternoons, Charlie and the kids would take Dale out to play, throwing the ball, brushing him, and giving him treats. They all — dad, kids, and dog — loved the time equally, while I loved the few quiet moments alone inside. Since Charlie's death, Dale wasn't getting the attention he was used to.

Bryce was sitting with Grandpa on the steps outside his house. They were all smiles, sipping root beer and licking Fudgesicles. The exact scene I was hoping to find!

"Looks like Dale needs some playtime, doesn't it?" I said. "After you're finished, let's play fetch with him in the backyard. Do you remember hearing Daddy talk about the dogs on his milk route?"

"Yes, but can you tell me again?" Bryce said, licking the last bits of a dribbling Fudgesicle from his fingers.

"He almost always took dog treats with him in his truck. When Daddy pulled his big truck onto a farm, the farm dogs would come running straight for the truck, their tails wagging, knowing your daddy was going to play with them and give them a treat. He told me he loved them all, but he had a few favorites. If they behaved themselves and stayed with him the whole time he was filling the truck, he'd reward them with a taste of milk when he unhooked the hose. He said they were so eager to taste that yummy milk that he had to jump out of the way of their tongues and paws because they got so excited."

Bryce had stopped licking and was watching, a big smile on his face, as I described his daddy.

Grandpa chuckled. "Used to do the same myself."

"Can I give Dale some milk when we go back to the house?" Bryce said.

"Sure. Daddy would have liked that."

It was getting easier to share "Daddy stories" with the kids. I'd just told an entire story and hadn't felt choked up once. Progress.

After I put the kids to bed that night, I sat down, phone in hand, to call Dan. Initiating conversation with a man on the phone felt strange to me — I couldn't remember having done it before! *Conservative* was practically my middle name. I had been married my whole adult life, I hadn't worked outside our home in years, and I had limited interactions with other adults outside my small sphere of church and family. Though everything I'd thought I knew had changed several weeks ago and my wallflower mentality seemed to be fading, I wondered if my newfound confidence could get me through this phone call.

I swallowed hard and made the call. It lasted less than two minutes.

"Hi. This is Marie Roberts. Is this Dan?"

He told me he was glad I'd called back. "Your Aunt Shirley, my ex-mother-in-law, suggested that when I drop off the gifts I should bring my kids over to play with your kids. Would that be a good idea?"

I liked it. He and my dad could play in the backyard with the kids, and I would stay in the house with my mom, perhaps avoiding conversation completely. Perfect. Maybe my new sense of life purpose and freedom was strengthening me from the inside out.

We decided to meet at my parents' house the next Wednesday evening. As I hung up, I told God that Dan had better not bring me a "self-help-through-tragedy" book. In the past three weeks, my library had blossomed, now containing a burgeoning load I didn't have time to read. I was thankful for the overflow of support, but my problems were not going to be solved by any book other than the Word of God.

I surprised myself by looking forward to the dinner at my parents' home. It was an opportunity for my kids to have an ordinary evening, playing in the backyard with my dad and some other kids. I'd been worrying that the kids were getting lonely. Since the shooting, we hadn't socialized at all. And try as I might, I knew I wasn't as much fun as their daddy.

Charlie's schedule had had room in it to play with the kids almost every afternoon. He usually left each evening around 7:00 p.m. to start his milk route, so we were all accustomed to his absence at bedtime. I put the kids to bed on my own every night for over seven years. Charlie would return home around 4:00 or 5:00 a.m. Once Carson grew to be a toddler, he would wake Charlie every day around noon. If I didn't watch him closely, he would sneak into our bedroom and wake his dad much earlier. The smile on his face and gleam in his eyes as he patted his daddy's cheek and kissed his head were too much for Charlie to resist. No matter how tired he might be, he always responded in love toward his son. Then, when the older kids got home, they usually had time to play with their daddy before dinner, after which Charlie went off to work again.

Wednesday evening arrived. The kids and I enjoyed one of my mom's delicious meals. Dan and his children were to arrive after dinner. *This will be a good time for the kids,* I thought. I'd been silly to worry over it like I had. Carson, especially, always lit up at the sight of new playmates. I anticipated the kids' squeals of delight. Lately, Bryce had seemed lonely and Abigail unusually quiet. A few hours of lively conversation and outdoor fun would be good for everyone.

Dan and his children, Nicole, age fourteen, and DJ, age seven, arrived just as we finished dinner. Introductions were easy. Mom and Dad knew Dan, and once I saw him, I remembered his open, friendly face. It felt as though I already knew this family from the many stories I'd heard. The kids bounced to the backyard, Dan and my dad following close behind, and Mom and I were kitchen-bound. She washed, I dried, frequently stopping to watch the exchange outside.

As a parent, I'd always treasured moments when someone else chose to invest time and energy in my precious ones. I was content to be with my mom, the soundtrack of laughter playing in the background.

"Mom, finding the energy to be playful just eludes me these days. I feel like I'm forcing it. For weeks now, it has been a daily challenge, like walking through quicksand, to handle all the responsibilities of a single parent. Chores, bills, yard work, paperwork."

"That's only natural, Marie. You've lost your partner in running a family," Mom said. "You're going to have to let some things slide to find time for what's most important. You don't have to keep a spotless house, and it's okay if some chores just wait. You'll get through this."

"Charlie was always such a playful dad. I worry that we don't have as many giggles in our lives."

Just then, the laughter from the backyard pulled me to the window, and I watched Dad and Dan playing like kids themselves.

"God is their Father, Marie. He's taking care of them."

She was right. My kids were okay, and I would be too.

Everything went according to plan until my mom said, "Go call everyone in for dessert."

"Mom," I complained, "I don't feel up to a conversation."

"It would be rude not to visit for at least a few minutes. Go on."

I felt like a twelve-year-old reluctantly following my mom's orders, but I went outside to invite everyone in for cookies and iced tea. The troop of seven all raced for the kitchen, Dad and Dan included.

Fortunately, the conversation that night barely needed me; the kids filled the time effortlessly. Dan and his children were thoughtful, kind, and compassionate. There were no awkward questions or tense moments. As they prepared to leave, he brought in a white basket filled with lovely handmade quilts, DVDs, and books for the kids. Then he handed his business card to my parents and me, offering help if we had a need he could fulfill. I took it but laughed to myself. *I don't ask for help, and I will certainly not be needing the information on this card.*

My middle child had other ideas. Playing with friends was his favorite pastime, and he and DJ had hit it off well. Over the next few days he insisted that we get together again, pleading for a playdate with DJ. I put him off. I turned him down. But my five-year-old had his mind made up.

I considered calling another friend from school instead, but I found myself incapable of dialing the phone. What did other parents truly think about our family now? Would they be reluctant to send their children to the home of a murderer? Would I, in their place? Beyond pleasant surface exchanges, what were the families of my children's friends whispering? My children had received no invitations to friends' homes since the shooting.

Bryce continued to ask for DJ. Finally, his determination overcame my resistance, and eventually I wondered why I'd said no in the first place.

I emailed Dan, thankful now that the business card I'd scorned provided an alternative to a phone call. We made plans to meet after church the following Sunday at a park.

This was a brand-new situation for me. The thought of meeting another man, even with our kids in tow, felt awkward. I was simply doing it for Bryce. If I had my way, we would stay at home, but this was not about me. *I will always lay down my life for my children.* It was a phrase that resonated through my heart each morning, defining the day ahead. And if I would lay down my life, surely I could tolerate a playdate for my kids. What was wrong with me? Still, I told my parents and Charlie's about it, just so I wouldn't feel like I was doing something "in secret." Then I put it out of my mind. It was late October, and given the implications of all the anniversaries we would face in the next eight weeks, I had more important things to think about.

And indeed, our lives flew from one emotion-filled "remembrance day" to another. Each of them had at one time been celebrations, but no longer. Our tenth anniversary came and went on November 9. Somehow I got through it without a grief-stricken meltdown. Elise's ninth birthday was next on November 14. God's gentleness with me was intensely real, expressed so beautifully in the cards and letters of encouragement and prayers still flowing into our home. I received them that week as a birthday gift from heaven.

Thanksgiving loomed before me. Holiday celebrations had always held such significance for our family. The hole left by Charlie seemed deep and black as the day approached. Imagine my shock when I received an invitation to take my children and parents on an all-expense-paid trip to the south of France for Thanksgiving!

I had a dear friend, Michelle, who was a missionary in France, along with her husband, Ben, and their daughter, a few months older than Carson. When Michelle heard the news of the shooting, she shared it with her missionary parents and her brother, who, in an act of God-inspired generosity, offered to pay for our trip as a time of healing. We leapt at that opportunity, were able to get expedited passports from the passport office in Philadelphia, packed our bags, and soon found ourselves in a picturesque little French village, warmed by the love of friends and fascinated by the area's history and culture. A French family in Michelle's church opened their home to us, and together we enjoyed strolling through the village and stopping at the local bakery to enjoy fresh-baked croissants. At Michelle's home, we celebrated Thanksgiving by baking pumpkin pies and making homemade bread. Our time was peace-filled and leisurely, and we returned home rested and restored.

It was another Holy Exchange — a dreaded holiday redeemed by a generous gift of new memories to last a lifetime.

The next hurdle to clear was my twenty-ninth birthday on December 5 and Charlie's thirty-third, December 7. My children and I quietly celebrated my birthday with my parents, and on Charlie's birthday we shared memories, looked at picture albums, and wept and laughed together.

My daily prayer was for healing peace for us all.

Christmas was coming fast. *Lord,* I prayed, *get us through just one more holiday, then speed us to the end of the year. Surely 2007 will bring a new beginning.*

The community continued to surround our family with love and grace in tangible ways. God stirred the heart of one special woman, Tiffany, who organized a "giving tree." Local families were invited to stop by Bart Fire Hall one day in early December to place a gift card, ornament, or note of encouragement for us on a Christmas tree. We were invited to the giving tree party at the end of that day, so my children and I, accompanied by my parents, walked to the fire hall together. The last time I'd taken this walk with my parents had been for the gathering with the Amish community and first responders. Though this time I felt a little nervous, I was far more at peace than on that occasion. Abigail, Bryce, and Carson, excited to be invited to a party, held hands with my parents and did their best to hurry them along.

When we arrived, I was stunned to find the tree adorned with an abundance of gift cards for grocery stores, gas stations, Target, Walmart, and local restaurants. There were so many Christmas cards and notes tucked into the tree that I knew I couldn't read them there. I would read and treasure them in the weeks and months to come. One of the most precious gifts we received that night was a lovely handmade oak rocking chair crafted by an Amish man especially for Carson. It sits, today, next to our fireplace as a constant reminder of God's grace.

The tree's beauty penetrated my senses. The soft, vibrant green needles and the fragrance of pine radiated life and pure, selfless love. I was overwhelmed.

My dad, Tiffany's dad, and several other men helped bring the tree to my home and place it in the stand. The lights twinkled in the darkness and filled the room with a sense of wonder.

Charlie and I had loved the holidays and enjoyed building family traditions. He and I had exchanged ornaments each year since the first Christmas we'd celebrated together. When we became parents, we included the kids in that tradition. They each received at least one ornament from us every year. My own personal collection included items I'd made in preschool and those I'd received as gifts over the years from my grandparents and parents. Decorating together as a family was a highlight of Christmas preparation, and we all loved retelling the story behind each ornament as we hung it on our tree.

I'd been fearing how I would handle the tradition this year, but God, as always, had a Holy Exchange in mind. Overwhelmed by the goodness of our community, I felt truly joyful as the children and I adorned the tree with our own collection of ornaments. This year, of all the ornaments I'd personally collected over the years, I hung only those given to me by Charlie. The kids placed theirs on first, filling the front of the tree; and I added mine around the sides. The back of the tree, facing the corner, we left bare. In the past, I'd given greater direction to spread the ornaments out evenly, but this season, that didn't seem important. The children were happy with the result, and I was thankful for their exuberance.

I tucked them into bed that night feeling like our world was a little closer to normal. Afterward, I sat in the glow of the giving tree, allowing the Giver of all good gifts to shine his light into my darkness. Healing is a continual process, and this was one more step toward it. After an hour, I could hardly keep my eyes open and went to bed. I fell quickly into a sound sleep, a gift in itself.

About 2:00 a.m. I was awakened by a loud crash. I knew from the sound that the tree had fallen over. I lay for a moment wondering if I could just ignore it and go back to sleep, but I didn't want the kids to get up in the morning and find their masterpiece sprawled across the floor.

To my amazement, they slept through the crash. I was thankful, and I kept the lights low and tried to work quietly so that I didn't disturb them. I straightened the tree and crawled underneath to tighten the clamps attached to the stand. It was clear why this had happened: the weight of ornaments across the front had tilted the tree forward until it fell. I fixed it as best I could and started to slide out from underneath it, but before I cleared the branches it started to tip again. I grabbed the trunk quickly, steadying it just in time, avoiding another collapse.

"Now what do I do?" I said to the darkness. I was stuck there. If I crawled out, it would fall. *This is fabulous. I can't stay in here all night, and there isn't anyone to help me.* I started to think of outlandish ways to secure the tree to something, undoubtedly inspired by the many episodes of *MacGyver* I'd watched as a child.

Then, to my delight, I saw Abigail's jump rope lying nearby. Grateful that she hadn't put it away, I was able to reach it without letting go of the tree. I tied one end to the trunk and the other to our front door knob, glad that we rarely used that door. Success was mine! Now I could go back to bed.

First, I scanned the floor for fallen ornaments and broken pieces. To my complete disbelief, there were only two broken ornaments, both from "my side" of the tree. Although the tree had fallen forward, not one of the kids' ornaments was broken.

I picked up the two broken ornaments and checked to see which they were. After all, every one of the ornaments Charlie and I had exchanged had a memory attached.

My jaw dropped. I double-checked to be certain of what I'd seen. The broken ornaments were the very first and very last ones given to me by Charlie.

And at the precise moment I noticed this, I heard the words *It is finished* echo through my heart and mind.

"It is finished." I repeated the words aloud, trying to affirm the essence of this statement inside me. *I know what you're talking about, Lord. Charlie and me. It is finished. I don't know what to do with this message right now, but I trust you to lead me through it.*

I went to the kitchen and found an empty glass jar. Gently, I placed every piece of those two ornaments in the jar. I cradled this treasure in the palm of my hand and carried it to my bedroom, where I placed it on my dresser. I crawled back into bed and within moments was peacefully asleep.

15

whispers and shouts

I suppose all the great love stories, the truly memorable ones, sweep us away with wide-eyed wonder and leave us thinking, "I didn't see that coming!" So why should God's love story for my life be any different?

When I share face-to-face what happened after the horrendous tragedy that shattered so many lives, I am always careful at this point in my story how I reveal what God did next. The jolt sometimes brings a raised eyebrow, often a look of perplexed disbelief, and sometimes even a bold declaration of disapproval. Thankfully, every now and then I get that rare eyes-wide-open-throw-the-head-back-out-loud-laughter "God is *too* good!" response.

I confess. That is my favorite response.

I also confess that when God revealed to me the next step in his plans for my life, this was not the response I gave.

In the aftermath of the tragedy, the biblical account of the conversion of the zealot Saul to the apostle Paul took on new meaning for me. Like him, my life was hit with a lightning bolt from heaven. The simultaneous infusion of heartrending pain and heart-healing grace was in every way earth-shattering. I was forever changed. I saw the world through new eyes. I lost patience for the things that don't matter and gained a heightened sense of urgency for what *does* matter.

In that context, it may be easier to grasp my newfound confidence in the whispers and shouts of God in my life. The God who showed up in my living room after Charlie's call, who met me at the window at my parents' home as I watched the Amish men embrace my father, who stood beside me at Aunt Linda's, at the graveside, in my bedroom, at the fire hall, and in Rosanna's hospital room, had earned my trust in a way I'd never known possible.

I now spent early mornings with Jesus and my Bible, reading the life-giving pages of the Word, meditating on its treasures, allowing them to seep into the center of my heart. This became the foundation of my day. Sometimes God revealed his stunning love in a way that kept me mesmerized for days. Other times I bathed in the words, letting them wash over me.

And one particular day in early November, he blew my mind!

But to understand the miracle of that day, I have to rewind to the planned playdate in the park for my children and the children of Dan Monville.

In response to Bryce's pleas to play with Dan's son, DJ, when I emailed Dan, we chose a local park where we would meet after church the following Sunday, October 29. I mentally prepared myself, listing potential conversation topics that would steer clear of the shooting or my adjustments to single motherhood.

I planned (some might say *over*planned) activities for the afternoon, collecting balls, baseball gloves, bubbles, snacks, and juice boxes. *I can do this.* Deep breath.

Saturday afternoon turned gusty, with winds blowing over 30 mph, and even higher winds forecast for the following day. My heart sank. *We can't play outside in this weather. Carson would probably blow away!* This seemed an easy out. *Let's reschedule,* was my first thought, quickly followed by the realization that my son would not find wind to be a suitable reason for cancellation. He would mutiny. How could I cancel our plans, ignoring his need for the comfort of a playmate?

I called Dan. He had an easy answer. "Why don't you and the kids just come over to my place? We can play games indoors instead."

I almost dropped the phone.

Throughout my teenage years, I didn't have guy friends. Nor had I ever, in my adult years, gone to a man's house to "hang out." Charlie and I had couples as friends, of course. But apart from Charlie, I'd never simply socialized with a man. I felt awkward at the thought. Playdates? Sure, I'd taken my children to others' homes and hosted their children at mine many times, but only with other *mothers*, never a father. A voice inside chided me. *Single adults get together, kids play, snacks are eaten all the time. It's not a big deal. Grow up and get over yourself. You are not a teenager. You have to follow through on this whether you want to or not.* My stomach churned, knots formed, apprehension grew deep within. Where are the CliffsNotes for sudden single-parent living? Ha! The joke was on me — they were probably in one of those many books given to me that I wasn't reading. *Soothe my fears, Lord,* I prayed.

Just to cover my bases, I mentioned the coming get-together to my parents and Charlie's. Integrity mandated shared knowledge; I had nothing to hide.

After church, I drove the kids to Dan's place. We ate sandwiches and played games. *This is easier than I thought*, I decided. *Why was I so worried?* A kid at heart, Dan loved games as much as the children. He also had a gift for conversation, and I soon believed he could probably talk to anyone about anything. With five kids between us, our conversations varied from favorite sports, pets, and movies to knock-knock jokes and superheroes. The mental list of safe topics I'd prepared was unnecessary. I breathed a sigh of relief.

That day, in the few moments devoted to conversation between the two of us, Dan was full of questions about the milk business, and I asked him about the career path that had led him to his current company.

Hours passed. Soon enough we were heading home. The smile on my son's face brought one to mine. Maybe — I hoped — this had been enough, and he wouldn't ask to play again. The day hadn't gone badly, but this new suddenly single life presented all kinds of dilemmas I was *not* ready to deal with.

The following week, I got a call from the high school soccer coach, John Girvin, my dad's cousin. He asked if he could drop off a little something for Bryce, a gift from the soccer team. Touched, I said yes.

The next afternoon Bryce was playing in the yard. Suddenly he came tearing into the house. "Mom, a big bunch of guys just pulled up in the driveway," he yelled. We stepped outside just in time to see what looked like the entire soccer team unloading a collapsible soccer goal and a supply of soccer balls.

Coach Girvin approached us grinning. "Hey, Bryce," John said. "I'm the coach of the high school soccer team. The guys have been thinking about you and your family. They heard you're a soccer player and thought you might like your own goal for practice."

Bryce looked dumbfounded, but he didn't have time to answer because he was suddenly engulfed by a swarm of lean, strong players in uniform. In a matter of seconds, Bryce was running and kicking balls, having the time of his life. I tried to find words to thank John, but he shrugged it off and joined his team.

I went back inside and watched from the window, tears streaming, my heart nearly breaking for joy. This mother, who'd felt incapable in so many ways to be what my son needed, was reminded that God is the Father of the fatherless. As for Bryce, I'm sure he was relieved. He'd tolerated his mom's feeble attempts to kick the ball around the yard long enough. Now these skilled players were teaching him the tricks of the game.

The following Saturday, my dad took Bryce to his soccer game. When the game was about to begin, Dad saw nearly the entire high school soccer team, led by Coach Girvin, heading straight for Bryce.

"Hey there, Bryce," the coach said. "My team had so much fun playing with you the other day, we wanted to come cheer you on today."

Bryce, confused, looked at my dad, then back at the coach. "Me? The team came to see *me* play?" I wish I'd been there to see his face!

"That's right, little man," said one of the boys. Then they all crowded around him giving him high fives like old friends.

Dad looked at his cousin John, who explained, "My boys wanted to do something for your family. They know what it means when a dad comes to a game to watch them. Since Bryce's dad is gone, they plan to come to all his games this season."

At the game's first water break, Bryce ran over to my dad — who suddenly realized that he'd forgotten to bring Bryce's water bottle. "Sorry, Bryce. All I've got is my thermos of coffee. Want a sip?"

"Sure!" Bryce didn't mind a bit. And for the rest of the game, Bryce took sips of coffee at every water break.

Coach Girvin laughed. "Bryce should have that thermos at every game! Looks like it makes him unstoppable, he's scored so many goals!"

But I know it wasn't the coffee. It was the thrill of having a team of young men calling his name and cheering him on from the sidelines.

True to their word, for the rest of the season, at every Saturday morning game, Bryce played to the sounds of "his team" cheering him on.

As for the supply of soccer balls — Bryce still has them (all well-worn) in the garage.

By mid-November, the six weeks since the shooting had brought me to a place of great dialogue with God and deep trust in the intimacy we shared. Though many days I longed to hear a human voice giving counsel and perspective, God's promise in James 1:2 – 5 spoke loudly to my heart.

> Consider it pure joy, my brothers and sisters, whenever you face trials of many kinds, because you know that the

> testing of your faith produces perseverance. Let perseverance finish its work so that you may be mature and complete, not lacking anything. If any of you lacks wisdom, you should ask God, who gives generously to all without finding fault, and it will be given to you.

I needed God's wisdom to rebuild our lives and parent my children, and daily I sought it. Daily I listened for it. I asked, he answered. It was becoming more and more natural with each passing day. Until, that is, the day I heard him say what felt like an earthquake, shaking me to the core of my being and leaving me trembling with the aftershocks.

"Dan Monville is the man you're going to marry."

I sat in stunned silence in my living room, Bible open on my lap, deafened by the accelerated rhythm of my heart.

Where did that come from?

"Lord, that sounds crazy!" I said. "It's too soon. Don't you know what all the books and all the counselors would say? What would people think? What would Dan think? I barely know the man!" I couldn't comprehend why God would think this was an appropriate time for a conversation with me on marriage.

Or *was* this God's voice?

I trusted God — but I was aware that perhaps I could not trust myself. After all, I'd been through a major life trauma. Maybe my perceptions were misfiring. I wasn't going to accept this declaration as truth without a thorough investigation.

I spent the next three days in prayer and fasting. I didn't sleep. My conversation with God consumed me. I argued with him. But finally I heard the words that stopped me: "You asked me to do big things for you. Why can't you just take what I'm trying to give?"

He spoke with such authority that I rested in that strength, feeling great peace. There would be no more questions.

"Okay, if Dan is the man you intend for me to marry, you'll need to make it happen, Lord. I won't argue with you anymore, but I'm not going to make a relationship happen. I won't pursue anything. I won't initiate one email or phone call. Dan will have to take the initiative, because I'm not!"

I took some consolation in the fact that God didn't say *now*; he simply said I would marry Dan. *Well, forever feels like a day to him. It probably won't happen for a long time.*

At the time of this conversation with God, mid-November, I hadn't seen Dan since the end of October. The day before Halloween he'd called to ask if I thought my kids felt up to trick-or-treating. I took him up on it, and the kids had a great time. I was grateful that the kids and I could make new memories rather than grieve old ones. Not only did the kids have fun, but I was pleased that Dan got to know Sean, the husband of my good friend Deanna, whose kids were making the candy rounds along with ours. When the topic turned to jazz, we agreed that the following week the four of us, myself, Dan, my friend, and her husband, would attend a jazz concert, not as couples on a date, but as friends.

We had a terrific night on the town.

Since then, Dan and I had exchanged just a few emails.

And now, this message from God.

Even the thought of marriage made me uncomfortable. I was just beginning to get my footing as a single mom. I wasn't looking for a husband. *Lord, I don't want to even dream about a husband,* I prayed. Dreaming involved risk taking. I was certainly too empty, too hurting to think of taking risks.

Again, I sensed the Lord speaking to me: "Approach me

empty-handed, free from past attitudes and disappointment. Don't define and limit me. Do you trust me?"

Lord, I can't do this life without you. Trusting you means I have no control, no guarantee, and no certainty of anything — yes, I trust you. I trust you a million times over. I trust you in all the ways I don't see you. I trust you with everything I have and all that I lack.

Even so, marriage seemed like a fairy-tale daydream, and my reality was far from a fairy tale. So I tucked away in my heart God's announcement and spoke of it to no one. *They'd think I'm a lunatic! I'd think I'm a lunatic if I were anyone else hearing about this conversation with God!* Besides, there was much to do and few spare minutes to ponder anything beyond the daily demands. I would simply get on with my life and see what God would bring to pass.

It was after that shocking revelation that I'd taken the trip to France, and there, to my surprise, received an email from Dan the day before Thanksgiving asking if we could talk by phone. Our conversation the following day left me confused. He had wanted to talk so he could tell me that he needed to cut off all communication for a while. He said that he wasn't doing that just with me — he was stepping back from a lot of friendships, maintaining only those in his closest circle until the end of the year.

On one hand, I was sad. Maybe the promise I'd felt was not being confirmed in Dan. I knew, however, that God would take care of me. If Dan wasn't the man I was to marry, I was okay with that. I'd promised God I wouldn't do anything to make our relationship happen. And though I was still riding the ups and downs of grief, I had survived enough of it so far to be sure that being a wife was not a requirement to finding joy. In fact, I was beginning to enjoy my growing self-confidence, my new identity. Maybe I'd been wrong about what I'd thought I'd heard from God — and if so, that was fine. I decided to let it go.

In the following weeks, I survived Elise's ninth birthday, my twenty-ninth, and Charlie's thirty-third. Then came the giving tree night. The broken ornaments, the "it is finished" moment. Since October 2, it seemed that my life had been one dramatic, inexplicable event after another.

As Christmas approached, I was on the hunt for some new traditions for my family of four. I'd often heard of Hershey's Christmas Candylane, a display of lights and seasonal celebrations at Hersheypark, an hour away. I thought we could walk around, enjoy hot chocolate together, and ride the train through the park. Many others must have had the same idea, as lines were long. We tired of the crowds and atmosphere quickly — a reminder to me that my kids, though seemingly back to normal, were still working through their recovery from grief. When had they ever been eager to leave an amusement park?

On the way home, Abigail asked if she could watch the American Girl Christmas movie that evening, a movie she'd watched several times the previous week.

"No, Mom," Bryce said. "I don't want to watch a *girl* movie."

"Bryce, let's do this for Abigail tonight, and then you won't have to watch it again for a whole year!"

He thought for a moment and then said, "Okay, if I sit quietly and don't fuss about it, can you get me a new dad for Christmas?"

I gulped. *That* came out of nowhere! "Well, Bryce, it's not like going to the grocery store and buying a box of cereal. I can't just pick one off the shelf!"

In his five-year-old way, he went on to list the qualifications this man must possess: "I know — he has to love you, we have to love him, and he has to love God."

I had to confess, he had the requirements right.

I was thinking fast. "I'm not sure I know how to get you that gift, but do you know what we can do? We can pray and ask God to do something about you wanting a new dad." He seemed satisfied.

I was mystified. My memory of the "it is finished" moment suddenly burned inside me with real intensity. This wasn't just about me — this was a deep desire within Bryce's precious heart. I prayed as I drove. *Whatever you are doing, I'm sure you will prepare the way. Doesn't every child need a mom and a dad? My kids need a dad now more than ever.*

Was there somewhere a man brave enough to love our family, strong enough to stand with us, and yet tender enough to reach into the broken places of our hearts? *Why would any man choose to sacrifice his life like that? If he marries the wife of Charlie Roberts, he'll be criticized harshly for it. God, whoever he is, I hope you've prepared him for what he's getting into.* My heart whispered a prayer for insight.

And God whispered back, "I'm not doing this just because it's best for your family. You are perfect for him too!"

The words startled me. I hadn't thought about the *blessing* a husband would receive by marrying me, only the challenges. But I sensed God telling me otherwise. Our family of four would be exactly what this man longed for and needed. I would be giving something wonderful to him even as I received all he gave to us! I needed a husband, my kids needed a father; this man needed a wife, and he needed my children. It was Christmas, a season of giving, and somehow God still called *me* a gift.

Will this chosen man be Dan Monville, undoubtedly in the distant future? Or another man? Or am I still too traumatized to trust my perceptions of your voice? I strove to keep myself from clinging to one particular outcome. I trusted God, but I was too skittish to fully trust my perceptions. Time would tell.

As Christmas drew closer, I was certain that our Christmas would be subdued, since I was still too tender in the face of such great loss to manage the usual tradition and celebration. To my amazement, a generous donor unexpectedly gave us a substantial financial gift. We decided to use it to help us find a way through Christmas by going on a Disney cruise. I extended the invitation to my family and Charlie's as well. My parents decided to stay home, since they had just made the trip to France over Thanksgiving and wanted to spend the day with my other siblings. Charlie's family decided to accompany us. Brothers, sisters-in-law, parents, grandparents — they all drove to Florida while I chose to fly, fearing that a twenty-hour car ride with three young children would be a difficult beginning for a vacation.

The children and I arrived at the dock and waited in line for over an hour to check in. We were four weary travelers, tired and hungry from the trip. I was struggling to keep it all together and wondered, as I stood in line trying to keep the kids excited about what was to come, if the trip had been a mistake. The crew member who greeted us, noticing that we were from Pennsylvania, asked a question that made my heart sink: "Do you live near where that Amish schoolhouse shooting happened?"

Stunned, I heard myself lying. "No, another part of the state." I've never made a habit of lying, but I just couldn't bear the weight of a truthful response.

I quickly decided, even so, that coming on the cruise had been a very good idea indeed. Still, the trip had its highs and lows, and there were moments that broke me. For one thing, there were couples everywhere, strolling hand in hand, giving one another dreamy looks of love over candlelit dinners. There were dads splashing in the pool and entire families playing, eating, and resting together. But not my kids — they had no father. It seemed as though every time I thought I had myself together, another impact of the shooting would send me staggering again. I'd thought such days of grief were behind me, but I was discovering the repetitive nature of grief. Even within a floating city of several thousand people, it is possible to feel completely alone.

One night at dinner my sense of loss and the weight of my solitary parenting responsibilities were suffocating. I felt as though I would completely lose it if I didn't get a couple of minutes to myself and regain some sense of composure. I asked Charlie's family if they would excuse me, and I went to look at the pictures taken by Disney photographers the day before. Just the break I needed.

As I stood in line to look for pictures of my three children, I was crying out, *I need you, I need you now, I am so alone.* But I felt no reply from heaven. Holding back hot tears, I breathed deeply, trying to convince myself that I could do this. God would help me.

A few moments later, the woman in front of me turned around and began to talk. She had brought her daughter and grandchildren on this cruise, she said, because they had just gone through a very difficult divorce and needed to get away if there was to be any hope of a joyful Christmas. Then she asked what brought me on the cruise. Feeling a sense of shared emotional trauma, I told her that my husband had died almost three months before, and I was there for the same reason. No sooner had I spoken the words than she wrapped her arms around me, pulled me close, and gave me the most vibrant hug. I didn't tell her what that hug meant, but it saved me. She was Jesus with skin on in the moment of my greatest pain.

Once again God had reached down from heaven, touched me, and changed my emotional reference point. My Shepherd carrying me in his arms, right there in the middle of the ocean!

16

laughter

It was 9:00 p.m. and my kids were sleeping peacefully on this January night. I sat on the recliner in our dimly lit family room, the fireplace flickering in front of me. I was waiting for a call from Dan Monville.

Other than Dan's Thanksgiving call, I couldn't remember a single time in the past ten years when a man (aside from guys in the family) had asked if he could call me. I felt a strange mix of emotions. His email had said that he wanted to share what God had been doing in his heart. I'd talked about Jesus with lots of people; this was one of my favorite topics. But this time, I sensed that Dan's call would cover more than his spiritual thoughts.

God always keeps his promises. God had told me over six weeks ago that I would marry Dan Monville. At the time, I had questioned my perceptions of that message and had told God that I would do nothing to make that happen. It was in his hands, not mine. As I waited for Dan's call, it was hard to push those thoughts aside. Was it possible that God had been talking with Dan in the same way he had been talking to me? If he had, then how would Dan start this conversation? I tried not to get ahead of myself.

I thought back to the night over eight weeks before when Dan and I and some friends had gone to the jazz concert. It hadn't been a date, just a group of parents socializing. But I remembered that I'd felt entirely comfortable with him.

In the weeks leading up to Thanksgiving we had exchanged a few brief emails, and then we'd had that odd call on Thanksgiving Day, but those things were enough to make me wonder if God was working in Dan's heart too.

The phone rang. I let it ring several times so that I wouldn't seem overly eager to begin the call. I didn't want him to know I had been waiting with the phone in my lap. The thought made me laugh. I was acting like a silly teenager. I said hello.

Our conversation began with simple things — the weather, the day's activities. It felt comfortable. Then he went a little deeper, sharing past struggles, the way Jesus had broken through his darkness, and the revitalized relationship with God he now had. Dan was telling his story.

I had heard bit and pieces over the years through my family — about his first marriage and divorce, and about his kids, but there was a lot I didn't know. Dan shared custody of Nicole and DJ with his ex-wife. He spoke from the depths of his heart — mistakes and regrets, discoveries and growth, his part in the failure of his first marriage, past struggles with alcohol addiction. He hid nothing, and I instinctively trusted him. In this first real conversation, he was vulnerable and authentic, giving me the opportunity to see him for who he truly was. Talking about his feelings seemed to be second nature. Definitely different from my conversations with Charlie!

Talking with Dan was easy. While the circumstances of his life were different from mine, I could hear similarities in heartbreak.

"Marie," he continued, "I want to share with you what God's

been doing in my heart the past six months and how I got to where I am now." I sensed a shift in his tone, a slight nervousness. "Back in the spring, I felt God promising that I was going to have a new wife and a full-time family again. I had no idea who she might be because I wasn't dating anyone. But I couldn't deny the promise or push it away."

I smiled. *That* sounded familiar. I felt a rush of excitement building inside me.

"When I came to give you those things at your parents' house that first night," he said, "I certainly wasn't looking for a date. I was on an assignment that, frankly, I felt uncomfortable about. I didn't want to impose on you during your grief.

"On my way home that night, my heart was pierced. I felt walls fall down that I hadn't even known were there. While I didn't instantly think that you might be the woman God had in mind for me, I knew that there was a change inside me — an understanding that I was now ready to commit to a deep, loving relationship — a marriage and family."

He was speaking so fast at this point that there wasn't even room for me to comment, but my eyes were growing wider. At least I wasn't the *only* one who'd had these sudden astounding messages from God!

"I was astonished when I met you that night," he said. "Nothing about you was what I'd imagined. I could see Jesus in you — confidence, grace, and love. Totally unexpected. When I looked at your circumstances, the loss of your husband and how it had happened only weeks before, I saw your miraculous healing and recovery and ... and ..."

I was on the edge of my seat, listening. If he thought he was astonished that night, he should have seen me right then!

"... and I was stunned. Marie, you are radiantly beautiful, inside and out."

I'm sure I blushed crimson. He stopped for a breath, and I sensed him relaxing. I, on the other hand, had fireworks exploding in my heart. He found me radiantly beautiful inside and out? He thought the regular me, the post-trauma me, the everyday Marie Roberts was something special? Apparently so — and he spoke it with quiet sincerity.

"To top it off," he went on, "each time we got together with the kids, you seemed to enjoy being with me. This was not what I had expected.

"I asked God to show me why this was happening. I assumed he was just showing me I was ready to move on in my own healing, that I was ready to really feel and love again, to prepare myself for marriage. Not with you, because how could that be right? Still, seeing you, I felt this change in my heart, and I didn't know why."

I wished I could see his face as he spoke.

"So I asked God to show me who he had in mind for me. As I pursued the Lord in November and December, he closed every door I thought might be open. I felt him clarify that it wasn't anyone in the circle around me and that, instead, he wanted to open a new door to a new relationship. I kept praying, asking who this woman was.

"Marie, I felt him tell me it was you."

My heart leaped, and a sense of absolute wonder invaded me. God was merging his whispers to me with his whispers to Dan, and through them he was shouting a single word — marriage. It seemed like the time for me to say something, *anything*, but I was speechless!

It was just as well. Dan launched into a series of disclaimers:

"When I started to realize the feelings I was developing for you, I needed to talk about it and process it. I needed a gut check. So I chose a few trusted people — friends from church, my mom and sisters, my pastors, accountability partners I'd chosen during my singleness. What I heard back were mixed reactions and many reservations. A few challenged my ability to hear the voice of God and questioned my reasoning. I understood that completely, of course. I'd have said the same thing to them. You had just been widowed through a horrible tragedy. You needed time. We barely knew each other. Really, we had nothing more than a budding friendship."

I laughed inside, wanting to tell him all the things God had spoken to me, but he kept talking. I had to bite my tongue and wait a bit longer.

"But God's message had been so direct, so clear. I was confused and knew I needed to hear the voice of God above everyone else. So I've spent the past six weeks pursuing the Lord very intentionally, solidifying the foundation of my relationship with him, and dealing with my heart. That's why I haven't contacted you through most of November and December. I needed time alone with God. I needed to find confidence in the words God had spoken to me."

Dan's words thrilled my heart not because he was talking about his love for me, but because he shared his primary commitment to God. Nothing was more important to me. But Dan didn't yet know what I was thinking. How much courage it took to let these words leave his mouth!

Now, it seemed, he was done. It was my turn. How shocked would he be to hear that his story was no great shock or surprise to me? In fact, it made perfect sense.

"Dan, back in November, one morning when I was spending

time reading the Bible and praying, I felt God whisper to my heart, 'Dan Monville is the man you are going to marry.'"

My words, kept bottled up inside me during Dan's soliloquy, now came pouring out in a rush. I told him of my subsequent three-day fast, my time of arguing with God, and how God had put an end to it. I pictured Dan on the edge of his seat, mouth hanging open, eyes wide with wonder and, I imagined, considerable relief that not only did I not think he was crazy, but instead we'd both had this remarkable experience individually with God.

Several hours of deep conversation followed. It was as if we pulled back the veil that had covered our lives. We so easily stepped into the next phase of our conversation that I am still amazed, looking back over the years, by that mysterious exchange. We agreed that this road would not be easy. There would be many around us eager to offer their counsel, and not all would affirm our decision. We understood their skepticism. Were it not *our* lives, our *own* God-breathed messages, we would have viewed the circumstances differently. But God would lead the way forward, we were sure of it. Dan said that he was ready to embark on a relationship regardless of others' perspectives. I agreed. Our responsibility was to maintain our focus on God and center ourselves on his will for our families.

We were poised to enter a dating relationship with the intent to marry. We were on the same page concerning our children, not wanting to cause them any additional heartbreak. We were intentional about the process; we must date as a family. We did not want to be a statistic; we needed to be the exception.

I shared more of my background and story. We both wanted to see the truth of each other's heart — places once marked by failure, loss, and weakness. I explained that who I was as a child was not who I was now, that God had brought a radical transformation over my life in these past few months. I had begun to see myself in a new way and believed in following the voice of God, rather than pleasing the people around me.

I told Dan about the crates of mail I received each day, encouraging letters filled with prayers and Scripture verses. "I have to tell you," I said, laughing, "Jeremiah 29:11 – 14 is the verse I heard most often from others over these past months." I recited it for him:

> "For I know the plans I have for you," declares the LORD, "plans to prosper you and not to harm you, plans to give you hope and a future. Then you will call on me and come and pray to me, and I will listen to you. You will seek me and find me when you seek me with all your heart. I will be found by you," declares the LORD, "and will bring you back from captivity. I will gather you from all the nations and places where I have banished you," declares the LORD, "and will bring you back to the place from which I carried you into exile."

"These verses were a great encouragement to me, and they reinforced the words God was speaking to me."

"I know them well," Dan said. "In fact, I — "

But I interrupted him, because I knew exactly what he was going to say. "You're going to laugh at this, Dan. When we exchanged those few emails in November, I didn't understand what your email address, jer291114@something.com, stood for. So I asked my friend Deanna what she thought the letters and numbers referenced. She instantly recognized it as Jeremiah 29:11 – 14." He laughed. "So many people were praying that verse, declaring it over me, and now God is sending me this promise, in flesh and blood, in *you*."

After a while, our euphoria over God's phenomenal intervention in our lives calmed and our conversation grew serious again. We began to discuss what, if anything, might hinder our relationship. Our children were our first priority, we agreed. Our concern went beyond the future of two adults; it encompassed two families.

I lost all track of time, lost in a sense of wonder at the potential for a mutually fulfilling, deep relationship. It was a feeling I had not felt in a very long time. But as satisfying and joy-filled as I felt, I cautioned myself. The decision to explore our relationship through family dates, even in light of the stunning messages God had given us both, didn't mean that marriage was a foregone conclusion. We'd had so little time together. One conversation was hardly enough for me to fall head-over-heels in love with Dan Monville. I'd heard his words, and he'd heard mine. Now we needed to see their fruit.

Dan and I planned our first family date for the following Sunday. Our kids — all five of them — immediately leapt at the idea of an outing together. We asked them for suggestions of what they would like to do. Much to my dismay, they unanimously picked swimming. To the kids, this seemed like the perfect winter afternoon outing, but it was way outside my comfort zone. I didn't want to go on our first date in a bathing suit! But I was doomed — we had let them choose and couldn't overrule them now.

We met at a nearby indoor pool. I was curious to see how the afternoon would unfold. Bryce seemed the complete opposite of DJ — Bryce ran, DJ walked. Bryce was rambunctious, DJ was calm and steady. I wondered if Dan would be able to relate to Bryce. Abigail, quiet and reserved, would be a challenge for him, and Carson, at twenty-one months, was a much younger child than Dan had been accustomed to in quite some time. Could he handle it? How would the kids interact with one another? The answers to my questions came soon enough.

Dan's daughter, Nicole, was a delight. I enjoyed chatting with her, getting to know her, and observing her relationship with her dad. I liked the tenderness and laughter I saw. Carson, ever playful, loved splashing in the water. DJ and Bryce were quick to jump in and play games together, diving to the deep end of the pool to retrieve dive rings and sticks. Abigail, although tentative, seemed to be enjoying herself. After giving her a bit of time to warm up, Dan encouraged her to join in with the boys. He gave tips on going deeper and swam alongside her on her first attempts to reach the bottom of the pool. She succeeded, all smiles, returning to the surface with dive rings in hand!

The One who knew my every thought and answered even the simplest prayer was thrilling my heart.

As the afternoon came to a close, we heard the cries of happy children: "Just five more minutes, please?" We said goodbye and got into our cars. I was interested to hear what the kids would say on our drive home, and I wondered what was being said in Dan's vehicle as well.

I was pleased that, as we drove, my three were bubbling with excitement over the afternoon and the time we'd spent together. Between bursts of laughter and chatter, there were moments of contented silence, during which we became aware of the delightful feel of tired muscles and the rumble of hunger in our bellies.

One day at a time, God, I prayed, *you will show us the way and guide us into your path. Right now I'm not planning for a lifetime, I'm simply enjoying a moment.*

As Dan and I told those closest to us of our family date, many questioned our wisdom, while a few approved. But Dan and I knew that the Creator of this vast universe was beginning to re-create something within our hearts, and he was not doing it based on everyone else's perspective. He didn't ask me to respond to any voice aside from his. I was responsible to him alone. *I will embrace what you are doing. Show me your wisdom, fill me with your love, but let me always choose obedience.*

We made plans for a second family date.

Dan and I were dating with the intention of marriage. I have to confess that I know how odd that is. But my life had been nothing *but* odd since October 2. Being different was my new normal.

As we spent time together, I was discovering why my heart was destined to fall in love with this man God had chosen. We were two separate instruments learning to play love's beautiful symphony together. The music began softly, a simple melody. But as we continued to play together, a depth and warmth emerged, a harmony far lovelier than my solo performance.

Early on in my conversations with Jesus after becoming a widow, I'd talked to him about the way God had knit me together in my mother's womb. *Why*, I asked him, *was I fashioned with such an intense desire for family, a husband and children, only to know the tremendous ache of loss in both areas?* Now I felt his reassurance, as if he were telling me, *You were made to be a fighter, a survivor. Yes, the road is long and hard some days, but you won't give up. You refuse to live a life contrary to my will. You will experience victory in the face of adversity.*

I was amazed. *You believe in me that much, Lord?*

The truth of 1 Corinthians 15:57–58 came suddenly alive for me.

> But thanks be to God! He gives us the victory through our Lord Jesus Christ.
>
> Therefore, my dear brothers and sisters, stand firm. Let nothing move you. Always give yourselves fully to the work of the Lord, because you know that your labor in the Lord is not in vain.

God filled me with hope. He believed in me. The Creator of the universe, the Giver of life, the One who walked on water, who healed every disease — he believed in *me*!

With those words, confidence surged through me. This changed everything. Listening to the whisper of the Holy Spirit in my heart, I had been finding a communion that brought life in a dimension I couldn't have anticipated. To the Author of life, "impossible" was nothing.

I thought back to my prayer a few months before — *Jesus, if there isn't a man on earth who could handle the circumstances of my life, I'm okay with knowing it will be you and me forever. But if there is a man, then bring me just one — I'm not dating.* I had to laugh in delight. God had freed me to love myself in deeper ways, and that in turn equipped me to love others — my children, this man who had entered my life, and his children as well. And because of God's work in me since the tragedy, I knew the end of the story: Jesus wins every time. His love always prevails.

As we continued our family-style dates, more and more I saw a man filled with integrity and intentionality. He connected his heart to mine as well as to my children's hearts, but he also connected us to the heart of the Father. It was clear that he spent time in the presence of Jesus — he reflected that love upon us. I stood amazed at all he had gone through as God was preparing him to become everything we needed. While I wasn't thankful for the heartbreak and agony he had experienced, I admired the way he had chosen to yield himself to it, allowing God to use it as preparation for this season, for us. I recalled the leap God had invited me to take a few months earlier — to love my life. *I do love my life, Lord, I truly do, and I love all you've done with it.*

In the early weeks of our relationship, surrounded by our children in bowling alleys and pizza parlors, and sitting in circles on the floor playing board games, it was easy to see there was great potential to love life with Dan. Although eleven years older than I was, he was filled with youthful effervescence and often ran circles around me. He was still a kid at heart, full of childlike wonder. He saw the world as a glass half full — a great fit, since that's also how I see it.

I saw in Dan what I had asked God to do in Charlie. It took my breath away to realize that God was honoring each of the prayers I'd had on my prayer list for Charlie — a deeper relationship with God, an ability to identify his thoughts and feelings and work through them with God and with me, a deep joy for life that could rise above life's losses. Not one prayer had gone unheard or would remain unfulfilled. Those answers hadn't come in the way I had initially hoped or expected, but they were coming now in Dan. With a sense of awe for how God works, I realized that I had been praying for Dan for years without knowing it. This wasn't the way I would ever have wanted it to happen — my prayers had been that Charlie, my husband, would know such fulfillment. My heart had cried out for years for what I believed God wanted for our family.

God, however, always creating us for our future, already had a plan for how we would redeem those prayers.

It was no minor plan. Redeeming those prayers would require everything I had thought I knew to be realigned, as I clutched tightly to all that God created me to be: his beloved daughter, wanted and loved, delighted in by my Father. The ultimate love story. It wasn't just a plan; it was a kiss. Heaven's kiss.

Experiencing heaven's kiss, I began to anticipate love's first kiss, believing it would convey more than a million words could. I waited, believing it would completely take my breath away.

17

the basket

Our five-year-old yellow lab, Dale, missed his master. He'd been Charlie's dog from the moment we brought him home as a puppy in our fifth year of marriage. Born on a local Amish farm, Dale had always loved to play outside and never missed an opportunity to chase one of the neighbor's cats when it dared to venture into our yard. But in the four months since Charlie's death, Dale had lost some of his playful exuberance.

Often at night I put Dale out on our gated deck, which suited him fine and gave me the opportunity to prepare the kids for bed peacefully. One evening in mid-January, after getting the kids in bed, I opened the door to let Dale back in, and to my surprise, he wasn't there. I pulled on my winter coat and circled the yard, yelling his name, as a sinking feeling grew in the pit of my stomach. He didn't come. A light snow was beginning to fall.

In the past, one call from Charlie had been enough to bring Dale galloping in an instant. Dale didn't always come when I called, but he never left the yard except for a quick jump over the porch gate to chase a neighborhood cat. Even though he always returned within moments, he had jumped that gate more often since Charlie's death, which made me wonder if Dale was looking for him. Charlie had typically left for work midevening, the time Dale seemed to want to be outside.

I went back inside. "Lord, please bring Dale back," I prayed. "We all four need his boisterous romping around this house." For the next two hours, I went out every ten to fifteen minutes, calling and looking for him. I saw no tracks in the newly fallen snow. I put food in his metal dish and rattled it around, hoping the noise would beckon him home.

At about 11:00 p.m. I opened the door to call him again and found him lying on the doormat, bleeding and broken. At first glance, I thought he was dead. He was completely still, lying in a pool of blood, his stomach broken open. It looked as if a car had hit him. A surge of panic swept through me as I knelt and stroked his neck. What a relief to feel his warmth! He lifted his head and looked into my eyes with such pain that I gasped. He didn't make a sound, not even a whimper.

"It's okay, boy," I said, trying to soothe him. "I'll get a blanket." I dashed into the living room and grabbed the blanket we kept draped over the back of the couch, covered him, then ran for my phone. I called my parents. Mom answered. I could tell from her voice that I'd woken her.

"Dale's been hit by a car," I blurted without even a hello. "Can one of you come over to stay with the kids? They're sound asleep, and I want them to stay that way."

"We'll be right there," Mom said.

Then I called my neighbor. "I think Dale's been hit by a car," I said, my voice beginning to shake. "Could you come over and drive us to the emergency pet clinic?"

Within ten minutes, Mom and Dad were there, along with my

neighbor who helped Dad load Dale into the back of my neighbor's pickup.

As we sped through the darkness, I silently called out to the One who was holding my frailties together. *Why? Why this, and why now? I don't want Dale to die too.* I hoped the injuries weren't as bad as they looked but feared the worst. *Jesus, save him! We can't lose Dale now. He's all we have left of Charlie!*

The thirty-minute drive to the clinic seemed to take hours. When finally Dale lay on the examination table, I stroked his head, but his eyes conveyed a message I could not bear to see. He was in pain, and the life within him was fading from his eyes. My tears flowed freely, falling all over him and leaving tiny splashes on the sterile metal table. The vet ushered me into the waiting room and soon returned, his eyes sorrowful.

"Mrs. Roberts, Dale's been hit by a car, and it's a very grave wound. I've done what I can to clean it up and make him comfortable, but you have two choices. We could attempt to keep him alive through the night with immediate surgery. If he makes it through the night, he'll need more surgery if he is to have any chance of recuperating, but his injuries are massive and his chances are not good. Your other option is to let him go. I could put him to sleep now and end his suffering."

I didn't want to lose Dale. Charlie's dog was a bit of the past still mingling in our present.

Through my tears I forced myself to speak. "If he were your dog, what would you do?"

"I would let him go. Dale would have to endure great agony to survive — multiple surgeries and a painful recuperation." This was not what I wanted to hear. As much as I wanted him to live, as much as I knew the kids would miss him, I couldn't force him to endure such agony. The best choice was to let him go, to set him free from the torture of his body.

Within minutes, Dale slipped quietly into peaceful sleep, forever.

I barely remember the ride home, except for the constant tears and useless efforts to try to work out in my mind how to explain this loss to my children. I remembered God's words to me when I asked him to "fix" the loss of Charlie. *I am not going to fix this. I am going to redeem it,* he'd told me. How would God redeem the loss of Dale?

It wasn't that I didn't understand that families lose pets every day. I'm sure the veterinarian who treated Dale could have told me dozens of similar stories just from recent weeks. It was the *cumulative* loss we'd experienced, and the need for my kids — and me — to have something familiar and real and cuddly to hold on to, something full of life to remind us that life goes on. Dale had functioned beautifully in that role — up till now. His loss would leave a hole far beyond the void usually left by a missing pet.

I returned home in the early hours of the morning, knowing I wouldn't sleep much that night. I lay in bed heartbroken, crying out to the God who, while loving us, allows us to be pierced by the pain of this world. *Why? Everything we had of Charlie is slipping away, no matter how hard we try to grasp it. What am I going to tell the kids? How can they endure this loss on top of losing their daddy?* God saw my heart; he knew my anguish. There was no reason to hide my words from him.

As I emptied my grief, placing it before him, I did what I'd been learning to do since the day of Charlie's death. I worshiped God. I didn't understand why he was allowing this loss, but I'd experienced the light of his presence these past four months, and

I knew he was present. As I worshiped, he filled me with trust. Surprisingly, I drifted off to sleep.

A few hours later the alarm went off. My pillow was still damp with tears. I decided that if the kids didn't ask about Dale, I wouldn't tell them until they came home from school. That would give us the evening to recover together.

My stomach was in knots as my heart constantly cried out, *God, please don't let them ask about the dog this morning!* We had sixty minutes until it was time for the bus. I felt like the clock was working against me, as though time stood still. I did my best to keep them busy but knew that there was no way I could prevent them from asking about the dog. Usually it was a challenge to keep him from complicating our morning routine, since he was so full of energy, eager to greet the day and each one of us. Surely they would ask about his absence. But I prayed on.

As departure time approached, I began to breathe easier, holding on to the hope that God was covering us this morning and answering my prayers. We walked to the bus stop, very close to success. I struggled to hold back my own tears, but I was determined to maintain focus. God knew I needed him to hold me together and keep the kids' attention directed elsewhere.

The bus finally arrived; Abigail and Bryce were off to school. "Thank you, Jesus," I prayed as I walked home with Carson in my arms. Tears streamed silently down my cheeks. I entered the house, set Carson down, closed the door, and leaned back against it as if trying to keep the sadness of the world from breaking through. This new challenge seemed to threaten me out of proportion to the loss of a pet, demanding strength from emotional muscles far too overused. *Father, you've got to do something about this. I can't handle it on my own.*

God replied in the most unexpected way. Within moments, someone knocked at the door. I knew my face was splotchy from crying, not the way I wanted to look when welcoming unexpected company, but I had no time to fix it. I opened the door.

A friend's warmth greeted me: "Marie, I'm so glad you're home!" Christine and her husband were the pastors of the church where our prayer group met. She stepped in, saying, "I'm sorry it took me so long to bring this to you. Someone dropped off this basket for you at the church several days ago. My son had chicken pox, so I couldn't bring it over until he was better." She held out a basket.

Christine didn't seem to notice my puffy eyes. I ushered her to the kitchen counter and opened the basket. To my amazement, there were three stuffed puppies inside, a note of love from a stranger, and a container of chocolate chip cookies.

I was overwhelmed. "Let me tell you something," I said. "Last night our dog was hit by a car. He died early this morning."

"Oh, Marie. No!"

"I haven't even told the kids yet. But I can't believe how God used your delay to bring this gift at the perfect moment. If you had brought these puppies last week, it would have been nice, but it wouldn't have meant as much as it does now. Just moments before you knocked on my door, I was calling out for God to do something, and in an instant, here you are. When I tell the kids that their dog died, I can tell them that God knew it was going to happen, and that he loved us all enough to send something to take away some of the sting. And you know what? It's not even about what's in the basket — it's about the fact that he loved us enough to send it on the very day we needed it." Fresh tears of joy now mingled with those of grief.

Christine seemed speechless that God had used her to answer my prayer. She offered a few gentle words of sympathy and comfort, gave me a hug, and headed home to tell her husband.

As soon as she left, I ran for the phone and called Dan. We had talked the night before when I was searching for Dale, but not since. I couldn't wait to share the beauty of God's provision in the midst of this loss. I expected to get his voicemail, but he answered; he had the day off. I explained the past eleven hours — through the moments of shocking loss and into the grace of God.

I could hear amazement in his voice as he said, "Marie, God has given you an immediate answer to prayer to demonstrate that he is present and that he will carry you through this difficult time." He asked if Carson and I wanted to spend the afternoon with him. I agreed, thankful that I wouldn't have to be alone, as Mom had offered to have Bryce over for the afternoon. A few hours later, joined by his daughter, Nicole, and one of her friends, we spent the afternoon laughing together. Unexpected joy lifted the heaviness from my heart as I realized that God was pouring his good gifts into my life not only in the form of stuffed puppies and chocolate chip cookies, but also in a dear man and two lighthearted teenagers.

Now, as I planned how I would share this heartbreaking news with the kids, I expected God to redeem their evening just as he had my afternoon. We conquered homework right after school and ate dinner a little early. Still the kids didn't ask about Dale, which amazed me. I asked them to sit with me in the living room.

"I have bad news and good news for you today," I said.

Abigail and Bryce both stiffened. Their eyes searched mine. I was sure that they were remembering when I told them their dad was dead.

"Last night, after you were asleep, Dale must have run into the road. He was hit by a car and was hurt very badly."

"No!" cried Bryce.

"Not Dale!" Abigail said. "Where is he?"

My heart ached so badly, and my tears started pouring. I told them about the trip to the vet and the difficult decision to let Dale go.

Abigail, Bryce, and Carson all burst into tears. I allowed myself to cry with them, and we held one another close, rocking. As we wept, a most unexpected emotion washed over me — relief. I was relieved that they were openly crying. This was a normal, healthy emotional response to the loss of a family pet. But it was even more than that. It was a time of unrestrained tears shared by all four of us together, and it felt cleansing.

After a few moments, as their cries began to quiet, I spoke again. "But now I must tell you the good news, and you will be as amazed as I was! Before any of that ever happened to Dale, God knew that it was going to happen, and he started a plan to heal the sadness in our hearts. Wait here. I have something to show you."

I unwrapped myself from the tangle of arms and legs, went to my room, and returned with the basket. I sat on the couch again, and my three children gathered close. Slowly, I lifted the lid and took out the three stuffed puppies, which were immediately snatched into hugs and snuggles. God's comfort, dressed in brown-and-white fur, wrapped around our hearts.

"God had a special plan all laid out," I explained. "A week ago, he inspired a lady we don't even know to buy you three puppies and put them in this basket, along with chocolate chip cookies. He led her to drop the basket at Christine's church and ask Christine to bring them to us. Christine kept them at her house until this morning, and then, even though she didn't know about Dale, God prompted her to bring them to our house today. Do you know what? After you got on the school bus, I was crying and praying for God to help us because we would all be so sad, and just then, Christine knocked on the door and handed me this basket! God planned this special surprise to remind us that he is with us. He cares that we are sad and he loves us, even in our saddest times."

My heart swelled so much that I found it hard to swallow as I watched each of them press their faces into the brown-and-white fur, clinging tightly to their new puppies. This chance to speak the truth of God's tender care for them brought a surge of gratitude for my heavenly Father. Though we were all sad about Dale, the kindness of others was shining the brilliant light of God into our lives, right there on the couch.

We enjoyed the cookies as a bedtime snack that evening, huddled together on our couch. Grief mixed with love and thankfulness in the midst of pain. Watching my teary-eyed children munch those cookies, I pondered the importance of a proper perspective — head lifted, eyes looking forward, even if those eyes are filled with tears. I looked back over the grief we had endured together. How breathtaking to see how far we had come in balancing life and loss, allowing the expression of real emotion while at the same time celebrating God's acts of tenderness.

Our dog, Charlie's dog, was gone. Charlie's absence felt more pronounced without Dale's playful presence. The silence grew louder. It was as if, after going through such a deep loss nearly four months before, this loss brought a resurgence of emotional intensity for the kids and me. But as much as we knew pain, we also knew great joy, as if in feeling the one we were more capable of experiencing the other. I felt the sting of Dale's loss to the core — and the tenderness of God's compassion just as strongly.

In the days that followed I reached for that which God continued to give — the love of Jesus in the form of Dan. Family dates continued to create a bond between the seven of us. Dan and I marveled at how smoothly all of the relationships were growing. Still, we needed time for just the two of us to form the foundation of what would become one cohesive unit — the bond that we believed would eventually unite us as husband and wife.

One Friday evening not long after we lost Dale, my close friend Deanna and her husband, Sean, invited the kids over, giving Dan and me an opportunity for an elusive "date night." To my surprise, he offered to cook, promising that it wouldn't be something from a box or can. I confess, I had previously spied out the contents of his kitchen cupboard, so I was only cautiously optimistic, unsure if his idea of "from scratch" would be the same as mine.

I felt like a nervous teenage girl as I dressed for the evening, scouring my closet for just the right look: casual but special, not too ordinary, but not over-the-top. Since Dan was cooking, I'd offered to drive to his apartment. I arrived around 6:00 p.m. and stood outside his door poised to push the doorbell, nearly laughing at myself for having butterflies in my stomach. Finally, I pushed the button.

Dan opened the door, his eyes alight with happiness, and welcomed me in. Candlelight flickered from every direction — candles on the dining table, the kitchen counter, the end tables in the living room. Jazz filled the air. He welcomed me with a warm hug, and soon, while Dan put our dinner on the table, we were chatting as usual — about our week, about the kids, about the kindness of our friends to give us a night for just the two of us.

Dan's creation, shepherd's pie, was better than I'd expected! He mentioned over dinner that we were listening to a custom playlist he'd compiled from his favorite music, specifically for our evening alone together. Music, candles, dinner ... would he kiss me tonight?

For me, a kiss says something serious about a relationship. It's not an insignificant exchange freely given, but rather something reserved for the one sharing hopes and dreams — God's chosen one for me. I'd been anticipating our first kiss, expecting God to use it to speak deeply inside my heart. I believed that our kiss would either confirm for me that Dan was the one or warn me if I was wrong about God's choice of Dan for me. Call me a hopeless romantic, a believer in fairy-tale kisses — guilty as charged!

When we finished our dinner, Dan changed the CD. "I compiled this CD too, Marie." He stepped toward me at the dinner table, held out his hand, and shocked me with his next question. "May I have this dance?" he asked tenderly.

I gulped, suddenly flustered. "I can't dance!" I protested, shrinking back as the image of myself as uncoordinated and awkward swept over me.

Dan didn't miss a beat. "Marie, *everyone* can dance," he coaxed gently.

"Not everyone! Dan, you don't understand. I really can't dance. I have no experience."

He looked at me in surprise for just a moment, then said softly, "All you have to do is follow my lead. I promise, it will be simple. We'll just do a box step together. I'll lead, you follow."

It was an invitation I couldn't pass up. Besides, I could see he wasn't planning to take no for an answer. His hand took mine, and he pulled me toward him, face-to-face, placing my hands on his shoulders, his hands around my waist. They felt warm and strong. The romantic music begged my feet to move. I was nervous but began to relax as he gently led me around his living-room floor without disaster. "See, you *can* do this," he said. His eyes smiled. I liked being in his arms, floating around the room.

The music played around us, but we were silent. Many words went running through my head, yet none of them came out of my mouth. Dan's silence was unusual, since he always had something to say. We simply moved in unison, our cheeks touching gently.

As the third song began to play, I lifted my eyes to his. They seemed to glow, warm and inviting. The glow warmed me. Dan leaned closer; I stayed still. Our eyes closed, and our lips touched. It took my breath away. I don't know what I'd expected, but this certainly exceeded it. My heart blazed in a way it never had before.

Every question, every doubt, every uneasiness was settled for me in that instant. I knew Dan was the one. I felt peace and confirmation. I was ready to set the date and order the dress!

As the kiss ended, the words "I love you" came out of my mouth before I even had a moment to contemplate their impact! I was more than a little surprised at my boldness. I felt myself flush. Although I had not planned to say it, I meant it with all my heart. I was on a thrilling adventure with Jesus! I felt total commitment to his plans, at least as far as I understood them. I was ready to run into the wind, embracing headlong all he had in store for our families.

Poor Dan. Wonderful Dan. Clearly he'd had the evening perfectly planned up to the moment of the kiss, but he was unprepared for the result! He looked stunned and suddenly seemed tongue-tied and uncertain — which, I must confess, I found adorable!

"I love you too," he said quietly. Then he took me by the hand and led me to the couch.

"Marie, I am enjoying every step of our relationship. But I believe it's really important that we not rush it. We've both heard from God about our future, but we don't know his timing yet. You need time to heal, and I need to give you that time, even if you don't think you need it. And we both want to be certain the kids are ready before we take the next step. The very last thing I want us to do is get ahead of ourselves. Do you understand?" Dan's eyes, filled with tenderness, were locked on mine. I did understand, and I knew that this man could be trusted to seek God's perfect timing.

What followed was a rich conversation. Dan saw our relationship as a process unfolding. He was finding joy in each discovery along the scenic route to our destination. I was confident that we were both hearing from God and advancing in solid pursuit of his heart, based upon the direction we felt led to go — and in that confidence, I was ready to dash straight to the altar. The melody echoing over me, while perhaps set to a faster tempo, needed the steady beat of Dan's thoughtful march. Neither approach carried greater weight or importance than the other. We were discovering each other's true makeup. We had so much to learn about one another: ideas to be understood and shared in confidence, preferences to explore.

Just as I was attempting to get to know the man God placed inside my world, Dan delighted in discovering me. It was as though we were in the midst of a great game of hide-and-seek. I even enjoyed discussing our differences. Neither of us insisted on "being right." We were simply seeking to be understood. Each revelation led to new understanding. A new adventure was unfurling before our eyes.

When our evening drew to a close, I nearly floated to the car. We'd been transparent with one another, nothing hidden, no pretense, no games. While I felt certain that we were destined to marry, I trusted that God would reveal the right time to Dan. Amazingly, I felt deeply content with that. I sensed that we were wrapped in the safety of God's arms, a place we could enjoy and treasure.

My God was a God who had a basket of soft stuffed puppies hand-delivered to my door at just the perfect moment. Surely if he gave such careful attention to our family's grief over the loss of our dog, how much more attention would he give to the perfect timing of declarations of love and proposals of marriage?

God's perfect timing became a new theme of the deep trust God was growing in my heart. I had no idea that, in just a few weeks, God would reveal yet another lesson to me to cement my trust in his timing.

Dan and I continued dating as a family activity and in a variety of ways, being purposeful in our plans, looking for opportunities that would encourage connections, strengthen new bonds, and develop trust. I loved the time spent with DJ and Nicole. God nourished each seed planted, in both their hearts and mine. Dan invested himself in Abigail, Bryce, and Carson, and they drank it in, thirsty for the love of a man who was looking out for them and showering them with positive attention and happy moments.

One day, just a few weeks after the loss of Dale, a package arrived in our mail crate. I'd picked up the crate while the children were at school and left it on the kitchen counter. When Abigail got home and spotted the package, she asked if she could open it. I was a little hesitant, not sure what the package held but confident that God would protect us from harm, so I agreed. As she lifted the flaps of the box, she broke out in a wonderful smile. In seconds, she was holding in her arms a purple Care Bear sent just for her.

My jaw dropped as a memory flashed through my mind. The previous summer, well before Charlie's death, Abigail had asked for the exact same purple bear one day as we browsed through a store at the mall. I had said, "I'm not spending twenty dollars for something that's going to lie on your bed and collect dust." She'd been unusually disappointed, which led me to wonder if I'd been overly harsh, but I saw no reason to change my decision. What was done was done. No one knew about her desire for this purple bear but her, me, and God.

Now, months later, God was showing both Abigail and me that he had been there in the store that day, and he remembered her. I was an imperfect parent, doing my best to discern when to give and when not to. But God was the perfect parent, knowing exactly when to shower us with evidence of his love. God had prompted a stranger to send Abigail her purple Care Bear!

"Mommy, look!" Abigail's voice exploded with joy. "How did this get here? How did they know I wanted this bear?"

I was undone. "God did this," I said through my tears, "just like he did with the puppies. He knew what was on your heart and wanted *you* to know he cares about you." Tenderness enveloped my daughter and me in that moment, as we shared in the revelation of divinity once again reaching out and touching humanity.

The One who knows all that happens within us is big enough to use the smallest gifts to make an extraordinary impact on our hearts.

18

the question

One Sunday night in late January 2007, as we returned home from an evening family date with Dan and his kids, Bryce's voice piped up from the backseat with a question that took me by surprise: "Mom, can you ask Dan to marry you?"

I laughed. "No, Bryce. Girls don't ask boys to marry them."

He had an answer for everything. "Okay, well, then just ask him to ask you to marry him."

I loved his simplistic view of the world, but I was thankful that Dan and his kids weren't in our car, as I'm sure my face turned several shades of red. But the conversation between Bryce and me that followed confirmed my suspicions: He loved Dan too. Abigail, while far more reserved than Bryce, smiled and nodded as she listened.

I savored the moment. Marriage, a husband, a father for my children — it was coming faster than I had ever expected. The kids' expressions reminded me of my prayers: *They have to love him like I do*, I had prayed. *Open their hearts to love and trust again.*

As their mom, I wanted to make the best decision every time. I was far from perfect, I knew, but even so, my choices, wise or foolish, had a tremendous impact upon their lives. That responsibility was continually on my mind. I was shaping our present, directing their future. I wanted them to have confidence in all that God had planned. And yet there was an obstacle: They had been broken. Trust and love, once given and received freely with their daddy, had been suddenly shattered. I believed God was restoring hope inside their hearts, just as he was in mine. This conversation in the car was a reassuring glimpse that their hopes for the future included Dan, Nicole, and DJ.

Though our children were embracing the growing bond between our families, there were others in our lives far less enthusiastic. Out of deep respect for my entire family, my side and Charlie's, I'd been careful to keep them informed that Dan and I were dating. I understood the cautions I was hearing. Had I been on the outside looking in, I too would be speaking words of caution. I could see that it might appear that I was traveling at light speed through events that needed to be taken in slow motion.

What they hadn't experienced was God's powerful presence and guidance for me and Dan simultaneously, even though neither of us had been aware of how God was working in the other. And although it was true that Charlie had been gone for only four months by this time, in those months I felt I had lived two lifetimes worth of pain and grief and two lifetimes worth of deepening faith. I continually laid it at the feet of Jesus, knowing that only he could free me from the pain of the necessity to "prove myself."

The words of God were my counsel. Hosea 2:14 – 15 says:

"Therefore I am now going to allure her;
I will lead her into the wilderness
and speak tenderly to her.

There I will give her back her vineyards,
and will make the Valley of Achor [a place of trouble] a door of hope."

Since Charlie's death, God had been teaching me to love the wilderness almost as much as I loved the mountaintop. Both were a part of God's love story written into our lives. I was certain that God was giving me back my "vineyards" in Dan. It shouldn't have surprised me when I began to see a much-needed new strength being chiseled into my soul. I had always been a people pleaser. Now it was clear that simply pleasing Jesus was my priority.

With that perspective, rather than getting defensive, I welcomed questions from those who had shared a deep bond of relational trust with me over the years. These friends didn't come to tell me I was wrong; rather, they cautiously assessed my reasoning. I could see their desire to protect and shield me. So I shared with them what God had been doing in me, in Dan, and in the kids, and I asked them to pray. I welcomed every request for God's wisdom for us all.

I will never forget my mom's irrepressible joy one afternoon as I sat at her kitchen table.

"Marie," she said, "you know that Bible-reading plan I've been working through? The other morning, I was reading in Genesis 30, the story of Rachel. She'd been unable to bear children, so, as they did in those days, she chose her servant girl, Bilhah, and gave her to her husband, Jacob, to sleep with. Bilhah bore a son for Jacob and Rachel. You will never believe what verse 6 says she named her son, and why."

I had no idea where Mom was going with this story, but she was so excited I couldn't wait to hear.

She read, "'Then Rachel said, "God has vindicated me; he has listened to my plea and given me a son." Because of this she named him Dan.' Marie, I felt God telling me that he has chosen Dan to redeem your loss of Charlie. The biblical Dan took away the shame Rachel felt and restored joy to her life. Dan's love will take away your shame, redeem your status, and restore your joy."

In my mother's words — my practical, protective, God-honoring mother — I heard God's confirmation that it was his voice Dan and I were following. I would press on, steadfastly maintaining my grasp upon the joy and peace sustaining every step.

January turned to February. Hours, days, weeks moved too slowly for me. I wanted to push it faster. I was in love! Dan and I had settled into the realization that we were, indeed, heading toward marriage within the year. We would need to find a new home where we could make new memories with our children. We began searching but without telling the kids, since we wanted to share the news of our engagement first. And so far, there was no official engagement. Dan had not yet actually proposed.

Valentine's Day was approaching, and I couldn't help but wonder if it would bring a ring to my finger. Meanwhile, Dan and I found time here and there to house hunt. After touring a number of homes, we liked best the first one we'd looked at. The listing agent for that house called our Realtor early Friday afternoon, the weekend before Valentine's Day, to say that she was expecting another offer. If we wanted to make an offer, now was the time to do it.

We were stunned. This wasn't the timing we had planned. I wanted my children to be able to stay in their current school until summer break, and then begin their next grade in their new school. Was this God's way of ensuring that they'd be settled in before their change of school? We asked God for wisdom.

We decided to put in an offer. Our Realtor called the following day — the offer had been accepted!

A brand-new home awaited our family, every detail custom designed by the One who knew our deepest needs. It was almost too much to take in.

We were content to wait on sharing this news with the kids and our family, wanting to do everything in proper order — marriage first, house together second.

It dawned on me that I, as a loving parent, knew the home I was preparing for my children — new dad, new school, new house, new life — but *they* didn't know because it was not yet time for them to know. Dan and I would reveal it at the perfect moment. How much more does our heavenly Father have our future planned — a future filled with good gifts, every need met, every purpose fulfilled? And yet we won't know those details until God chooses to reveal them at the proper time. My children didn't need to worry about the big questions of housing and schooling; they could trust me as their parent to care for their needs.

God grew larger in my finite mind that day. My trust grew with him.

Dan was a thoughtful romantic, constantly surprising me with expressions of love — handmade gift certificates to wash my car or rub my shoulders, unexpected flowers, cards tucked under a pillow on the couch. One day he scheduled an e-card to be delivered once an hour for an entire day. Because of that, I held high expectations for the quickly approaching holiday. To my dismay, there was snow in the Valentine's forecast. That might interfere with Dan's ability to visit, since I lived in rural Georgetown and he lived just outside of Strasburg, about ten miles away. It also meant shoveling — a task that had fallen to me as a child while my dad worked, and as an adult when Charlie worked. The prospect of snow annoyed me.

In continuous motion, my brain never stopped, always thinking, preparing, and planning. *When will he ask me to marry him?* I had a family reputation for typically unraveling secret plans prematurely through too much thinking. I did want Dan to surprise me, but for that to happen I needed to stop pondering and analyzing every move, which seemed impossible.

Dan and I had registered for a marriage conference held the weekend after Valentine's Day. The program included special sessions for engaged and remarried couples. Eager to do all we could to form a deep, stable foundation, we signed up. I didn't want to attend without a ring on my finger. Dan knew this, so I was sure the pivotal question would arrive before the conference. Maybe he would ask on Valentine's Day!

February 14 arrived as predicted, covered in snow. *This is going to ruin everything*, I pouted. I might not see Dan at all this day. Instead, I would spend it shoveling — and playing outside with the kids, which was, at least, a bright spot.

As any mother of young children in a snowy climate will confirm, it takes a lot of time to sufficiently dress three children for an afternoon of playing in the snow. But it was worth it — I enjoyed every second of their rosy cheeks, their laughter, and their snowballs, sleds, and snow angels. I had planned a special meal of a few of their favorite dishes in celebration, on this day devoted to love, of my love for my three children. I couldn't change the weather or its effect on my spending time with Dan, but I wasn't going to allow it to ruin the beauty of all that lay before me.

But all was well: Dan surprised us when he pulled into the driveway with a carload of shovels and salt. In no time, he had cleared my walkways and driveway. While thankful for his help, I was disappointed that he couldn't stay for dinner. He needed to get home before darkness fell and the predicted winds picked up, making travel more treacherous. Before leaving, he handed out candy to the kids — and handed me a bag of Hershey's Kisses. "Think of me while you're eating these tonight," he said with a sly grin. It was a sweet thought, pun intended — but not quite what I'd hoped for on this Valentine's Day. I reminded myself to love the moment and let go of my expectations.

Lord, you're graciously guiding me through the firestorm of the shooting and the wilderness left in its wake. You've taught me to trust, to expect to see you at work, to love the moment, confident that you are always creating us with the future in mind. Yes, I see how silly my current impatience is in light of all you have done for me. Help me trust you with Dan's timing as well. I prayed it and meant it.

Living it was another matter. Oh, what love can do to us!

Daily routines consumed the rest of the week. Life felt good — unless you were expecting a moment of revolutionary change in the form of one little question.

Friday came. The conference drew closer by the hour, yet there was still no ring. I was frustrated but determined to put the frustration behind me and glean what I could from the conference.

Our one-hour drive to the conference was made in complete silence. I knew I had to do something to break the tension and to soothe my disappointment. As we pulled into the parking lot, I said, "I'm not getting out of the car until everything is okay. I'm not going into a marriage conference with a problem hanging over us."

Dan said, "It didn't go according to plan. There's nothing I can do. I'm sorry that I've disappointed you."

I could tell by his comments and his tone of voice that he was up to something, and I felt guilty for inflicting him with my disappointment. I apologized. I would have to continue working on the virtue of patience.

Saturday night was listed as a "date night" on the conference schedule. That was no surprise — it had been explained in the basic information we were given when we'd registered weeks before. Guys were strongly encouraged to plan a romantic date to share with their wife or fiancée. The conference leaders explained that this was to be an evening of heartfelt sincerity. Knowing Dan, I anticipated nothing short of perfection.

The conference ended for the day at around 5:00 p.m. Saturday night.

"We're heading back toward Lancaster," Dan explained. I tried to tease out of him the special place he had chosen for us.

And he told me. Out of the immense selection of great local restaurants available to us, we were eating at a sports grill place at the mall.

He has to be joking, I thought, figuring that he was up to some fantastic surprise.

And I *was* in for a surprise. He pulled into the parking lot of the sports grill. It was not a joke. First, I'm not a sports fan, and second, I did not want to eat in a loud environment with televisions blaring hockey and other sports. As he put his name on the waiting list — they didn't take reservations — I tried to give him the benefit of the doubt, knowing he was a romantic, but as the minutes passed, my ability to be gracious wore thin.

He suggested that we do a little shopping each on our own while we waited for our table. He made a purchase and decided to take the bag out to the car, leaving me to browse on my own until he returned. I had told my close friend Deanna that I was expecting Dan to propose tonight, and now I dialed her from my cell and filled her in on the frustrating details of how poorly the evening was going. She listened and commiserated but encouraged me to give Dan the benefit of the doubt. I'd *been* giving him that benefit every step of the evening thus far, I explained, my exasperation clear in my voice.

When we were finally seated at our table, Dan rushed through dinner, not even offering to order an appetizer or dessert! Had he missed the entire idea of the special date emphasized at the conference? I fumed inside. *I would rather have dessert than dinner! What is his problem?* He hurriedly paid the bill, and when we got out to the car, he made a move toward opening my door, but I scooted around and beat him to it. If he was in such a rush, I'd help bring this night to a close.

"Would you like to drive past our new house?" Dan asked. We hadn't been back in the week since submitting the offer.

"I don't think so," I replied. "The snow's over six inches deep, the place will be dark, and we don't have the key yet." I was dressed for a special date, I thought — not an outdoor adventure!

But Dan insisted. He pulled up to the curb, got out, and walked up to the house, making fresh tracks in six inches of pristine, powdery glory. I waited a minute, wondering if he was serious. His feet were clad in heavy men's shoes and socks; I wore ballet flats.

He turned and motioned for me to join him. I waited a moment more, then opened my own car door and tried to place my feet in the tracks he'd made.

We stood in silence for a few minutes. Light radiated off the snow, casting a glow that seemed to dispel the darkness of my frustration. Dan reached for my hand. He offered warmth — I was cold. This exchange, while simple, melted the coldness still lingering in me. God had sent Dan to love me, a gift unexpected and wondrously delivered.

Suddenly my heart was pierced by guilt. In the past few hours, Dan had tried to create a beautiful evening. And while it hadn't been what I'd envisioned, at least it had held purpose and love. I had no right to say it lacked beauty and delight.

Then, as I turned and looked into Dan's eyes, he dropped to one knee and pulled a velvet box from his pocket. "Marie, will you marry me?"

I was speechless! I reached for him, pulled him close, and said, *"Yes!"* He slid the ring onto my finger. Then, shaking his head, he said, "You have no idea how hard this has been!"

Dan Monville saw the worst of me on the night that forever shaped our destiny. I am still amazed at his courage to persist in the face of my attitude.

As we stood on the porch together, his arms wrapped securely around me, he began to pray. He dedicated our lives, our family, and our marriage to the Creator of all. His words cascaded over me. I was home.

On the drive home, Dan shared the tale of his misadventures to find the perfect ring and plan the perfect proposal. He had ordered several different styles in the past weeks, but in each case he'd felt that they weren't quite right and sent them back. The ring he'd given me had been scheduled to arrive days before, but the winter storm had delayed deliveries. He had planned to propose much sooner than this night, he explained, relieved to finally be able to let me in on what he'd been going through. The reason he'd chosen the sports restaurant was because it was close to the jewelry store, and the ring is what he'd taken out to the car when he'd abandoned me in the mall.

The more he explained, the faster he talked, and the more adorable he was to me. I laughed, buzzing inside with excitement and amazed at the love and attention to detail he'd invested. He laughed with me.

"And poor Deanna!" he said, still laughing.

"What about her?" I couldn't imagine what he was referring to.

"We've both been calling her all evening," he said, laughing even harder at my shocked look. "I called her this morning and told her my plan for the night. While you were calling her complaining, I was calling asking her to calm you down."

"No! Really? Oh, Dan, she was in on it? She knew about the ring?" We laughed ourselves silly telling each other what she'd said.

It was a night I will never forget!

I wore my ring to the conference the following morning but took it off before I picked up the kids at my parents' house later in the day. Dan was off work on Monday, as were our children for Presidents' Day. We had already planned breakfast together at my house. We would share the news with them then — not just the engagement, but the house as well.

That morning when we told them, our kids erupted in enthusiastic celebration, fireworks exploding in each and every heart.

I will always be in awe of you, I prayed.

19

seven candles

I took a deep breath and dialed the number for one of Charlie's brothers. It was important to me that Charlie's immediate family hear the news of my engagement directly from me. I could only imagine how difficult it might be for them. Would they feel I was trying to replace Charlie? Trying to usurp their part in the lives of Abigail, Bryce, and Carson? Not at all—I wanted my children to remain deeply connected to Charlie's family so that they could discover more of who their father had been and enjoy their connection with him.

Charlie's brother was glad to hear from me, and we spent a few minutes catching up on the kids. Finally, I told him of my engagement. I held my breath through what felt like a very long pause, realizing how fearful I was of his disapproval.

Finally, I heard a sigh. "Marie, if you've found a silver lining in this very dark cloud, then you should grab hold and take it for everything it's worth."

"Thank you." Overcome with sweet relief, I could barely get the words out.

My call to Charlie's grandparents brought a huge surprise. Because they spent winters in the warmth of Florida, I hadn't seen them since they'd joined us on our Christmas Disney cruise. I told his grandmother the news about Dan as gently as I could.

"Marie," she said, her voice filled with reassurance, "do you know what my husband said to me on the cruise? He said, 'I sure do hope God brings Marie a new husband soon. The burden of raising a family alone is weighing on her so heavily.'"

Charlie's grandparents had been hoping that God would send me a new husband? I never would have anticipated such a response.

My mom and dad welcomed Dan with open arms and open hearts, as did many of our friends and family. There were some, however, who didn't welcome our news. Dan and I had expected words of caution and concern, and we heard some — but we never heard one that we hadn't considered ourselves!

Marie, maybe your sense that God is telling you to marry Dan is more wishful thinking than the Lord speaking.

Dan, is she the right woman? Maybe. But this is the wrong time. What's the hurry? She needs more time to heal.

Marie, you've never really dated anyone other than Charlie and Dan. You could be just latching onto the first man to give you attention and mistaking that for love. Take your time. Date other men. Then decide once you've got more experience.

Dan, it might be that Marie is just desperate for financial support and a father for her children. Be cautious. You don't really know her that well.

Marie, your loneliness and your drive for comfort and security may be clouding your judgment.

Dan, you can't really trust Marie's judgment to make a major decision so close to a traumatic event.

Marie, Dan could be a user, taking advantage of your need for security to fill a gap in his own life. You need to put him to the test of time.

When such concerns were expressed by loved ones and trusted friends, we took the time to listen and to give an account of God's leading. We prayed together and independently for God to lead us in our timing, and we trusted that he would. We didn't set a date when we got engaged. We were committed to taking one step at a time and waiting on God.

But we did encounter a few people, just a few, who were vehement in their opposition. At times like that, I was glad I had friends like Dara.

Dara first wrote to me the week after the shooting, introducing herself as one who, like me, had been widowed at a young age with small children. Dara and I continued to write each other, and she became a wonderful confidante. She commiserated with me over my months as a single mom, and then she became a wise, experienced sounding board as Dan and I moved forward into dating.

When, years earlier, she'd met the man who later became her second husband, she too had felt at times like she'd been thrown back into her teenage years, smitten with fresh love that sent her emotions skyrocketing into the stratosphere one day but left her filled with doubts the next. Knowing that Dara had weathered those highs and lows and had now been happily married for many years encouraged me to keep my perspective and my sense of humor.

One day I opened my email inbox, and Dara's name brought a smile. I'd recently written her about my hurt feelings when someone let me know in no uncertain terms that I was irresponsible to be pursuing a relationship with Dan, thinking only of myself and not of my children. That accusation had stung more than most, because I thought this person knew me better than that. I *was* putting my children first, as was Dan, and we continued to see confirmation from the Lord, and from our kids, that they loved being together and were already starting to feel like family to one another.

I opened Dara's reply.

> *Marie, you have clung to God and pulled thru beautifully, lady. God knows your heart… You're his friend, his for-real friend, who didn't turn on him and accuse him of causing your pain but loves him thru it… and that's the most awesome thing any of us can do. You know, when someone suffers a loss I often wish I could give them back what they lost but "awesomer." Right? And this is exactly what I think God's thinking when he looks at you.*

Dara always encouraged me to focus on God's wisdom, not my own, and not the thoughts of those around me. She was right. God in his generosity had exchanged my trauma for the "awesomer" gift of Dan Monville. I needed to resist my old identity as a people pleaser and embrace the fact that God's journey for me was so unconventional that there would always be some people certain they were seeing what was best for my future more clearly than I.

Throughout the rest of February and into March, Dan and I entered a season of pre-marriage preparation.

When we sensed God's leading that the time was right, we talked through many potential dates and, as did many others that year, selected 7/7/07.

Once I confirmed that my kids would be able to continue attending their current school until the end of the school year, we decided that Abigail, Bryce, Carson, and I would move into our new house in mid-March.

Three heartwarming events occurred before we moved out of our Georgetown home on Old Grandpa's acreage, and they became sweet memories for the closing of that chapter of our lives.

The first was on a snowy day in February. We awoke to a heavy blanket of snow. The children were eager to suit up in their snow gear. I wasn't as enthusiastic because I knew I'd need to shovel our driveway — not my favorite pastime.

As we were eating breakfast we heard what sounded like a farm tractor in our driveway and all rushed to the window. There we saw, to our amazement, a neighbor clearing our driveway. His act represented to me the many kindnesses of my Georgetown neighbors.

The second event came on moving day. Once again, we had snow — and discovered that the moving truck had nearly bald tires! Imagine how touched we were when an Amish neighbor appeared with a skid loader and cleared our driveway in a heartbeat. My first thought was of the Amish men who had embraced my father on the day of the shooting, saying, "You are a part of our community, our neighbors. This tragedy doesn't change that." This kind Amish neighbor was reaching out to serve the widow and children of Charlie Roberts. Another scene of grace written into our lives.

The third, on that very same day, was just as remarkable. As we scurried around packing our final belongings into boxes, there was a knock on the door. I opened it to find an Amish woman with a beautiful smile, holding a basket.

"I wanted you to know that we will miss you," she said. "I thought you might enjoy some bread and cookies for such a busy day." We were still being held in the embrace of the Amish, and the parting was bittersweet.

As we drove out of Georgetown that day, I knew I wasn't leaving Georgetown behind. I was carrying it with me, and I still do to this day. I am forever bound to those good people.

The sense of new beginnings made us nearly giddy with excitement as we worked feverishly to unpack boxes, hang pictures, and personalize our new space, with the help of Dan, Nicole, and DJ, who would move in after the wedding. Dan and I continued to marvel at how easily the children worked together, already acting like a family.

Though there was much to miss about Georgetown, our new home in Lampeter had some distinct advantages. Strangers were not on the lookout for "the shooter's wife." Gone were the questions I sometimes heard that made my skin crawl, such as "How do you sleep at night knowing what your husband did in the schoolhouse?" or "Did Charlie have life insurance? Do they even cover this kind of death?"

And what a relief to be able to let the kids play outside without worrying about the continuing parade of people who still, months after the tragedy, seemed determined to seek us out. I didn't miss the sight of people driving slowly by my house, pointing and staring. I didn't miss the numbers of unknown cars turning around in my driveway. I had found it so troubling that some days I kept the curtains pulled, even though I love sunlight.

But God, as he often does, used such experiences to serve a purpose — they became an opportunity to talk with each of the children about the tragedy and how we were recovering from it. I understood all too well that sorrow sometimes tucks itself away and gnaws at the soul, so it's best to not let it remain hidden. I prayed fervently for wisdom to encourage in my children's lives the spiritual tools that would equip them to deal with grief.

In response, God prompted me to invite them to join me in a treasure hunt. I challenged them to spot with me the presence of Christ. We found him in gifts sent by those we'd never met, cards awaiting our discovery in the mailbox each day, kindnesses shown to us, and the beauty of nature. And most importantly, we found him in the love we shared with one another.

Just before Easter weekend, the news media heard of my engagement. The newspaper headline read, "SHOOTER'S WIFE PLANS TO REMARRY." I was devastated. In the eyes of the media, I was just "the shooter's wife." But I had a name, a heart that beat and bled, and hopes and dreams outside the events I did not choose.

The article included a number of details, including Dan's name, a forecast that our wedding would take place in July — or maybe October. The writer also put his spin on the past months' events in my life.

Dan and I knew when we read the article that our wedding date would have to change. I didn't want to be a front-page story, and I didn't want reporters storming our wedding ceremony. I simply wanted to get married like any other normal person, far from the spotlight of national media.

God's timing is impeccable. He stepped in once again in a huge way. A stranger blessed our family with an Easter trip to Disney World, including airfare, hotel accommodations, meals, and park passes. God's provision took us out of the area, protecting me from the days of newspaper stories of the engagement and reporters at my doorstep wanting further information. The Easter trip became a wonderful object lesson for the entire family that

God offers provision for every situation. What a treasure for our family treasure hunt!

Dan and I changed our wedding plans to ensure privacy from the media. We called eighty-five of our closest friends and relatives, telling them to reserve May 25 for an evening celebration, and that we would reveal the location just two days before the event. There would be no printed invitations or programs. We made every choice with the goal of honoring the union God had provided and eliminating the media from the celebration. We chose the lovely Mulberry Art Studios for our 5:30 p.m. celebration, and meticulously crafted a wedding ceremony celebrating the beauty of God's great goodness in each of our lives. I asked Charlie's dad to join my dad in escorting me down the aisle. It brought joy to my heart that he accepted, making Charlie's family a part of this celebration. We were collectively uniting seven into one divinely ordained family unit.

For Dan and me, this union brought with it not only the promise of multiplied blessings in the years to come — it also wrote the words "redemption and restoration" over our pasts. Our greatest expectation was the goodness of God poured out afresh in our lives. Our stories could have been vastly different. The extravagant love of a Father for this daughter and this son was rewriting the heartbreak of the past. I could not get to the end of this limitless love from a God who redeems brokenness with new life.

On the day of our wedding, Abigail said to me, "God has done so much good that it makes the bad stuff not seem so bad." She was right.

On the altar that day, seven separate candles burned. Individually they seemed small, but together, after we each tipped our candles to the wick of the one tall white candle, their flames, combined, shone with brilliance.

20

release

We all love "happily ever after" endings. God's love story written for all who believe in Jesus Christ promises exactly that, but not until we stand face-to-face with him in heaven. Until then, God continues to write new chapters. How easy it is for us to get caught up in our present, expecting our "now" to be the fulfillment of all we've hoped for.

Walking down the aisle to blend two families into one on our wedding day wasn't the close of my story. It was the opening of a new chapter. I loved the insight that God instilled in me in the week following the shooting — that he is always creating us with the future in mind. What, then, did my future hold?

What I didn't yet know was that God had so transformed me through the experiences of the previous months and so reshaped my understanding of who I am that I would emerge with a new vision for my life. God was in no hurry to whisk me to that point, however. He knew I needed time to rest in the joy of my new family.

In the first months of our marriage, Dan and I focused on creating a nurturing and secure home life where all of us could continue to heal and bond. We jumped into the challenges normal families face: balancing schedules and activities, accomplishing household responsibilities, and finding time to develop our relationship as husband and wife — dating in the midst of five kids. We gladly laughed ourselves through it. It was surprisingly easy to weather the adjustments of blending two families. May to August was a delightful blur of new home, new siblings, new routines, new neighbors. For all seven of us, it was a fun adventure to find our new normal. Perhaps it seemed so easy because when you've lived through a tsunami, an occasional rainstorm seems insignificant by comparison.

Late August broke the spell.

"Will all the kids in my class know about my dad?" Bryce's voice told me this question had been troubling him. "Would they like me if they knew?"

We were on our way home from buying school supplies. Car rides were always great times to find out what was on Bryce's mind.

I gave myself a few moments to consider the questions I'd been wondering myself. I felt such a tremendous burden for my kids. I fiercely wanted to protect them from the consequences of Charlie's actions. But that was a God-size, not a mom-size, job. I could cover them with prayer and do my best to equip them to respond to the challenges they faced. I reminded myself that the rest was in God's capable hands.

"If this wasn't your life, how would you feel if one of your friends had to go through what you've been through?" I asked him. "Look at it from someone else's perspective. If one of your classmates had a family tragedy, you would want to help him, wouldn't you? You care about your friends. And that is how a true friend will act."

This conversation with Bryce was really a continuation of

what I expect will be a lifelong conversation about integrating the tragedy into our lives and relationships.

The first anniversary of the shooting was looming large. From the resurgence of media calls, we knew that Nickel Mines and Georgetown were about to be invaded again. We were advised by counselors to leave town over the anniversary to avoid the intrusion of media upon our lives. Once again, I declined every media request. The media, I knew, would reduce our horrific experiences into a few quick sound bites or staggering headlines, and I didn't want my family subjected to that. What purpose would it serve? My first priority was the healing of my children, and I didn't see interaction with the media as something that would further that goal.

So we planned a one-week cruise to Bermuda with our family of seven, Dan's mom, Charlie's parents, and some of his extended family. I was thrilled that Charlie's parents could go with us, so that we could continue to blend our family with love from all sides.

Up until a year ago, I had only taken one round-trip flight on an airplane. Because of my dad's work schedule, I didn't grow up going on yearly vacations. It seemed that since the shooting, God was making up for lost time and missed opportunities!

Even away from town, however, a sickening sense of dread grew stronger as October 2 drew closer. When the day dawned, I was a wreck inside. I held back tears through breakfast, while we disembarked, and as we waited to board a bus to a nearby beach. But once I was seated, I lost my tenuous grip on my emotions. While my children chatted happily with one another and Dan marveled at the crystal blue water, his wide eyes glued to the scenery through the windows, I too kept my face toward the window, hoping that no one noticed the stream of tears flowing down my face. The pain that had been lurking in the shadows of my soul rushed to the surface.

The thought of the Amish children, mothers, and fathers facing this anniversary of their loss that day tore at my heart. Wrenching sadness over Charlie's choices, shame for not somehow knowing, and fear for my children's emotional well-being overwhelmed me. I tried in vain for self-control, then realized that I had to simply let my tears do their work of washing out the clinging grief. Rather than resisting it, I had to let it come, offer it to God, and open myself to his cleansing power.

"Marie, are you angry at Charlie?" It was a question I'd heard from loved ones and counselors many times. I heard it again on this day.

"No, I'm not angry. It's not that I've never felt anger, but when my emotions surface, I take them before the Lord. He is the Comforter. It was anger that led Charlie to his violence, so allowing it to take root in my life is unthinkable. My children need a compassionate and steady mom, not an angry one, and my desire is to give them everything they need."

I remembered that even in the immediate aftermath of the shooting, feelings of anger surfaced only a few times. In those flickering moments, I felt angry that Charlie had stolen the lives of innocent children, robbed Amish families of their precious young ones, robbed my children of their father, and abandoned me to answer for it all. But those times of agitation were always overcome by the gentleness of Jesus. He invited me to a deeper place, characterized not by anger but instead by great anguish and sorrow within my heart. I saw his suffering at Gethsemane differently now — choosing to bear undeserved burdens. As I allowed myself to experience sorrow, God comforted my heart as only he can. So

I honestly told the counselors and my family that I did not *feel* angry.

Today, I asked myself the same question — and found that my answer hadn't changed. Grief and sorrow flooded my soul on this first anniversary, but not anger.

Later in the day, while my family splashed in the waves on a gorgeous beach that should have made my heart smile, I was focused inward, recalling the wisdom in 2 Corinthians 1:3 – 7 that I have tested and found to be true:

> Praise be to the God and Father of our Lord Jesus Christ, the Father of compassion and the God of all comfort, who comforts us in all our troubles, so that we can comfort those in any trouble with the comfort we ourselves receive from God. For just as we share abundantly in the sufferings of Christ, so also our comfort abounds through Christ. If we are distressed, it is for your comfort and salvation; if we are comforted, it is for your comfort, which produces in you patient endurance of the same sufferings we suffer. And our hope for you is firm, because we know that just as you share in our sufferings, so also you share in our comfort.

We live in a fallen world in need of a Savior. Wars, pestilence, cruelty, natural and man-made disasters — all of them grieve me and, I believe, grieve God. God wasn't the source of the sin. Rather, he is the source of salvation from that sin. The tragedy of the shooting doesn't shake that understanding. Jesus has not invited me to a place of anger, but rather to share with him in his sufferings and experience his healing presence and redemptive power. My life is a beautiful testimony that such transformation can occur. I may not have believed it possible in the aftermath of the shooting, but it is the truth.

I settled into *that* beauty and, grateful for the evidence of God's comfort in our lives, watched Dan and our children playing together in the waves. We had come so far in just one year.

~

I tried not to watch the clock that day, but there was no fighting it.

8:15 — Charlie and I walked the kids to the bus stop.

8:40 — I kissed him goodbye on his way out the door to work — or so I'd thought.

11:00 — his call.

Then the police, my flight to my parents', our arrival at Linda's.

Like a movie with no soundtrack, it played all day. Was I doomed to be "the shooter's wife" forever?

Then came renewal and fresh perspective. In Jesus, it always does. I emerged from that one-year mark with a clearer understanding of the pain I still carried. It showed itself in anxious thoughts about my children and self-doubt about my place in the world.

Perhaps my most important discovery during this time of contemplation was a whisper from the shadows inside me as I wondered at God's rescue. He'd stepped into my crisis so dramatically — but why me? He had done something extraordinary, and he'd done it for me. I felt unworthy. I realized that there were still deep wounds inside, more healing necessary. I needed to find the truth of who God created me to be; I needed his vision for my life.

I needed still greater confidence in his love. I longed for his words of truth to drown out the shouts of condemnation and accusation I still heard. Rather than frightening or discouraging me, that realization spurred me on, together with Dan, to remain steeped in God's Word and take the long view of healing.

I revisited every scene of grace and every lesson learned over the past year, and I landed not in despair, but in worship. Where else *could* I land? Jesus had brought healing into my heart and restoration to our family. He had given me an amazing husband who loved our children unconditionally. We'd grown from a family of four to a vibrant family of seven. I had experienced driveway embraces and the wall of grace, the giving tree, a basket of puppies, and countless acts of love from my community, including the mountains of cards placed in my hands. My heart was full of joy amidst the sorrow, and I was undone by the tender redemption of God.

As if those and other scenes of God's light in the darkness were not enough, he added to our lives three tangible symbols of his gentle love. Today they abide in the lively yard that surrounds our home.

The first is a rosebush. When we moved from the home I had shared with Charlie, I ever so carefully dug up the three rosebushes Charlie had given to me, taking great pains not to damage the root system. Together, Dan and I transplanted them to the yard of our new home. Now, years later, one bush survives, a living witness of our story. Its roots are grounded in the soil of Georgetown, its thorns speak of the pain we bore, and each year its new blossoms declare that God brings new life from death. Each summer when its fragrant, peach-colored blossoms appear, I snip the first perfect one and place it in a vase on Abigail's dresser. After that, we share the blooms all summer. A bittersweet reminder of past love, present in our lives all over again.

The second symbol was a housewarming gift from the Amish family I took to visit Rosanna's family in the hospital. Among their many skills, they are shed builders. Shortly after we moved into our new home, they delivered the gift of a handcrafted shed. My youngest affectionately called it our barn and wanted to fill it immediately with cows and sheep. The children of the builder came along that day and jumped on our trampoline with my kids. Their squeals of laughter, I am sure, could be heard all the way to heaven. This was a gift I could not have planned for or even known to hope for. It stands today as a symbol of grace in its most extraordinary capacity — a storage shed for memories of God's entwining one Amish family with my own.

The third symbol of God's great exchange of life for death is far more active and wiggly than the first two.

One early February day, my parents joined Dan, my three kids, and me as we visited an Amish family whose lives had been deeply affected by the tragedy at the schoolhouse. We spent the afternoon chatting in their living room, and then they invited us to explore their barn. There we found a litter of tiny pink newborn puppies snuggling with their mother. As my kids peered into the stall, oohing and aahing over the newborn pups, the farmer mentioned that they had two puppies from a previous litter that were old enough for sale. That was all the kids, who shared Charlie's love of dogs, needed to hear! They were shown the puppies, and in a heartbeat, Bryce scooped up one and Abigail the other. They both began begging to take a puppy home.

The one chocolate lab we already had seemed enough for me, and I hadn't planned on expanding our animal population. They held the puppies as we walked around looking at the horses and cows, and our hosts explained the milking equipment and feeding process to the children. A large operation, it brought back a flood of memories of years sitting beside my dad in the front seat of his milk truck, visiting the Amish farms on his route. I thought of Charlie's dream of becoming a milk truck driver and how much he'd loved his job. Every memory was a happy one.

As we prepared to leave, the begging began.

"Please, we'll do anything!" the kids cried, still cradling their puppies.

Abigail declared, "I'll do chores."

Bryce said, "I'll take it out for walks."

Carson chimed in, "Me too!"

Dan grinned at me. He knew how this would end.

"Bringing home a puppy is not a quick decision," I said. "You'll have to let Dad and me pray about it first."

Several days later, on Valentine's Day, we surprised them with the gift of one of the puppies. Abigail named her Eden, and she quickly became one of the family.

Today, Eden bounds through our yard, lavishing irrepressible love on every member of our family. She's not perfect, and often she challenges us, but even so she is another reminder of the continual Holy Exchange and of God's redemption of our lives. The words of Isaiah 51:3 explain Eden's purpose:

> The LORD will surely comfort Zion
> and will look with compassion on all her ruins;
> he will make her deserts like Eden,
> her wastelands like the garden of the LORD.
> Joy and gladness will be found in her,
> thanksgiving and the sound of singing.

How fitting that she was born on an Amish dairy farm — a new life from a family that had been touched by the deaths of October 2, 2006.

~

In light of all I had experienced since the shooting, perhaps one of the most beautiful things about the next year and a half of my life with my new family was this: There was nothing earth-shattering or dramatic to tell! My family continued to grow in both outward stature and inward resilience.

These were days of slow and steady living, when my roots had the chance to reach down into the rich soil of the new home into which I'd been transplanted.

Dan was God's instrument in my healing, a steadfast source of encouragement and affirmation, grounded in the Word and in love with God. Dan saw more in me than I could have dared to believe on my own. When the time was right, God would use Dan to spur me to reach beyond my comfort zone and dream.

One spring day in 2008, Dan came through the door breathing a sigh of relief. "Nicole is becoming a more confident driver."

I laughed. "Or are you becoming a more confident passenger?"

He smiled uncertainly. "I'm getting there."

I asked, "Who do you think will graduate first? Nicole from driving lessons or Carson from diapers?" Dan declared it to be anybody's game. Potty training and driver training spanned the spectrum of normal growth, from childhood through adolescence, and I loved it all. *In the aftermath of the shooting, I'd have never dreamed our lives would be this whole*, I thought.

A few days later, I told Dan about a weeklong worship school, led by worship leader and songwriter Rita Springer. I thought that a week focused on growing in worship might further the long-term healing process I was living. Even as I mentioned it to Dan, I couldn't see how I, as a wife and mom of five, could make it work. But Dan wouldn't take no for an answer. Four months later, I set off on a week that would change my life.

Dan and the kids took me to the airport; I didn't know how to leave them. Aside from my honeymoon with Dan, I had *never* been away from my children for an entire week. I sat at my gate waiting to board the plane, fighting back the tears. But somewhere in the vast skies between Pennsylvania and North Carolina, a shift occurred. I started to focus less on all I would miss at home and more on the anticipation of what God had in store for me in the next seven days. As I met the other dozen women attending the conference, I was excited but nervous. How would they respond if I revealed my past?

Dinner the first night was full of awkward introductions as everyone chatted about their lives — husband, children, family dynamics. These women knew nothing about me or my story, and as I avoided their questions I realized how veiled I'd become with strangers since the tragedy. Explaining our blended family of seven brought a typical question: Are you divorced? My response — "No, my first husband died" — brought even more questions, and there was no easy way to answer, except to say, "Maybe I can share more of it this week."

I knew there was no way to avoid the inevitable.

But these women became my new friends. Their love of God and care for one another were genuine. It took two days for me to decide that I *wanted* to tell them about my life. This was a completely new feeling, stirred, no doubt, by their friendship. They liked me for who I was, even though they didn't know one thing about me. I had encouraged Bryce not to worry that the story of his family would hinder new friendships, and I knew that I would find the same to be true for myself in this gathering.

Nervously, but wanting to be transparent, I asked Rita if I could share the following day.

The following afternoon Rita introduced me: "Marie would like to share how God has been working in her heart."

My mouth went dry, but I stood and walked toward the front of the meeting room, heart pounding, reminding myself that this was a safe place. I stood before them and opened my mouth, not quite sure where to begin. So I went straight to the heart of the matter.

"My first husband was the man who committed the Amish schoolhouse shooting."

I stood silently for a few moments and searched their faces. Compassion looked back at me. Not repulsion or accusation. Their gentle eyes invited me to say more, and I did. As I spoke, the stigma associated with the label "the shooter's wife" was released. The shadow I'd been carrying to veil my identity was lifted, and I revealed my experience of God's unfathomable grace to me in the wake of the shooting. That day, I caught my first good look at the new identity God had been sculpting inside me. I shed the heavy garment of Charlie's choices and received a luxurious robe of love and acceptance. I felt lighter.

When I finished my story, the women stepped forward and encircled me, laid hands upon me, and prayed with authority. They declared the healing balm of Christ upon each wound and every hidden place. Jesus' presence rested tangibly upon the room. I couldn't move and had no desire to. Love I could feel and truth I could see brought an awakening that touched the core of my being. The label was gone.

Over the next few days I began to see myself more clearly. While "the shooter's wife" wasn't who I was, it *was* a part of my life that God was going to use. God began stirring in me the ability to dream of how he might use me in addition to my roles as wife and mother. Something was sparking within me, but it was not a full-fledged inferno — not yet.

At the conference, we were given a writing assignment, and as I wrote, my deepest thoughts poured out as never before. I offered God the deep suffering within my heart. I didn't know what he would do with it, but I knew that his comfort was transforming those wounds.

When I came home from that school, the desire to express myself continued to grow. Just as I'd learned new things about myself through painting at Linda's, I was discovering new growth as I wrote words upon a page.

I sensed God telling me, *"I've written a story upon your heart. It needs to be released."*

God had already begun to open doors for me to share my story of his work in our lives. Local church groups began calling me with requests to speak at women's events, Sunday evening services, and banquets. Rather than declining those invitations, I now felt eager to reveal the beautiful way God had met me in places of brokenness, released light into my darkness, and ignited hope. He had done it for me, and he would do it for others.

One day I received an invitation to speak at a local event called Community Day to be held at Solanco High School, my alma mater. When I thought of the girl I'd been a decade before when I'd walked those halls, I realized how drastically I'd changed. *That* Marie never would have been comfortable alone on center stage, but now I felt ready for it. This was the first time I would share my story at a community event open to the general public, and I wondered how people would respond.

To my surprise, a few days before the event, I received a phone call from someone who knows my family. This person questioned my choice to talk openly about our lives, believing that it wasn't in the best interest of my children. I'd felt led by the Lord to accept the opportunity, but this resistance spun me onto a spiral of self-doubt. I hung up the phone upset and unsure of myself. *Lord,* I prayed, *did I not hear you right? I thought you wanted me to tell the world what you've done for us. Am I hurting my children by accepting this invitation?*

The Lord was kind. Thirty minutes later the phone rang again — a divinely appointed call from an Amish man who'd lost a child in the schoolhouse. "Marie, we just heard you'll be speaking about what the Lord has done in your life since the shooting. My wife, my children, and I will be coming, and we'll be bringing a few others from our community too. We want to support you." My heart lifted. God had confirmed his leading and released me to speak.

Before I took the stage on the night of my presentation, Dan and I saw several Amish couples with their children enter the auditorium, and we went to greet them. "Dan and Marie," one of the men said, "we want you to know that we support you and your family. You are brave to tell your story. It will bring hope to many."

I stood on the stage, illuminated by bright lights. "My name is Marie Roberts Monville. I am here tonight to tell you about the light of God that broke through my darkness." I felt a supernatural peace as I spoke — totally unafraid — as if I were sitting across the table from a friend.

Fall 2011 arrived, bringing with it the fifth anniversary of the shooting. Media requests poured in. Strangely, I sensed for the very first time a quiet urging from the Lord to carefully consider my response rather than automatically declining. The Lord's message from my week of worship school echoed in my mind: *I've written a story upon your heart. It needs to be released.*

The *Lancaster Sunday News* was planning to devote an entire section of the paper to the fifth anniversary of the tragedy. They requested an interview.

Lord, I prayed, *if I agree to go public and speak about the experiences of our family, what about my children? I don't want them exposed and hurt.* But as I prayed, my perspective changed. I found myself asking God a different question: *Lord, I hear you. Show me how my telling the story of you at work in our lives will release life inside my children.*

I now saw a grand purpose in my telling the story. I wasn't afraid anymore.

To the Lancaster reporter, I responded, "I don't feel comfortable with an interview. But if you will agree to publish a written statement from me, in its entirety, I will send you a few paragraphs."

They accepted.

It was time to begin writing.

I've been writing ever since, revisiting the great deeds of the Lord. Filled with vision and purpose to share the story of God's light in the darkness of the Amish schoolhouse shooting, I was filled with joy.

Until I received another terrifying call and darkness once again threatened to consume the light.

21
father of light

"Marie, I'm at the hospital with your dad." Mom's voice sounded worried. "We saw a cardiologist this afternoon, and she was concerned about Dad's frequent bouts of pneumonia. She sent him for an emergency CT scan. The doctor found a mass in his left lung. They're admitting him now."

Screaming inside, *No, this can't be happening,* I rushed to the hospital to be with my parents.

Dad's diagnosis: lung cancer. The tumor was the size of a plum. Rounds of chemotherapy and radiation would begin — the ultimate fight of his life. I was terrified — was I losing another precious member of my family? My mom needed her husband. My kids needed their grandpa. And I needed a dad.

I sat in my dad's hospital room, looking back on special memories. Dad hoisting me into the cab of his truck when I was just a little girl, teaching Charlie to maneuver a truck, cheering Carson as he caught his first fish, playing passenger in the lawn mower cart while Abigail drove, throwing a baseball to Bryce and DJ, sowing seeds of quiet love into Nicole, just as he had done with me. I could still see Dad embracing Dan as his own son.

Poignant moments of Dad's solid presence during the tragedy

were etched in my mind as well. Dad packing my car to flee my home, weeping in the arms of an Amish man, radiating strength and steadiness beside me in the car, loving on my kids at Aunt Linda's, holding Bryce's hand as we entered the church for Charlie's funeral, standing next to me at Charlie's graveside.

I was, once again, looking grief in the eye, realizing that it might be about to pour into my future. I didn't want that grief — I didn't want my dad to suffer; nor did I want my mom and family dragged through the pain of more loss.

Yet this simple truth remains: Grief comes in this life.

Over the next five months, my dad battled cancer with radiation and chemotherapy. Our family rallied around him, serving him and each other in the ways each heart knew best.

"Mom, let's take Grandpa a milk shake. Would he want black raspberry, peach, or vanilla?" Bryce loved ice cream and hoped it might be just what his grandfather needed. I would call Dad to find out what he was hungry for today. Treatments altered Dad's sense of taste, and eating became a daily challenge.

We visited Dad frequently. "Marie, will you pray for me?" Dad often said. "Something special always happens inside when you pray over me." Prayer felt like the best gift we could give him, and I was honored to pray words of love and life for the man who'd poured both into me.

We made every effort to enjoy our moments together — Dad showed off the produce ripening in the garden and teased about the challenge my mom faced in keeping up with the bumper crop of tomatoes. Sometimes we spent evenings watching a program on television or talking about the people he'd met at the doctor's office. His heart was burdened for many who seemed to be in difficult places.

In September 2012, five months after the initial diagnosis, test results showed only a shriveled hollow where the cancer had been. What relief! We praised God together, and in private, I wept with joy and thanksgiving.

Now that the hardest part was past, he could begin rebuilding his body and his life. My parents planned some time away at Rehoboth Beach in mid-October. Dad didn't have much energy after his harrowing treatment regimen, but he loved being with my mom. They texted pictures of their rides together on the shuttle service from the hotel to the boardwalk and called to share details of their trip. They were happy, in love, and thankful for this gift of time. I saw their relationship with new eyes as they lavished tenderness and joy on one another. What fun to see my parents so in love after more than forty years of marriage!

This joy was short-lived. Test results in late November showed the cancer was back. This time there was no hope for a cure, short of a miracle.

"Marie, I'm sorry to give you this news over the phone," my mom said. I couldn't imagine it would have been any easier in person. "The doctor said your dad has only months of quality life left."

This was not okay. My dad loved life and wouldn't give up on it easily. We were fighting for victory. We would live whatever time we had left with Dad to the fullest and never stop praying and believing for miraculous intervention.

"Marie, I'd like you to do something for me," he said one day in early December when it was just the two of us. I was visiting Dad at the hospital because he had taken a turn for the worse, suffering from pneumonia and a blood infection on top of the cancer.

"Would you do some shopping for me? I have a few ideas of what I want your mom to find under the tree on Christmas morning."

We had fun working on his list, and I was gratified to play a part in his Christmas secrets for Mom. I hoped it would not be my last Christmas with him.

"Dan," my dad said on another visit, "will you teach me how to play a few games on your iPad?" I heard the two of them laughing together during the "lesson" and suspected they were far busier commiserating over the challenges of life with their wives — suspicions confirmed when I caught them nodding conspiratorially while saying to one another, "I know *exactly* what you mean!"

Dad wasn't simply trying to build happy memories. He tackled difficult conversations too and prepared our hearts for what we would do if he lost this battle. "If I don't make it out of here, can your mom come live with you?" he asked.

"We will do anything she needs," I said.

"I want Dan to have my truck," he continued. "He needs a more reliable vehicle, and Bryce needs more room for his sports gear on the way to practice. And besides, you guys need something to haul building supplies for Carson." (Carson was always planning some kind of building project in the basement. He and my dad had been working together, pounding nails into scraps of wood.) "And, Marie, I want you to have my snowblower."

Isn't that just like him? I thought. He knew how much I hated shoveling snow. Always looking out for his little girl. My heart was breaking, and I told myself to be strong and not cry for once. "Dad, the way you love our family is amazing. But just concentrate on getting better." I tried to sound optimistic. His body was deteriorating, but his heart was vibrantly alive.

Knowing that death is coming does not ease the pain it brings.

On December 24, 2012, at 8:00 a.m., my dad passed from life on earth into the embrace of heaven.

My dad loved well. He left a rich legacy for my family through the gentleness with which he spoke, the thoughtful plans he laid out for our family, the steadiness of his strength, and the depth of his love. I've never been more proud to call him father than when, at his physical worst, he radiated love best.

He was only sixty-one when we lost him. Too soon. I wasn't ready to let him go.

I don't like this invasion of grief that has gripped me, and some days I don't want to look for the beauty within it. The mystery is that it finds me anyway. It grabs my face in its hands and points the way so I don't miss one act of God's grace.

The night before my dad died, Dan and I spent the evening with my parents. I snuck into the room when Mom wasn't around and handed Dad the wrapped packages one at a time. He wrote her name on each tag, and I placed them under the tree. I thought back to my teen years when Dad, his brutal work schedule keeping him from shopping, would sometimes ask me to buy Mom gifts or pick out a card for him to give. Back then I groaned inwardly at his requests. This time, it was pure joy to be his hands and feet of love. Had not Dad been the hands and feet of Jesus for me?

Life had come full circle.

In my fresh grief, I fall back into the arms of an understanding God, the One I long to understand more deeply as Father.

Oh, Father to the fatherless, I cry, *life without my dad crushes me. So I wait for you in the same way I've waited before. I stand, arms lifted high, head bowed low, welcoming the One who fathers me.*

God answers.

"To this I will appeal:
the years when the Most High stretched out his right hand.
I will remember the deeds of the LORD;
yes, I will remember your miracles of long ago.
I will consider all your works
and meditate on all your mighty deeds.
(Psalm 77:10–12)

Remember, remember, remember.

I began telling you my story with an audacious promise:

No matter how tragic your circumstances, your life is not a tragedy. It is a love story. And in your love story, when you think all the lights have gone out, one light still shines.

You've seen how God, in his bounteous grace, pierced my darkest moments with his light. Over and over again he broke through my pain, revealed his presence, and restored my hope.

He is doing it still.

My dad is gone. God didn't *eradicate* the darkness, but once again, he pierces it. I need only live in expectancy of seeing him at work.

God didn't grant my every hope. Instead, he calls me to love the moment, confident that he is creating me with the future in mind.

He didn't *fix* the tragedy. He *redeemed* it. I am now and forever a redemptionist, confident that, in Christ, nothing is wasted, but all will be transformed to spiritual gain.

He didn't *prevent* the loss — not with Elise or Isabella, not with the Amish girls in the schoolhouse, and not with Charlie or Dad. But, oh, how he *sustains* me through it.

On this side of heaven, for all of us, God doesn't always spare us the loneliness, remove the pain, or still the storm. So I ask you:

How often do we miss his light because we fail to look for it?

How many times do we turn away from the tiny flicker that reveals his presence because we shut our eyes tight, insisting that he remove the darkness?

What is your story? Mistreatment, injustice, torment, suffering, grief, or even the worst of what humanity can do to one another?

Or is it a love story of the Creator God sustaining, intervening, redeeming, and restoring?

Live the love story! Fall into the embrace of forgiveness. Hide in the shelter of his wings. Step inside the wall of grace. Live in the expectancy of seeing him at work. Leap into his mysterious will. Receive the gift of love. Be released to respond to his call.

Tell the world your love story.

And when again the lights go out, you too will see that one light still shines.

acknowledgments

Dan — Your love lifts me to new heights, your friendship settles my soul, and your pursuit of God lights the darkness around you. To me, you're like Jesus with skin on — selfless love and beautiful redemption.

Abigail — You are strong and wildly beautiful in every way. You are the embodiment of a promise made and my dream come true, and this is only the beginning.

Bryce — You run and jump and breathe deep the kingdom of God. You are exactly what the world needs.

Carson — You fly to places I've never been and see the world from a viewpoint beyond my comprehension. You open eyes to see God fresh.

DJ — You are deep mysteries and wonder, and those who know your friendship feel the vibrant warmth of gentleness. You are a gift.

Nicole — You are the best-kept secret; laughter, full and free, celebratory; a protective defender; and you light the way for those who follow your dance. Never stop!

Mom and Dad — Without your love I would be nothing. The mix of Dad's quiet tenderness and Mom's straightforward boldness has given me wings, taught me to fly, and allowed me to find my own way. Mom, my heart is grateful that we are on this journey together. Dad, I miss you more and more, for a million different reasons, and each day I rediscover why I've always treasured you.

Ken and Kristin — You hear our hearts even when we haven't said one word — you get the jokes; you are true family. Thank you for sharing life with us.

Vicki and Ethan — The path before you, while not easy, promises your own grand adventure. I'm with you all the way.

Roberts Family — A unique journey of finding light in darkness forced itself upon you; may you continue to see Jesus writing new chapters in your love story.

Kelli and Shawn, Jennie and Chris, Elise, Fred and Leann — You've encouraged my heart when it was weary, lifted me when I was low, and celebrated every victory. You are the King's finest servants and my ever-faithful friends.

Dean and Lindsey — You give extraordinarily without reservation or second thought. I'm watching with eager eyes, waiting to see the ways in which God brings the harvest for all you've sown.

Russ, Kimi, and Abby — Your support of our family is steadfast, even in the sorrowing places. You are our forever friends!

Hannah — Your texts always came at just the right time! You love with a grace-filled gentleness that gives life.

Joe and Joan, and the Power Hour ladies — Your friendship gives a glimpse of heaven!

Kate — Your love is a treasured gift; thanks for listening, protecting, and loving!

Dara—You simply and authentically live the love of Jesus. Your ability to reach my heart with precise accuracy drew me into the embrace of pure love and opened my eyes to see God in new ways. You have an amazing ability to feel the wounds of another and bring divine healing. You are a gift to the world around you.

Deanna—Your family didn't just stand with us, you climbed into the chasm and steadied us as we made the long trek out. You chose to shoulder our burden and rejoice in our beauty. My heart will be forever grateful for your friendship.

Dawn—Your willingness to yield to the Father is inspiring. The words you speak release hope, bring light to dark places, and communicate intimate love straight from God's heart.

Pastor Dave, Pastor Herb, and Christ Community Church—The gentle strength of Jesus surrounds my family through you.

Rita and my DIVE sisters—You have propelled my reach, sparked new dreams, and inspired undeniable belief. DIVE was the catalyst for the rest of my life, and I'm thankful our friendship did not end there.

Michelle—The sea cannot separate our friendship; your voice speaks the melody of a pure heart, and your ability to love profoundly sings of Jesus.

Anita—Your connection started it all; thank you for following Jesus and opening a door.

Wes—It's an honor to call you friend and a privilege to have you as my agent. Your encouragement has been profound, and I am grateful for this divinely ordained friendship.

Cindy—From the very first moment, I knew you heard my heart. It has been a joy to work together. You embody the tender brilliance of Jesus.

Dave—You and Cindy have a beautiful partnership; you are a perfect complement to one another. I am thankful for your wisdom and investment in my story.

The Zondervan team—It is an honor to work with those

who truly live the love of God. Sandy, you believed in the message behind each page and saw the love stories others will be inspired to write. I am forever grateful for your gentle encouragement. Alicia and Heather, your passion to reach the world with the love of God inspires me to dream with a limitless potential. Curt, your creativity is astounding; your cover design surpassed my hopes. Bob, thank you for your superb attention to every detail in the manuscript and production. Katherine Lloyd and Sarah Johnson, your expertise in interior design ensured that each page was elegant. I know there were many more individuals whose names I do not know who played a part in bringing my message to the world. Thank you all.

And to the countless others who have blessed our family with your love — I treasure each act of thoughtfulness.

Jesus — Without you, none of this is possible!

For information about Marie Monville speaking engagements, please contact Info@AmbassadorSpeakers.com or call 615-370-4700

Share Your Thoughts

With the Author: Your comments will be forwarded to the author when you send them to *zauthor@zondervan.com.*

With Zondervan: Submit your review of this book by writing to *zreview@zondervan.com.*

Free Online Resources at

www.zondervan.com

Daily Bible Verses and Devotions: Enrich your life with daily Bible verses or devotions that help you start every morning focused on God. Visit www.zondervan.com/newsletters.

Free Email Publications: Sign up for newsletters on Christian living, academic resources, church ministry, fiction, children's resources, and more. Visit www.zondervan.com/newsletters.

Zondervan Bible Search: Find and compare Bible passages in a variety of translations at www.zondervanbiblesearch.com.

Other Benefits: Register to receive online benefits like coupons and special offers, or to participate in research.